ERNST VON DOHNÁNYI

Ernst von Dohnányi

A Song of Life

BY

ILONA VON DOHNÁNYI

EDITED BY

JAMES A. GRYMES

INDIANA
University Press

Bloomington & Indianapolis

This book is a publication of

Indiana University Press
601 North Morton Street
Bloomington, IN 47404-3797 USA

http://iupress.indiana.edu

Telephone orders   800-842-6796
Fax orders   812-855-7931
Orders by e-mail   iuporder@indiana.edu

The paper used in this publication meets the minimum
requirements of American National Standard for Information
Sciences—Permanence of Paper for Printed Library Materials,
ANSI Z39.48-1984.

MANUFACTURED IN THE UNITED STATES OF AMERICA

Library of Congress Cataloging-in-Publication Data
Dohnányi, Ilona von, 1909–1988.
Ernst von Dohnányi : a song of life / by Ilona von Dohnányi ; edited by James A. Grymes.
p.   cm.
Includes bibliographical references and index.
ISBN 0-253-34103-5 (cloth)
1. Dohnányi, Ernst, 1877–1960. 2. Composers—Hungary—Biography. 3. Pianists—
Hungary—Biography. I. Grymes, James A. II. Title.

ML410.D693 D65 2002
780'.92—dc21
[B]
2001051663

1 2 3 4 5 07 06 05 04 03 02

CONTENTS

EDITOR'S PREFACE

Ernst von Dohnányi (1877–1960) was one of the most highly regarded musicians of his time. From a young age Dohnányi enjoyed an international prestige that brought him into contact with such nineteenth-century masters as Eugène d'Albert and Johannes Brahms. Dohnányi's technique and interpretive skills as a pianist and a conductor are legendary. He is also remembered as the composer of numerous masterpieces for piano, chamber ensembles, and orchestra. As a teacher and administrator, Dohnányi was responsible for the training of an entire generation of musicians in Hungary, including Géza Anda, Béla Bartók, György Cziffra, Annie Fischer, Andor Foldes, Boris Goldovsky, Edward Kilenyi, Jr., and Georg Solti.

Dohnányi's most significant contribution, however, may have been the integral role he played in developing the musical culture of Hungary. Despite this, his homeland turned its back on him in 1945 when he was falsely accused of being a Nazi sympathizer. Dohnányi was eventually able to disprove the allegations, but rumors would follow him for the rest of his life, causing irreparable damage to his reputation. It was not until 1968, twenty-three years after Dohnányi's expatriation and eight years after his death, that his name was finally removed from the blacklist in Eastern Europe. Since then, the Hungarian government has gradually increased its recognition of Dohnányi's contributions. In 1990 Dohnányi was posthumously awarded the Kossuth Prize, the highest award a Hungarian citizen can receive. Hungary has also named a music school and a street adjacent to the Franz Liszt Academy of Music after Dohnányi. The Hungarian Ministry of Culture is currently working toward establishing an International Dohnányi Research Center in Budapest.

As a result of both Dohnányi's damaged political reputation and his rejection of avant-garde techniques, his recordings and compositions were largely ignored in the latter half of the twentieth century. In recent years, however, musicians have begun to revise their interpretations of twentieth-century music history to include brilliant compositional and performance styles that, like Dohnányi's, adhered more closely to nineteenth-century aesthetics, and performers and audiences all over the world have begun to rediscover Dohnányi's musical legacy. Nevertheless, the effects of Dohnányi's blacklisting are still evident in the lack of information available on him. Until now, the only biography of Dohnányi has been Bálint Vázsonyi's distinguished work, *Dohnányi Ernő* (Budapest: Zeneműkiadó, 1971), which is in Hungarian.

In addition to filling a conspicuous void as the first English-language biography of Dohnányi, *Ernst von Dohnányi: A Song of Life* presents a unique perspective in that it was written by Ilona von Dohnányi (1909–88), Dohnányi's third wife. Consequently, parts of this biography are also somewhat autobiographical. As a writer, Mrs. Dohnányi contributed to newspaper columns, edited magazines, and authored historical novels in Hungarian, Spanish, and English. She also wrote biographies in Hungarian of composers Vincenzo Bellini, Gaetano Donizetti, Gioacchino Rossini, and Robert and Clara Schumann. Mrs. Dohnányi's published books on her husband include *From Death to Life* (Tallahassee: Rose Printing Co., 1960), in which she chronicled her struggle to come to terms with her husband's death, and *Message to Posterity from Ernst von Dohnányi* (Jacksonville: H. and W. B. Drew, 1960), which she described as a collection of Dohnányi's meditations.

The subtitle "A Song of Life" is derived from the translation of the title of Dohnányi's symphonic cantata *Cantus vitae*, op. 38. In addition to being his largest-scale composition, *Cantus vitae* was the work that Dohnányi felt best reflected his own philosophies. Although Mrs. Dohnányi gave the title *Cantus vitae* to a German version of this biography and entitled the English version simply "The Life of Ernst von Dohnányi," there is no better way to characterize Dohnányi's life than by invoking his most personal work. Furthermore, this biography is indeed a "Song of Life." The book can be divided roughly in half: the first half, which comprises Dohnányi's life through 1937, is the story of a great Hungarian musician who brought international prominence to Hungarian music through his own unparalleled success as a virtuoso pianist, composer, conductor, and pedagogue; the second half, which Ilona von Dohnányi personally witnessed, is the tragic story of a man ruined by malicious allegations, condemned by his beloved homeland, and blacklisted by his own profession. In 1953, however, Dohnányi was rewarded for his persistent struggle with a triumphant "redebut" at Carnegie Hall at the age of seventy-six. Mrs. Dohnányi ended the biography with this victory, adding only a brief epilogue explaining that Dohnányi continued to perform, compose, conduct, and teach up to his death in 1960.

Mrs. Dohnányi compiled the contents of this biography from a series of interviews she conducted with her husband in Tallahassee, Florida, during the final years of his life. For the documentation of Dohnányi's professional activities Mrs. Dohnányi relied on a collection of twenty-six scrapbooks assembled by Dohnányi's family. These contain concert reviews and programs dating back to 1889, when Dohnányi was twelve years old. Because there was a ban on the export of newspapers, books, and music from Hungary, Dohnányi's sister Mitzi sent the material through the Iron Curtain page by page in letters. Twenty of these scrapbooks are in the Ernst von Dohnányi Collection in the Warren D. Allen Music Library at Florida State University in Tallahassee, and the rest are in the British Library, London.

Both the copy on which this edition is based and an earlier draft of the biography are located in Florida State University's Dohnányi Collection. The cover page bears the inscription "Read in entirety and witnessed by me / 23rd August 1960" in Mrs. Dohnányi's handwriting. The Ernst von Dohnányi Collection also includes two unpublished German translations of the biography, on permanent loan from Dr. Seán McGlynn, Dohnányi's grandson. Throughout the present edition, every effort has been taken to preserve Mrs. Dohnányi's intentions, while clarifying the presentation. Much of the material that Mrs. Dohnányi originally recorded in a rather lengthy endnotes section has been added into the text, and selected letters, lectures, and newspaper articles have been included in this edition as Appendices A, B, and C, respectively. I have also added a chronological works list as Appendix D.

Throughout the preparation of this edition, I have made every effort to ensure that this biography presents an accurate chronicle of Dohnányi's life and musical thought. I have verified much of the information about Dohnányi's concerts and other professional activities by personally examining the sources that Mrs. Dohnányi used, most notably the reviews and programs in the twenty-six scrapbooks. In the cases of the numerous anecdotes about Dohnányi's personal encounters that cannot be substantiated, I have relied on interviews with those who knew Dohnányi, especially his stepdaughter Helen Dohnányi McGlynn and his protégé Edward Kilenyi, Jr., for corroboration.

I would like to express my gratitude to those who helped me prepare this edition. I will always be indebted to the faculty and staff at the Florida State University School of Music, especially Professor Douglass Seaton, who have given me a considerable amount of support and encouragement. I would also like to thank Head Music Librarian Dan Clark and his staff at the Warren D. Allen Music Library for their willingness repeatedly to grant me access to the materials in the Dohnányi Collection. Finally, I would like to thank Dohnányi's family, especially Helen Dohnányi McGlynn and her son Seán, for their warm encouragement throughout this project.

James A. Grymes

INTRODUCTION

This biography of my husband was a labor of love. In the event of accusations that I see my husband through rose-colored glasses, I make no denial; of course I do. Through those spectacles, however, I have made an honest and earnest effort to view his life in an impartial manner. It is probably inevitable that I have not been able to accomplish this, but in no place have I falsified an incident, person, or thing in order to make a better story. There is a literary obligation to one's readers to leave history unchanged, but when the subject is so close to one's own life and heart, the obligation transcends literary honesty and becomes a moral obligation. Of this, I make a serious claim: everything I have written is true and can be documented.

I hope that this biography of Ernst von Dohnányi will serve as a reference book for any student of music who is interested in him, his career, the musical life of his time, and those great musicians of the past whom he met and with whom he maintained friendships. But, in truth, it is not intended as such. It is, as I have said, a labor of love, dedicated to my ever beloved, unforgettable husband.

When I wrote this biography, Dohnányi was still alive. I learned the facts from him, and he himself approved most of the chapters. The first part of this book is based on dates, letters, and information given to me by Dohnányi himself. This made my work somewhat difficult, because Dohnányi did not like to talk about himself. Nevertheless, he insisted that I write everything down without adding any fiction or coloring it in any way. I drew the information from the second half of this biography from my personal experiences; I witnessed most of the events myself.

Ilona von Dohnányi

ERNST VON DOHNÁNYI

PROLOGUE

1877–1894

Ernst von Dohnányi was born on 27 July 1877 in Pozsony, Hungary.[1] To understand Dohnányi and his music, it is necessary to know something about his homeland, its history, and its attitude toward life.

Because Hungary has always been a small nation located near large powers, she has always had to protect herself from being conquered. From 896 through the thirteenth century, Hungary was ruled by the descendants of Árpád, who had led the Magyars from the Ural Mountains to take over the legacy of Attila the Hun. Hungary was invaded in the thirteenth century by the Tartars, who destroyed two-thirds of the country. In the sixteenth century, after a vain attempt to defend not only her own land but also all of Europe, Hungary became enslaved by the Turks. The united armies of Christendom reconquered Buda in 1686, on the same site where the royal palace of Budapest later stood.

After the Turks had been driven out, Hungary became united with Austria under the Austrian ruler Ferdinand II. The Austro-Hungarian alliance was advantageous in many ways to both countries. While Hungary was primarily an agricultural country, mountainous Austria was an industrial one. The Austrian monarchs, however, incessantly tried to incorporate Hungary into their Empire. This led to a long series of Hungarian insurrections; the fiery, freedom-loving Magyars refused to endure oppression. In 1848 Hungary fought a war of independence against King and Emperor Francis Joseph that she would have won had he not received military aid from the Russian Czar. Francis Joseph then took bloody revenge on his subjects, bringing Hungary to the brink of destruction. It was not until 1867 that he realized that it was wiser to make peace with his people. A peaceful period followed in which the arts, especially music, flourished in Hungary.

---

1. Dohnányi is sometimes referred to by the Hungarian form of his name, Dohnányi Ernő. Although he was baptized Dohnányi Ernő Jenő Frigyes, he called himself Ernst von Dohnányi whenever he was not in Hungary. Pozsony was also known by its German name, Pressburg, and is now Bratislava, the capital of Slovakia.

Pozsony was once the coronation town of Hungary, and the fire-scarred remains of the royal palace dominated the city. The ornate palace of the Archbishop, the Clarissa Convent, and other ancient buildings also stood as reminders of the Middle Ages. The ruins and buildings made the past an integral part of life in this city. In 1877 Pozsony's population consisted of about 48,000 Hungarians and Germans who proudly declared themselves Hungarians. The German citizens were proud of the important role that their city had played in Hungarian history and solemnly called Pozsony the *alte Königstadt* (old royal city). Although the names of the streets were written in Hungarian as well as in German and the theater performed its shows for half a season in each language, the official language was still Hungarian.

The Dohnányi family made significant contributions to their country throughout her history. During the years of Austria's attempts to incorporate Hungary into the Austrian Empire, the Dohnányis generously shared their property with the poor and helped alleviate the suffering of the starving people. The Dohnányi family was rewarded with a title of nobility in 1697, eleven years after the reoccupation of the Buda fortress. Their mercy and compassion are symbolized in the seal that accompanied the title. In the lower center of the seal stands a golden pelican feeding its children with the blood flowing from its breast, which it had cut open with its own beak. Over the entire picture an outstretched, masculine arm holds three arrows in a firm grip.

Ernst von Dohnányi was born at 12 Clarissa Street, where he spent his entire childhood. It was an old, three-story house built around a square courtyard. The house was entered through a heavy, arched gateway that seemed to belong to an ancient fortress. Across the street from the Dohnányi house stood the large, old building that had been the Clarissa Convent. In 1297 the Clarissa sisters came to Hungary at the invitation of the Hungarian king and occupied the building that had previously been the convent of the Cistercian nuns. In the eighteenth century, after the nuns had all died, Emperor Joseph II dissolved the order and turned the building into the Királyi Katolikus Főgimnázium (Royal Catholic Chief Gymnasium).[2] Dohnányi's father, Frederick von Dohnányi, was Professor of Mathematics and Physics in this Gymnasium.

Professor Dohnányi was "a strong, tall man, with a short, blond beard and grayish curly hair. Kindliness and amiability were expressed in his smiling eyes behind gold-framed glasses."[3] Although he possessed a strong pas-

---

2. In Europe, a "Gymnasium" is an institute with a somewhat more thorough and higher instruction than a high school, comparable to an American junior college.

3. This description of Frederick von Dohnányi is taken from Emil Kumlik, *Dohnányi Frigyes 1843–1909: Egy magyar gyrosíró élete és munkássága* [Frederick von Dohnányi 1843–1909: The Life

sion for music, he had become a teacher in order to support his widowed mother and his younger brothers. He had made this sacrifice without the slightest bitterness and applied himself wholeheartedly to his duties. He was fully aware that unless an artist could rise to the level of an Anton Rubinstein or a Franz Liszt, he would be unappreciated and could never become financially secure. The few hours that Professor Dohnányi could devote to music, however, made him very happy, and he had the gift of being able to maintain a fine technique with very little practicing. Because he was such a splendid cellist, he was often asked to play at charity concerts. He performed on separate occasions with Rubinstein and Liszt, and he was very proud of both of these events.

Professor Dohnányi was amazingly versatile. In addition to being a musician, he was a painter, a joiner, a turner, an electrician, and a glassblower. He had single-handedly manufactured all of the instruments, including the screws and nails, used in the physics laboratory of the Gymnasium. He also devised a new system of stenography. According to Emil Kumlik, who was one of Professor Dohnányi's pupils,

> He was a good professor because he was born a good man, and he did not lose this kindheartedness in the struggles of his hard and difficult life. His sense of humor also contributed to the winning traits of his character. He accomplished the requirements of three different professions: as a physicist he occupied himself with the eternal rules governing and uniting the universe; as a musician he paid homage to the cultivation of the universal beauty of art; and as a stenographer he was interested in the creation of an international system of stenography that could be readily learned and used by anybody.[4]

Professor Dohnányi was a congenial man who enjoyed spending time with his friends. In Pozsony it was a local custom that before dinner men would visit a certain beer garden to drink beer and talk about the happenings of the day. Professor Dohnányi would frequently take advantage of these opportunities to brag about his young son, who would sit for hours in a big armchair and listen with the gravest attention whenever his father played chamber music with his friends.

One day, just before a benefit concert in which he was to perform a Gavotte by Bach, Professor Dohnányi brought out his cello to practice. The three-year-old Ernst sat at his usual place in the big armchair. Suddenly he slipped to the floor, approached his father, and begged him to play the piece again and again. Professor Dohnányi was in a playful mood and granted the

---

and Work of a Hungarian Stenographer] (Budapest: Gyorsírási ügyek magyar királyi kormánybiztossága, 1937), p. 1.
    4. Ibid.

requests. For fun he placed the bow in the little boy's hand, and Ernst drew it up and down according to the rhythm of the melody while his father fingered the appropriate strings. This was the first sign of Ernst's interest in learning to play a musical instrument. Although Professor Dohnányi recognized his son's talent and foresaw the realization of the musical dreams that he himself had had not been able to fulfill, he refused to give him lessons out of fear that Ernst would become a child prodigy. Ernst's early musical education consisted only of enjoying music.

Dohnányi's mother, born Ottilia Szlabey, was an exceptional woman. Although she weighed hardly seventy-five pounds, her seemingly frail body harbored such an iron will and inflexible determination that she could control all her emotions, her words, and perhaps even her thoughts and feelings. She was one of the anonymous heroines of daily life who keeps vigil over the happiness, comfort, and purity of her household. She always suppressed her own interests and moods, instead acting for the well-being of the family. Her children saw her weep only once, when her own mother died. Even then she quickly wiped her tears as though she were ashamed of such a weakness. She never sat in a comfortable armchair, even in her old age; she preferred a hard seat without a back because she was unwilling to spoil herself with comfort.

Throughout his life Dohnányi was grateful to his mother for teaching him that words are often damaging and harmful; people are usually hurt more by words than by deeds. Mrs. Dohnányi also taught him about the Bible and Roman Catholicism, even though she was a Lutheran. From her, Dohnányi learned a kind of practical Christianity. He used to say,

> If people realized that the doctrines and ideals of Christ should be followed not only for their religious value, but chiefly because they are so practical, everybody in the world would live by those laws and tenets. They would realize how much easier and more pleasant it is to love than to hate, and what a waste of time it is to try to take revenge for our injuries upon others. Hatred consumes the person who is suffering of it. One feels much better if, instead of hating one's enemy, one wishes him well. I act as I do chiefly from selfishness, because this is the only way to be happy and well-balanced.

Dohnányi's paternal grandmother helped to make the home pleasant. She was a typical grandmother who kept herself busy all day in the house, sewing, mending, or knitting stockings for the children. She always felt cold and wrapped herself in heavy shawls. Whenever the children would run around the table, she would reproach them in her preferred language of German, "Kinder, macht's kein Zug!" (Children, don't make a draft!). Although the kitchen was run by Dohnányi's mother, his grandmother would enter the kitchen to prepare the *fánk*, a round pastry filled with marmalade. Dohnányi always swore that he never in his life ate such fine *fánk* as the one made by his grandmother. She was famous for making this cake and took the preparation of *fánk* very seriously. Whenever she was preparing *fánk* for dinner, she alone occupied the kitchen for hours. If someone happened to open the door, she would protest severely, because the cake might "catch cold." She jealously guarded the secret of her creation; no one in the family except Dohnányi's mother ever learned her recipe.

Dohnányi shared much of his childhood with his sister Mária, nicknamed Mitzi, who was a year and a half younger. Although they were brought up under strict discipline, they shared a playroom where they were allowed to play without restrictions. Mitzi was always a faithful companion for her brother, and her admiration for him increased with the years. In return, young Dohnányi always tried to play along with his sister, often agreeing to play with her dolls. They gave each doll a name and decided that some of them were obedient, while others were naughty. When the dolls were naughty, they were scolded. When the dolls behaved, however, they were rewarded. When the dolls became sick, Ernst and Mitzi turned into doctor and nurse to cure them. Once, the children decided to arrange an exhibit of pictures for the dolls. They had heard much about such exhibits and had even visited one. They took great care in the preparation of the paintings that were to be the focus of this great artistic event. When the pictures were ready, Ernst and Mitzi examined them critically, in order to choose the masterpiece that should win first prize. Suddenly, as though inspired, they dropped big patches of paint on a scrap of paper and smeared the various colors with candle wax. This picture, they decided, would win the first prize, and they hung it in a place of honor. One of young Dohnányi's favorite games was playing train. The two children would push chairs together and pretend that this was the train. Sometimes they would play with the simple railroad toys of that time. Even decades later, when Dohnányi would look into a shop window and see skillfully manufactured railroad toys, he would stop and say with admiration, "Today's children don't know what it means to possess such wonderful toys! I wish my sister and I had been able to play with them!"

The Dohnányi family spent their summer vacations in Breznóbánya, a small town in Upper Hungary, at the house of Dohnányi's maternal grandmother. Breznóbánya was an independent, royal city that had previously been a mining town. By the end of the nineteenth century, however, men sought gold in the mountains unsuccessfully. The town was nestled high among these mountains, surrounded by forests, and the air was fresh and cool. Dohnányi thoroughly enjoyed the beauties of nature that surrounded him. He would often travel by coach with his friends to the practice range, where the men of the town came to shoot at targets while their wives chatted and gossiped, leaving the children to play.

It was here in Breznóbánya that Professor Dohnányi, for his own amusement, began to teach his six-year-old son to play the piano. Although Professor Dohnányi was not an accomplished pianist, he was an excellent pedagogue. Throughout these lessons, young Dohnányi learned happily, as if he were playing a game. A year later his father also taught him to play the violin, but the boy was not as interested in this instrument. Nevertheless, he later became proficient enough to play second violin or the viola in orchestral and chamber ensembles.

When Dohnányi was seven years old, he asked for manuscript paper for Christmas and started to compose his first creations. A short *Gebet* (Prayer) was followed by six short pieces for violin and piano.[5] When he played them with his father, his heart throbbed with joy at the sound of his own music. Later, several piano works followed, including sonatas and pieces with characteristic titles such as "Bagatelle," "Etude," "Fantasiestück" "Impromptu," "Mazurka," "Novelette," "Pastorale," "Romance," "Scherzo," "Scherzino," "Scherzando," "Tarantella," and "Waltz." Dohnányi's talent manifested itself almost daily. Left to his own amusements, he read music as other children read books. In this way, at a time when most children are still concerned with fairy tales, he became acquainted with the works of Haydn, Mozart, Beethoven, Schumann, and other great composers.

Through his interest in various works, Dohnányi developed a marvelous ability of sight-reading and could play almost any piece the first time he saw it. This ability, however, once led to an unfortunate experience when István Thomán, the Professor of Piano at the Országos Magyar Királyi Zeneakadémia (National Hungarian Royal Academy of Music) in Budapest, had a concert in Pozsony and visited the Dohnányi family. Although the Dohnányis never made a spectacle of their son for visitors, Thomán had heard of the talented boy and naturally asked him to play. Dohnányi did not feel embarrassed and took his seat with perfect ease; he already possessed the poise that would accompany him throughout his life. He never experienced stage fright, perhaps because he never modeled his life after the opinion of others, but after his own principles. Although he knew that an important person would be listening to him, he chose, as usual, to sight-read a piece. It was an Etude in B Major by Stephen Heller. At one point in the piece, Dohnányi played an incorrect note. When Thomán called his attention to the mistake, Dohnányi became very embarrassed. His unhappiness increased when Thomán himself sat at the piano to perform. During a brilliant passage Professor Dohnányi reproachfully remarked to his son,

---

5. Other pieces written around the same time include an "Adagio" and seven untitled pieces for violin and piano as well as a sonata for cello and piano. See Appendix D for a complete list of Dohnányi's compositions.

"Do you hear the scales?" Dohnányi broke into sobs and wept so bitterly that they could hardly console him.

Professor Dohnányi eventually realized that he was no longer able to teach his son; the pupil had surpassed his instructor. When Dohnányi was eight years old, he was entrusted to the care of Károly Forstner, the organist of the Pozsony Cathedral. Forstner was affectionately called "Uncle" by Ernst and his sister Mitzi, who both took great pleasure in studying with him. Uncle Forstner had a sweet, well-balanced disposition and was endlessly patient with his pupils. He did not overburden them with finger exercises and long explanations of how they should hold their hands. He instead let them play as they wished and allowed them to develop at their own pace. Dohnányi, who was not at all interested in his school studies, eagerly looked forward to each piano lesson.

For a time Dohnányi's mother taught his elementary school studies at home. He learned to read and write at almost the same time as he started his piano lessons. When Dohnányi reached his eighth year, however, his mother found herself unable to continue his education, and Dohnányi was sent to a private school attended by a dozen children. The school had a young teacher whose method proved to be so successful that, after a year's work, Dohnányi passed an examination and entered the Gymnasium where his father was teaching. Before entering a Gymnasium, the students were supposed to have completed four years of elementary school studies.

Because Professor Dohnányi was teaching in the same school, Dohnányi went with him every morning. They usually left at the last moment, and Dohnányi would end up swallowing his breakfast while crossing the street, after they heard the ringing of the school bell. Although Dohnányi tried to apply himself to his studies, he was often less than diligent. Nevertheless, he was a good student; Professor Dohnányi kept a strict vigil over his schoolwork and kept himself informed, through his colleagues, of his son's progress. Professor Dohnányi had also instructed his wife to watch their son do his homework, and Dohnányi had to sit at his writing table in his room and pretend to study. When he heard the door open and his mother approach, he quickly bent over his books and murmured something as though he was studying. After his mother would leave, Dohnányi would return to scribbling his compositions on the staff paper that he kept underneath his books.

Every year the students of the Gymnasium arranged a celebration in honor of their Director, Emerich Pirchala, on 3 November, which was the evening preceding Pirchala's name day.[6] The programs organized by the

---

6. Instead of birthdays, European Catholics often celebrate their "name day" on the birthday of the saint from whom they took their name.

Gymnasium students consisted of songs, music, poems, and speeches. Although these performances were not open to the public, they were given a great deal of publicity. In 1886, when Dohnányi was barely nine, he himself contributed to such a celebration, playing the piano part of the Mozart G Minor Piano Quartet. This was Dohnányi's first public performance. Many years later, his sister Mitzi still recalled the occasion. Although he was slim, frail-looking, and somewhat pale, his playing was strong and vigorous. He appeared in short trousers and white stockings, with smooth blond hair and sparkling blue eyes. His performance was received with applause, and the other three members of the quartet, who were all older boys, lifted him high so that the audience might see him better. It was then, perhaps, that Dohnányi became convinced of his calling, for which God had given him this talent.

When Dohnányi was twelve, he agreed to perform a Quintet by Schumann with a string quartet from Pozsony in which Professor Dohnányi was to play the cello. Before this concert, which took place on 12 December 1889, Dohnányi contracted a severe case of influenza. He had such a high fever that he lay almost motionless in his bed. When Dohnányi realized that his parents had decided to cancel the performance, he became uncharacteristically excited and insisted that he would play. Dr. Kováts, the family doctor, decided that it was better to let him play than to let him become upset. When Dohnányi mounted the stage he seemed to immediately recover from his fever. The audience was enchanted, and repeatedly broke out into applause, hailing the young artist.[7]

Dohnányi gave his first solo performance on 28 December 1890 in the great hall of the Town Hall as part of a concert of the Pozsonyi dalegylet (Pozsony Song Society). He performed Chopin's Nocturne op. 31, no. 1, Mendelssohn's Scherzo in B Minor, the fourth and sixth of his own *6 Fantasiestücke* (6 Fantasy Pieces) for piano, and Liszt's Eighth Hungarian Rhapsody. Dohnányi played another one of his own works, *Scherzo,* as an encore.[8]

By his sixth year at the Gymnasium, Dohnányi had also begun to establish a reputation as a composer. For the 1891 celebration of Pirchala's name day, Dohnányi presented *Üdvözlő dal* (Song of Welcome), which was premiered by the school chorus and orchestra, conducted by Professor Dohnányi.[9] In the same year, Dohnányi wrote the background music for a

7. An article appeared in the *Grenzbote,* a German newspaper in Pozsony, on 13 December 1889; see Appendix C.

8. The *Pressburger Zeitung* published a review of this performance on 29 December 1890; see Appendix C.

9. This song, written for chorus, string orchestra, piano, and harmonium, was based on a text by Dohnányi's fellow student Marcell Jankovich, who later became a famous writer.

play performed by the girls attending Mitzi's school. He would dance with the girls during their lessons, flirting with them. Dohnányi also composed a Mass to commemorate the end of the school year. This Mass in C Major, which was written for alto and tenor soloists, chorus, string orchestra, and organ, was premiered on 8 June 1892 with Dohnányi at the organ and his father conducting. The Mass was performed throughout Pozsony, including performances on 19 June in the Blumenthal Church and 28 June in the Jesuit Church. The Gymnasium performed the Mass again on 29 June and 4 September 1892 and continued to perform the work even after Dohnányi's departure from Pozsony.[10]

By 1892 Forstner began to supplement Dohnányi's piano instruction with lessons in harmony. Forstner subscribed to the method of Karol Meyerberger, who had been a music theory teacher in Pozsony.[11] This method was so full of minute details that Dohnányi quickly became bored with the lessons; he had already learned the rules of harmony by studying the works of the masters.

Forstner also gave Dohnányi lessons on the Cathedral organ. Dohnányi gave several organ recitals in which he would play works by Bach, Mendelssohn, and Liszt, as well as his own compositions. Emil Kumlik was present at Dohnányi's first organ recital and described it in his book about Frederick von Dohnányi:

> I cannot distinctly recall in which year it took place, but I assume from certain signs that it was 1887 or 1888 when my teacher invited me to *the first organ recital of his son Ernst.* It took place in the Clarissa Church, which belonged to the Gymnasium, at ten or eleven o'clock in the morning. I clearly recall little Ernst, who wore short trousers and a dark blue blouse with a white sailor collar. He was a handsome, serene, somewhat pale, but healthy-looking boy.
>
> Many famous professional musicians were present, among them Károly *Forstner,* who was Ernst's first music teacher, and Charles Wiedermann. I noticed other professors in the choir and nave of the church.
>
> The boy's performance was an extraordinary success. If the audience had been allowed to applaud in the church, their enthusiasm would have been overwhelming. Everyone hurried to congratulate the father. Professor Dohnányi, however, was busy whispering into the ear of his son, who had just come through the nave of the church. Although it must have been some serious

10. Other religious works from that time include *Pater noster* for mixed choir, *O salutoris et Ave verum* and *Veni sancte spiritus* for men's choir, *Kyrie* for choir and orchestra, *Der 6. Psalm* (Psalm No. 6) for double choir, and *Ave Maria* for tenor and bass, solo violin, and string orchestra.

11. Meyerberger (1828–81) had once been a pupil of the famous Viennese composer and pedagogue Simon Sechter (1788–1867). Meyerberger had taught Professor Dohnányi as well as most of the music teachers in Pozsony.

criticism about his playing, one could note that the Professor felt a great joy and pride in the artistic achievement of his son. Forstner showed his great approval with a radiant smile.

What the little artist played, I cannot remember anymore. I was then a twenty-year-old journalist, much occupied with affairs of my own. . . .

"Well," the father asked me suddenly, "what is your opinion of his playing?" Ernst was by then animatedly chatting with other musicians.

"Unfortunately, I am no expert in music," I answered in embarrassment, with a modesty unusual for a young journalist. "But I do admire the *muscular power* with which your child plays."

"He does possess muscular power," the father said somewhat louder and very seriously, so that everybody standing around could hear his words. "But he also possesses something *else,* which doesn't dwell in the muscles, but *here!*" and he pointed to his heart. "If he continues, he will get far. But now, with *Forstner* we have to make sure that he *does not turn into a child prodigy.*"[12]

Dohnányi also had many opportunities during the summers to play the organ in Breznóbánya.[13] This organ had been purchased by the wealthy citizens for the Evangelical Church. It was a splendid instrument, with three manuals and sixty registers. In fact, it was much too big for the church; whenever the full organ resounded, the walls would begin to tremble and the windows to reverberate.

When he was in Pozsony, Dohnányi spent his Sundays playing the organ in the Cathedral, where he also played the violin and sang in the chorus. When Uncle Forstner was playing, Dohnányi would sit next to the organ and work the registers for him. In addition to his duties at the Cathedral, Dohnányi played the organ for the Gymnasium's Sunday Mass. He did not enjoy these performances as much as he did the ones in the Cathedral because the organ in the Gymnasium was an ancient, shabby instrument from the time of the Clarissa Sisters; it was probably as old as the convent itself. The pedal was worn, the "white keys" were black, and the "black keys" were yellow. It had eight registers and an atrocious hurdy-gurdy. It also moaned, groaned, and squeaked when it was played. There was, however, a small salary that was paid to the Gymnasium organists. Dohnányi earned five florint and four krajcárs for his yearly playing. This was the first money he obtained through music.

It is a strange coincidence that the boys who preceded and succeeded Dohnányi as the organist in the Pozsony Cathedral also became famous musicians. Franz Schmidt, who was two years older than Dohnányi, con-

---

12. Kumlik, pp. 79–80. Emphases in the original.
13. It was in Breznóbánya that Dohnányi composed his *Fantasie* (Fantasy) for Organ in C Major, which is his only solo work for the organ. He dedicated this work to Franz Reger, the organist at the Evangelical Church of Breznóbánya.

tinued his studies in the Hochschule für Musik (Academy of Music) in Vienna, of which he later became Director, and became one of the most prominent Viennese composers of his time. The other boy was Béla Bartók, who was four years younger than Dohnányi. Bartók was a frail-looking child; he was already suffering with the lung disease that would later cause him so much trouble. He was, however, also very talented. Despite the difference in their age, Dohnányi took much interest in his young colleague, and the two became close friends.

❧

Dohnányi's early musical training was augmented by the highly artistic and cultural environment of Pozsony. Beethoven's *Missa Solemnis,* which had been performed in the town during Beethoven's lifetime, was performed every year on St. Cecilia's Day. On every Good Friday Haydn's oratorio *Die sieben letzten Worte unseres Erlösers am Kreuze* (The Seven Last Words of Christ on the Cross) was performed. Pozsony had its own orchestra, which performed in the great hall of the Town Hall. Dohnányi took part in this ensemble as a second violinist. Although the programs usually contained works of composers from the eighteenth and early nineteenth centuries, the orchestra also performed modern works. For a concert that included Bruckner's Seventh Symphony, the composer himself came from Vienna to attend the performance. Dohnányi was fascinated by the clumsy figure of Bruckner, who drew an enormous red handkerchief from his coat pocket to dry his tears of emotion as he mounted the stage to receive the applause. Pozsony's opera company consisted of young actors and singers, many of whom later became well known in Europe. They performed operas by Meyerbeer, Verdi, Wagner, and Gounod. They also performed *Lászlo Hunyadi* by the Hungarian composer Ferenc Erkel and Beethoven's *Fidelio.* There was also a monument to Johann Nepomuk Hummel, who was born in Pozsony and was among the town's most famous sons.[14]

Most of the great musicians who gave recitals in Vienna also visited Pozsony, and Dohnányi attended many of their concerts with his parents. Solo performances took place in the Town Hall's beautiful Baroque hall before a very select audience. Even after Dohnányi had become a famous artist, he felt a strange embarrassment and emotion whenever he walked out onto that stage. "Each time," he explained, "I remembered those concerts, which I had heard in my childhood by those great, wonderful artists."

14. Throughout his life, one of Dohnányi's most prized possessions was his 1828 edition of Hummel's *Ausführliche theoretisch-practische Anweisung zum Piano-forte-spiel.*

One performance that left an especially deep impression on Dohnányi was given by Anton Rubinstein. Many years later Dohnányi said,

> I can still vividly recall a Rubinstein recital that I attended when I was seven years old. It is not the program that I can remember—I can recall only Mozart's Rondo *alla turca*—and it was not the playing of Rubinstein that made an unforgettable impression on me; it was the presence of Franz Liszt. From early childhood I had heard so much about Liszt that just his name had a magical effect. And this time I could see him! The concert was in the great hall of the Town Hall. From the back of the hall, I could see Franz Liszt standing to the left of the stage, next to the wall and under the candelabra. His tall figure and his sharp profile were distinctly visible to the audience. I can no longer remember whether he stood there through the entire concert or only during a part of it, but the whole picture is still clear in my mind.

Another recital that had a profound impact on Dohnányi was given by Eugène d'Albert. It may have been the memory of this superb performance that persuaded Dohnányi to turn to d'Albert only a few years later for his final lessons before launching his own career as a touring virtuoso. Dohnányi also heard Alfred Reisenauer and the violinists Joachim Wilhelm, František Ondříček, and Ede Reményi. Reményi, an immensely popular Hungarian violinist, had fled his motherland in 1849 when the Hungarian war for liberty had been lost to the united Austrian and Russian armies. He had immigrated to America, and nobody in Hungary heard from him for twenty years. When Reményi suddenly reemerged, he was received with great enthusiasm. He appeared in Pozsony, where he played the famous folk song "Fly, my swallow." Throughout this tour his playing touched many people's hearts. This was, however, Reményi's last tour in his homeland. He returned to the United States, and in San Francisco, with his violin in his hand, he collapsed dead upon the stage.

Among Dohnányi's favorite memories were those of concerts by famous singers such as Alice Barbi and Rosa Papier. Dohnányi was able to attend many of these events because a standing place cost only thirty-two kreutzers.[15] He would arrive early enough to occupy a place in the first row. By leaning upon the iron bar, he was able to enjoy the shows in a comfortable stance. Dohnányi was also greatly impressed by a performance of the court orchestra of Meiningen, conducted by Hans von Bülow. Dohnányi was especially pleased with the orchestra's response to the conductor. This, no doubt, was the beginning of his aspirations toward conducting symphony orchestras.

---

15. A kreutzer is a small copper coin formerly in use in Austria. It received its name from the cross (*Kreuz*) stamped on it.

❧

Dohnányi and his father sometimes spent a few summer weeks at the house of Karl Haulik, an elderly bachelor and a passionate amateur musician. Mr. Haulik's estate, which was in Herestyén, Upper Hungary, was a spacious, old country house. It had twelve big, somewhat gloomy rooms, many of which were hardly used. Whenever the Dohnányis came to visit, they would devote entire days to tours, hunting, or chamber music. They were often invited by Mr. Haulik's neighbors to parties that usually included musical entertainment.

Among these neighbors were the Szirányis, also wealthy estate owners, who threw parties for their neighboring friends every Sunday. Mr. Szirányi's sister, "Aunt Caroline," was one of those aristocratic Hungarian spinsters who preferred to speak the "elegant" French. She loved music, and when musical guests performed chamber music, she would nod with delight at every movement, "Charmant! Très charmant!" (Charming! Very charming!). Aunt Caroline frequently participated in the performances, playing the harmonium, while Dohnányi performed at the piano and Professor Dohnányi played the cello. They were often joined by the Szirányi's charming young cousin from Vienna named Miczi von Szirányi, who sang very nicely. This unusual quartet thrilled Dohnányi, who was enchanted not as much by the music as by the young Viennese woman. He accompanied her with awe when she sang Lieder by Schubert, Schumann, and Brahms. One day he composed a song for her, which was performed at the Szirányis.[16]

During one visit at Mr. Haulik's, Dohnányi met a Viennese painter named Ernst Stohr, who painted a pastel portrait of Dohnányi. When he heard the Piano Quartet that Dohnányi had composed when he was fourteen years old, Stohr exclaimed, "This work has to be performed in Vienna!" and took the manuscript with him when he departed for the imperial capital. Stohr arranged for Dohnányi's Piano Quartet in F-sharp Minor to be performed in Vienna on 11 March 1894 at a concert of the Ersten Wiener Volks Quartet (First Viennese People's Quartet), with the sixteen-year-old composer at the piano. Childhood seemed to be ending for Ernst von Dohnányi; the performance in Vienna was the first step of his career.

16. Dohnányi dedicated a *Lied* (Song) for alto accompanied by cello, harmonium, and piano to Miczi von Szirányi, who wrote the text. Other songs composed around this time include "Die verlassene Fischersbraut" (The Fisherman's Abandoned Bride) for alto and piano; "Zwei Liedchen" (Two Little Songs) for alto and piano; and "Das verlassene Mägdlein" (The Abandoned Maidservant), which he dedicated to Irma von Spányi, for alto and piano.

ONE

1894–1897

The year was 1894. A train advanced, puffing and fuming, toward Budapest. It contained no comfortable Pullman cars and no luxurious dining cars. Those who could not afford comfortable coaches had to travel on these slow passenger trains, which stopped at every obscure village while the travelers patiently awaited their destinations.

In a corner, at a window, sat the seventeen-year-old Ernst von Dohnányi. He was a fair-haired youth of medium height, and his figure was well proportioned: slim with broad shoulders. His complexion was light, and his features were well formed, almost delicate. His blue eyes had a frank and cheerful expression; when his lips smiled, his eyes smiled too. Those lips, however, showed determination. It is no wonder that many girls approached him with admiration and devotion. In return, he was interested in them; he was interested in everything that was beautiful. Someone once asked Dohnányi if he had been in love when he wrote one of his early compositions. He answered with his customary smile, "I was, and I always am, in love." With these words he did not mean an attraction for women only. He meant his love for art, nature, beauty, and all of humanity.

While looking out the window and observing the beauties of autumn—forests covered with gold and red leaves, fields of ripening grapes, and flowers in cottage gardens—a faraway look came into Dohnányi's eyes. He enjoyed nature, every bit of it, but at the same time his mind wandered to music. He was creating melodies; tunes were awakening in his soul. Most of his compositions did not come to life at the writing table, but sprang from his mind and heart while he was walking in the streets, listening half-attentively to the chatting of noisy company, or even sitting in a train, as he was now, apparently lost in observing the view. "I am never bored," he used to say. "I have my thoughts to keep me company." Melodies and ideas developed in his mind, and he wrote them down only when they took a definite shape. Perhaps that was why he was usually silent even in the midst of a crowd. "Schumann was even less talkative," he would say when people reproached him for his silence. "He expressed himself through music."

The train arrived in Budapest, and the boy was greeted by his uncle, Ernő Szlabey.[1] Although Dohnányi had been in the capital several times as a child, he was still fascinated by the vibrations and traffic of this constantly growing city. The thought of staying here and studying at the National Hungarian Royal Academy of Music was an exciting one. Dohnányi's uncle accompanied him to the room that had been rented for him on Hunyadi Square, one block from the music school. The place was simple, and the furniture was shabby, tasteless, and dull; his family could not afford a luxurious apartment. After his cozy home in Pozsony, Dohnányi felt disappointed. Then he resigned himself to it, just as later on in his life he would adapt himself to many painful situations without complaint. His philosophy was: "If I can alter a situation, I will. If I cannot, I must accept it and not grieve over it."

Dohnányi's first task was to enroll in the University to study the Hungarian and German languages as well as literature. This was not Dohnányi's desire; his only interest was in music. Nevertheless, he obeyed the wishes of his father, who wanted him to earn a diploma in a more secure profession. Six months later, however, Professor Dohnányi would realize the full extent of his son's talent and permit him to drop his academic studies. The process of matriculation consumed a great deal of Dohnányi's time. In addition, he met old friends from Pozsony, including a young man named Julius Zachár, who was only one year older than Dohnányi and had been his playmate during the summers in Breznóbánya. Zachár was already a student at the University, studying law.[2] He tried to persuade Dohnányi to join a fraternity to which he belonged.

It was several days before Dohnányi presented himself at the Academy of Music. Because of this negligence, he was not informed of the date of the piano examination for admission, and he consequently missed it. Professor Thomán, who had heard Dohnányi play in Pozsony and had been excited at the prospects of having such a talented performer as one of his students, sent a telegram to Pozsony inquiring why Dohnányi had not yet reported to his class. Professor Dohnányi dispatched a telegram to his son urging him to register at the Academy of Music immediately.

On 9 September 1894 Dohnányi shyly entered the office of the Director, Edmund von Michalovich, an elderly bachelor who had been a friend of Franz Liszt. Because of his musical talent as a composer, as well as his aristocratic lineage, Michalovich was the designated leader of musical life in

---

1. Ernő Szlabey was the General Inspector of the Hungarian State Railways and Dohnányi's uncle on his mother's side.
2. Julius Zachár later became Dean of the Law School and a Supreme Court Justice for the Austro-Hungarian Empire.

Hungary. He was jokingly called the "Musical Pope," because the Academy of Music in Budapest was considered to be not just a conservatory, but also the headquarters of musical activities in Hungary.

When Dohnányi arrived, Michalovich was deep in discussion with one of the professors. Dohnányi stopped at the door and waited until he was noticed. He became embarrassed when the Director, who was angered by this interruption, rebuked him harshly, "Who are you, and what do you want?" When Dohnányi introduced himself, however, Michalovich's attitude changed. He smiled and suggested that since the other gentleman present was a member of the piano faculty, Dohnányi could take his piano examination right there on the Chickering piano that stood in the Director's office.[3] Michalovich and the professor listened with increasing astonishment. They exchanged glances and informed Dohnányi that he was accepted. He was notified of the date of the composition examination.

On a sunny autumn morning, Dohnányi reentered the Academy with his compositions under his arm. He seemed calm and composed, as usual, but he actually felt uneasy in this dignified building where Franz Liszt had spent part of his life. Dohnányi was relieved when he noticed another student coming toward him. The young man, a youth of short stature and a bent back, dashed up to him with excitement. Dohnányi, feeling somewhat shy, found it difficult to talk to the student, who overwhelmed him with questions. He wanted to know where Dohnányi had come from and what he wanted. Dohnányi answered as well as he could and then ventured a question of his own, asking about the requirements for admission. The young man gave him the information, adding, "And you will, of course, also have to play Rischbieter." Dohnányi became alarmed; he had never heard the name of such a composer. "What does it mean to play Rischbieter?" he wondered.[4]

The stranger kept his eyes fixed on the compositions under Dohnányi's arm. When he could not control himself any longer, without asking permission he grabbed at the music with trembling fingers. As he skipped through the pages, his eager excitement turned into sad resignation. When he returned the music, his face showed admiration. "You will not have to play Rischbieter," he said respectfully.

This young man was Peter König, born in Steiermark, where the famous pianist Emil Sauer had discovered him. On the advice of Sauer,

---

3. This piano had been presented to Franz Liszt by the Chickering firm.
4. Wilhelm Albert Rischbieter (1834–1910) taught harmony and composition at the Dresden Conservatory. He was the author of several compositional textbooks, including *Über Modulation, Quartsextakkord und Orgelpunkt* (1879), *Erläuterungen und Aufgaben zum Studium des Kontrapunkts* (1885), and *Die Gesetzmässigkeit der Harmonik* (1888).

König had come to study at the Budapest Academy. Although he was the pride of the composition class, the previous summer he had experienced premonitions that an unknown talent would appear unexpectedly in the music school and that this stranger would overshadow his own works. He later confessed to Dohnányi that on the morning they first met, he had again felt this peculiar sensation. That was why he had addressed Dohnányi so confidently and had taken the liberty of examining his music. Although he had only skimmed the pages, he was immediately convinced that this was the person who was to become his victorious rival. In spite of their unusual first meeting, König and Dohnányi became close friends.

The composition examination was unusually long. When the committee saw Dohnányi's compositions, they exchanged glances and asked him to play a few of them. Then they asked him to improvise; they obviously had doubts about the authorship of the works. Dohnányi, skilled in the art of improvisation, was able to comply, and the committee was overwhelmed. He was accepted into the "Third Academic Class," which meant that he would be able to finish his studies within two years.[5]

Dohnányi's piano teacher was István Thomán, and his teacher for composition was Janós Koessler. Koessler, who was an excellent theorist and composer, had connections with many famous musicians, including Johannes Brahms. Koessler was one of those to whom Dohnányi would feel a deep gratitude and appreciation throughout his life. He was a first-rate pedagogue who taught his pupils a valuable discipline: self-criticism.

Dohnányi became acquainted with many outstanding musicians during his studies at the Academy. Most of the famous European artists would make annual visits to Budapest. Among these were Eugène d'Albert and Emil Sauer, who openly competed with each other for laurels. Dohnányi was also able to observe several legendary conductors; the Budapesti Filharmóniai Társaság (Budapest Philharmonic Society) frequently hired guest conductors such as Hermann Levi, Felix Mottl, Karl Muck, Edouard Colonne, Leopold Auer, and Hans Richter. The director of the Royal Hungarian Opera was Arthur Nikisch, who had come to Budapest after leaving the Boston Symphony Orchestra. Dohnányi had the opportunity to meet Nikisch and his wife, a fine singer whom Dohnányi accompanied in several concerts.

The experiences that the young Dohnányi particularly enjoyed, however, were the numerous concerts of chamber music that were performed

---

5. According to a letter Dohnányi wrote to his parents on 14 September 1894, he played the Largo from his String Sextet, the Scherzo from his String Quartet in A Minor, and his song "Das verlassene Mägdlein" for his composition examination. He had also played his *Romance* in A Minor as part of his piano examination. The letter can be found in Appendix A.

in Budapest. The Hubay-Popper Quartet, which gave several subscription concerts, was a permanent feature.[6] In addition to flourishing on the concert stage, chamber music was played in the homes of many music lovers. Once the musicians at the Academy discovered what a fine chamber musician and accompanist Dohnányi was, they often made use of his talent. In addition to growing familiar with much music, Dohnányi received financial remuneration that, combined with the money his parents sent every month, enabled him to live comfortably.

Dohnányi quickly became the pride of the Academy. Although he appreciated this distinction, he remained modest. He had a good sense of humor and shared a cheerful life with his companions, with whom he attended concerts and theater shows. They often met in coffee shops, especially in the one opposite the Academy called the Mücsarnok-kávéház (Art Gallery Coffeehouse), which became known as the meeting place of young musicians. Dohnányi made many acquaintances but was cautious in choosing friends. The word "friend" meant something special to him; he used it only to describe people for whom he had a genuine appreciation.

One of those he called a friend was Peter König, who rented a tiny room in Dohnányi's neighborhood. This room had probably been intended as a servant's chamber. It could be entered only through the kitchen and was so small that all the space was taken up by a bed, a washstand, a piano, and a chair for the piano. When Dohnányi came to visit, König would crawl into bed in order to offer his guest the only chair.

Another friend was Ludwig Lebell, a young cellist with whom Dohnányi made music, played billiards, and had long chats in the coffee shop. They also shared an occasional glass of wine or beer. Together they often visited a third friend, Emil Lichtenberg.[7] Since Lichtenberg came from a wealthy family—his father was employed at an insurance company—he had a nice home, where he was able to entertain guests. Dohnányi, who always enjoyed humor, used to compose, or rather improvise, little pieces for which Lebell would invent texts. They called these humorous pieces the "Academy Ballet." They were comical portraits of certain individuals, such as Director Michalovich and his secretary.

Once, when visiting Lebell, Dohnányi found only his roommate Hugo Morascher, an organ student, at home. Dohnányi glanced at the piano and saw the score of an Organ Concerto by Rheinberger. "This doesn't seem

---

6. Jenő Hubay (1858–1937) was an important personality in Hungarian musical life; he was an excellent violinist and professor of violin at the Academy of Music in Budapest. David Popper (1843–1913) was a renowned cellist and professor of cello at the Academy.

7. Emil Lichtenberg studied piano at the Academy. He later became a well-known conductor and was engaged at several theaters, including the Budapest Opera.

difficult enough for a concerto!" Dohnányi remarked in his usual teasing way.

Morascher flared up in indignation. "What? You dare to say this isn't difficult?"

Dohnányi smiled with calm self-assurance. "Well, I only mean that I could sight-read it."

"Phoo! You pianists think that playing the organ is like playing the piano. Liszt was a great pianist, but a poor organist!"

"Don't get so excited, my friend," Dohnányi tried to soothe him. Then he shrugged his shoulders. "You may put me to the test, if you wish!" Dohnányi departed and quickly forgot this incident. Morascher, however, did not forget; his pride was deeply hurt.

One day Dohnányi found Morascher practicing the Organ Concerto in the music hall. With a triumphant sneer Morascher exclaimed, "Well, here you are! Just in time. Now come and play! Play this part for me!" and he pointed to a passage. Dohnányi sat at the organ and played the passage perfectly. Morascher observed him with increasing astonishment, pointing at another passage and again at another. Dohnányi played them all with ease. Morascher became increasingly amazed and then troubled. At last he stammered, "You have played the organ before!"

Dohnányi laughed and asked, "Did I ever say I hadn't?"

❧

Dohnányi was invited to many parties, but he appeared most frequently at the home of the Kunwalds, a very musical family: Antal Kunwald was an excellent violinist with whom Dohnányi played sonatas, and one of the daughters, named Elsa, was a fine pianist.[8] A friendship developed between Elsa and the young Dohnányi that, with the passing months, grew deeper and deeper.[9]

In February 1895 the Academy hosted a festival in the honor of Karl Goldmark, which Goldmark himself attended. After a performance by the teachers at the Academy, a student performance of Goldmark's Piano Quintet took place in which Dohnányi played the piano. Goldmark, delighted by their playing, called out with enthusiasm, "This surpassed the performance of the professors!"[10] Although Goldmark and Dohnányi later

---

8. Elsa's brother Cézár later became a noted artist; he did a series of red-chalk drawings of famous musicians, and his portrait of Dohnányi still hangs in the conference room of the Franz Liszt Academy. Elsa's sister Margit would become the mother of the famous conductor and composer Antal Doráti (1906–1988).

9. Dohnányi later dedicated his *Vier Klavierstücke* (Four Pieces for Piano), op. 2, to Elsa.

10. Dohnányi related this event in a letter to his father dated 10 February 1895; see Appendix A.

became close friends, it must have been the February 1895 performance that inspired Goldmark to declare in his will that Dohnányi should perform in the world premiere of his Second Piano Quintet.[11]

Dohnányi's own Piano Quintet, op. 1, which he dedicated "with respect and friendship" to Koessler, was premiered on 16 June 1895 during one of the closing performances of the school year. This was a remarkably successful day in the young artist's life, and some of his best friends contributed to the triumph. Luis Berkovich played the first violin, while a friend named Louis Pecskai played the second.[12] A young American named Carl Hohlstein played the viola, and Ludwig Lebell played the cello. The Piano Quintet would later become Dohnányi's first published composition, and it remains one of his most popular works.

When the school season came to an end, Dohnányi returned home to his parents in Pozsony. Together they visited Breznóbánya to spend the summer months in the home of his grandmother. During this vacation, a letter came from Professor Koessler saying that Brahms was interested in Dohnányi's Piano Quintet and wanted him to come immediately to Bad Ischl to play the work. Dohnányi would have been more than happy to comply, but the trip would have been very expensive and Professor Dohnányi could not afford it. Instead, they sent the manuscript to Bad Ischl by mail.

Even though Dohnányi could not be present, Brahms's first experience with the piece was nevertheless successful. The famous Kneisel Quartet, who just happened to be visiting Bad Ischl as Brahms's guests, performed the Quintet for him with Arthur Nikisch at the piano. Brahms was delighted and later told Koessler, "I could not have written it better myself." In addition to this flattering remark, which was most unusual coming from Brahms, he also arranged a performance of the composition before the private audience of the Tonkünstler Verein (Composers' Association), of which he was President. Dohnányi, in his eighteenth year, traveled to Vienna to perform his Quintet.

In Vienna music was always at the height of its glory. The *Kaiserstadt* (imperial city), which was the Emperor's residence and the favorite city of the Austro-Hungarian aristocracy, was a place of culture, luxury, and entertainment. Perhaps nowhere else in the world did people amuse themselves with such enthusiasm; nowhere were balls so magnificent, and nowhere was music enjoyed so profoundly. It was in this Vienna of Novem-

---

11. On 1 March 1916, one year after Goldmark's death, the Rosé Quartet played the Quintet from manuscript at a concert in Vienna with Dohnányi at the piano.

12. Dohnányi knew Pecskai, who was a pupil of Jenő Hubay, from Pozsony, where he had accompanied him in a concert.

ber 1895 that the young Dohnányi ascended the concert stage three times in succession.[13]

Dohnányi arrived in Vienna several days early in order to be present at the rehearsals and pay Brahms a visit to thank him for his kindness. Brahms lived at 4 Karl Gasse, on the third floor. When Dohnányi rang the bell, the housekeeper opened the door and led him through the hall and bedroom into a room next to Brahms's study. It was in this simply furnished room, where Brahms's piano stood, that guests were usually received. Brahms, with his characteristic long beard, low, clumsy stature, short legs, and broad shoulders, greeted Dohnányi warmly and talked to him kindly in a deep, murmuring voice. Although the visitor was just a boy, Brahms, as was his habit, offered Dohnányi a seat on the comfortable sofa, while he himself sat on a chair.

They were chatting about the music scene in Budapest when Brahms remarked, "It is fortunate that you are studying in Budapest." When Dohnányi asked him why he thought this, Brahms grumbled over the musical conditions in Vienna, which he felt were extremely bad. "Whom would we have here in Vienna to teach you?" he asked in contempt. "What artists do we have now? Well, let's see . . ." He began to count them on his fingers. "Surely not our *Altmeister* [old master] Bruckner?" he asked in annoyance. Everybody knew about the bitter hostility between Brahms and Bruckner. There was a great contrast between the two artists not only in their personalities, but also in their compositional styles. Bruckner, as an Austrian, was closer to the heart of the Viennese. His works were more lyrical than those of the somewhat heavier, graver, and more reserved Brahms, who was from northern Germany. The Viennese had more difficulty in understanding Brahms's music.

One by one, Brahms recounted the notable musicians of Vienna, supplying a malicious remark for each. It was in his nature to oppose; people rightly called him a *Widerspruchsgeist* (spirit of opposition). They say that Brahms would remark sarcastically upon leaving a party, "If there is one among you whom I failed to offend, I ask him to excuse me." While Brahms so bitterly criticized the musicians of Vienna, he spoke to Dohnányi with a great appreciation for Koessler, praising him as a theorist and as a pedagogue.

Brahms then asked Dohnányi about his newest composition. Dohnányi told him he was writing a symphony. "Of course, in minor!" Brahms said mockingly. "First symphonies are always written in minor!"

---

13. Preceding the performance of the Quintet, Dohnányi gave two sonata concerts with the violinist Victor von Herzfeld, who was a professor at the Budapest Academy. Herzfeld played first violin in the performance of Dohnányi's Quintet.

"Mine, by chance, must be an exception, for it is in F Major," Dohnányi answered with a smile.

At the performance of the Quintet, Brahms sat in the first row beside Fritz Steinbach, who was a conductor from Meiningen.[14] Steinbach made flattering remarks about the work, but only to others. To Dohnányi he cautioned, "There are also some gifted young composers here in Vienna!"

An informal banquet was given after the concert. Brahms sat opposite Dohnányi at the table, while his neighbor was Professor Fischhof, a composer and pianist. After enthusiastically praising the Quintet, Fischhof started a conversation about the pleasant days he had once spent in Hungary. He even boasted of knowing some Hungarian sayings and made a great effort to quote them with precise pronunciation. Dohnányi, however, could not help bursting out in laughter over Fischhof's peculiar accent. Fischhof reproached him with severity. "I don't mind being criticized for my compositions," he complained, "but I can't stand being laughed at for my Hungarian accent."

Brahms quietly listened to this conversation. Then, with a frown, he turned to Dohnányi. "Don't believe him," he said with his usual sarcasm. "One always defends one's weaknesses. But his weakness is not his Hungarian; it is his compositions!"

Before Dohnányi left Vienna to return to Budapest, he paid one more visit to Brahms. This would be the last time he would see this robust man whose music he so greatly admired. When Brahms died on 3 April 1897, Dohnányi, accompanied by König and two other colleagues, was sent to Vienna by the Academy to attend the funeral. Because of his connections with the great musician, Dohnányi was chosen to say goodbye and to officially represent the Academy at the burial.

The year 1896 marked the celebration of the Millennium, an important festival in Hungarian history in which the country celebrated the thousandth anniversary of her existence. The important activities on this occasion included magnificent concerts, theatrical productions, exhibitions, and a gala procession in which the aristocrats marched in brilliantly colorful national costumes that were modeled after fashions throughout Hungary's history. The costumes were made of heavy, rich velvet or silk braided with gold and trimmed with ermine and lace. Their buttons were exquisite antique jewels. The ermine cloaks, which the aristocrats threw

---

14. At this concert, the first violin was played by Victor von Herzfeld, the second violin by Jarislav Czerny, the viola by C. Mayer, and the cello by Friedrich Buxbaum.

over one shoulder, sparkled in the sunshine, and the feathers of their caps waved in the breeze. Soldiers on foot and on horseback paraded in the various uniforms of the Hungarian Army. The peasants followed, attired in their traditional garb. The Millennium was celebrated in Budapest by festivities everywhere: in the parks, on the river Danube, and in the palaces. Special Masses were celebrated in the churches and commemorative concerts were given in concert halls, in which the Academy participated. Dohnányi appeared in several of these performances.

During these national festivities, composition contests were held in the name of the Emperor. There were four "Royal Prizes": the first prize of 2,000 florint was awarded for any work by a Hungarian; the second prize of 1,000 florint was for a symphony; the third and fourth prizes of 500 florint each were for a piece of chamber music and for an orchestral overture, respectively.[15] Although nobody won the first prize, Dohnányi won prizes for his Symphony in F Major, which was the symphony that he had mentioned to Brahms, and for his *Zrínyi* Overture.[16] There was a rumor that the committee had wanted to give the third prize to Dohnányi's String Sextet but was reluctant to give all three awards to the same composer.[17]

At this time Emperor Francis Joseph and his lovely and noble wife Empress Elizabeth were still in deep mourning for their only son Rudolf, who had lost his life in tragic circumstances.[18] As a result, they spent only a few days in Budapest. Years before Millennium, the compassionate and generous Empress had reconciled the Hungarian nation with their ruler. When she appeared pale and broken at the Millennium festivities, every Hungarian felt a deep pity for her that overshadowed their own happiness. A year later, in 1897, she was assassinated in Geneva by the anarchist Lucheni, who killed her believing that he was doing a favor for humanity.

❧

The school year 1896–97 was the last that Dohnányi spent at the Academy. At the Academy examination concert on 2 June 1897, Gyula Erkel conducted the premieres of Dohnányi's Symphony and *Zrínyi* Overture.

15. About two and a half florint were equal to one dollar in value.

16. Miklós Zrínyi was a Hungarian hero who had fallen in the war against the Turks. Although both the Overture and the Symphony received much praise, Dohnányi did not publish either of them. In fact, Dohnányi labeled his next symphony as his first.

17. The jury consisted of Edmund von Michalovich, Alexander Erkel, Raoul Mader, Julius Káldy, and Victor von Herzfeld. They awarded the third prize to Béla Szabados.

18. Very little is known about the mysterious death of Archduke Rudolph von Hapsburg (1858–89). Some say he died by suicide, and some, including Dohnányi, suspected murder. Since the only witness of the tragedy, a coachman named Bratfisch, mysteriously disappeared, no one knew the truth. Archduke Rudolf had shared with his mother an affection for Hungary that was unusual for Hapsburg rulers. His early death was a grave blow to the country.

At a student concert on 16 June, Dohnányi performed Liszt's *Réminiscences de Don Juan* (a Fantasy on themes from Mozart's *Don Giovanni*), which was considered by many to be the most difficult piece ever written for the piano. This performance was a tremendous success. "He is one of the titans of modern virtuosity," wrote the *Budapesti Hírlap*, "who, as soon as he appears before the public, will be ranked with d'Albert and Sauer. We can compare the power and sincerity of his performance only to these two masters." At the end of the performance, the audience rose, crowded around the stage, and kept on applauding, forcing the young artist to return to the piano and play encore after encore. As the *Budapesti Hírlap* wrote, "A Hungarian boy started his triumphal career on the stage of this school, to which the echo of his fame will always reverberate."[19]

The years he spent at the Academy would always remain happy and touching memories for Dohnányi. When he received his Artist's Diplomas in Piano and Composition on 27 June 1897,[20] however, he was eager to start his musical career. He was an optimist; throughout his life he felt impatience with pessimists, whom he said were never right. He believed that even if an optimist failed in his hopes, he still had time to become troubled, while a pessimist was constantly worried, very often without reason. Dohnányi eagerly anticipated the five weeks he would spend with d'Albert, who would put the finishing touches on Dohnányi's performance skills before his professional debut in Berlin.

※

On a serene day in July, Dohnányi boarded another train. This time he traveled to Munich and from there to Lake Starnberg, where Eugène d'Albert was spending the summer. Dohnányi stayed in Benried, about fifteen minutes' walking distance from d'Albert's villa, in a simple but pleasant Gasthof, which housed many colorful guests, including painters from Munich. There was only one aspect of his stay that annoyed the young artist: his window opened on a courtyard in which a local butcher exposed people to the repulsive sight of the weekly slaughter of pigs and calves. At first, this sight disgusted Dohnányi and upset his stomach. Just because it caused him such discomfort, however, he forced himself to watch until he became accustomed to the spectacle. It would have gone against his principles to turn away from an unpleasant situation without mastering it.

Although d'Albert was not a pedagogue, Dohnányi profited from his instruction. D'Albert listened to the pieces that Dohnányi was to play that

---

19. This article, which appeared in the *Budapesti Hírlap* on 17 June 1897, can be found in Appendix C.

20. Artist's Diplomas were also awarded to Peter König (Composition) and Gustav Schmidt (Violin).

autumn in Berlin as well as his new composition, *Variationen und Fuge über ein Thema von E.G.* (Variations and Fugue on a Theme by E[mma] G[ruber]) for piano, op. 4.[21] D'Albert made comments and sometimes even played parts to Dohnányi. When d'Albert had guests, he would ask the young musician to play. D'Albert would then perform passages himself, calling Dohnányi's attention to certain corrections in front of the guests. Before Dohnányi left, d'Albert remarked to him, "You can continue by yourself now. I have taught you all I can."

Dohnányi, feeling optimistic about his future, settled in Berlin. This city seemed to be the right place to start concertizing and to establish himself in the musical world.

21. This piece is based on a theme by Emma Gruber (later Mrs. Zoltán Kodály), to whom it was dedicated. Dohnányi had also dedicated his *Walzer* (Waltz) for piano, four hands, op. 3, to Emma Gruber.

TWO

1897–1905

Dohnányi launched his career with recitals in Berlin on 1 and 7 October
1897. He premiered his *Variationen und Fuge über ein Thema von E.G.*
on the first concert and the third of his *Vier Klavierstücke* (Four Piano
Pieces), op. 2, on the second concert. Although both performances were
well received by the small audiences as well as by the press, they were not financially successful for the artist because the concert agent insisted that
Dohnányi pay all of the expenses. Dohnányi's performance of Beethoven's
G Major Piano Concerto with the Budapest Philharmonic on 17 November, however, did prove to be profitable.

The conductor of the Budapest Philharmonic, Hans Richter, scheduled only two rehearsals for the 17 November 1897 concert. At the first,
which took place one day before the performance, Richter asked Dohnányi
what cadenzas he was going to play. When the young artist answered that
they would be his own, Richter looked surprised and asked to hear the cadenza for the first movement. Dohnányi obeyed, and Richter was thrilled
by the composer's talent. When they came to the third movement, Richter
wanted to hear its cadenza, but Dohnányi told him that he had not yet
completed it. "Well, it is high time you got it ready," Richter grumbled.
That evening Dohnányi went to see Richter in the Pilseni Sörcsarnok
(Pilsen Beer Hall), where the conductor was drinking beer with some
members of his orchestra. Dohnányi showed him the manuscript of his
cadenza for the third movement. Richter took it eagerly, but then burst
out into laughter. There was only a scribbled draft on the paper. "Nobody
could make sense out of this," he called out, still chuckling. Dohnányi
could; in the performance the cadenza turned out to be perfect, and few
knew that it was almost completely improvised. The audience responded
to the concert with great enthusiasm, and Richter engaged Dohnányi for a
performance of the Concerto with the Vienna Opera Orchestra in January.

Three days later Dohnányi played Liszt's *Réminiscences de Don Juan* in
Budapest. He followed this with a recital in Pozsony, for which he appeared
on the same stage where as a child he had often listened to famous artists.

Dohnányi's audience consisted of friends from his childhood as well as the Archduchess Isabella and her court.[1] Dohnányi was so overcome by memories that, for the first time, he felt embarrassed and experienced stage fright. Nevertheless, he was rewarded with the thunderous ovations to which he was becoming accustomed.

Dohnányi spent Christmas at home with his family. Although his parents had preserved the cozy, intimate home life of his childhood, one thing had changed. His kindly old grandmother, who had made the delicious *fánk,* had passed away. Dohnányi could not stay in his parent's house for long, however; he had to follow the demands of his career.

On 7 January 1898 Dohnányi played a solo recital in Budapest that was a musical as well as financial success. He then traveled to Vienna to play the Beethoven G Major Concerto with Richter and the Vienna Opera Orchestra. This concert, which took place on 9 January, was Dohnányi's greatest success yet.

That evening Richter invited Dohnányi to dinner at his home in the Viennese Villa Quarter. After dinner Richter, Dohnányi, and a local music critic sipped wine and chatted about their musical memories and experiences. They hardly noticed that hour after hour was passing. When night came, they were still together, immersed in conversation. Richter, smoking his Turkish pipe, began to talk about his favorite topic: Bach. He became carried away with emotion and rose from his seat, urging Dohnányi to play one of the organ fantasies. Dohnányi willingly sat at the piano and played Liszt's transcription of the G Minor Fantasia and Fugue. Richter listened as in a trance; then his eyes slowly filled with tears. "That was well played!" he called out in ecstasy. Richter also talked about Otto von Bismarck and Helmuth von Moltke, whose volume of correspondence he enjoyed reading. Richter, who had been a close friend of the Wagner family, enjoyed relating several anecdotes about Richard Wagner. Before the evening was over, Richter inquired about Dohnányi's future plans and engaged him to play Beethoven's G Major Concerto the next autumn during one of his "Richter Concerts" in London.

From Vienna Dohnányi went to Dresden, where he performed Liszt's E-flat Concerto with Jean Louis Nicodé on 13 January. Dohnányi then traveled to Berlin, which was the music center of the world. There Dohnányi met many famous musicians and attended numerous concerts. During his stay he made a piano arrangement of two waltzes from Leo Delibes's ballet *Naila.* He also resumed work on his Piano Concerto, op. 5, which he had begun at Lake Starnberg and was dedicating to d'Albert.

---

1. Dohnányi dedicated his String Sextet in B-flat Major to the Archduchess Isabella.

Dohnányi's work was again interrupted by a concert in Vienna on 12 April 1898, in which he played his Piano Quintet. This piece had been performed in Vienna three years earlier in the private Tonkünstler Verein hall. The 1898 performance, however, was for the general public. The performing artists this time were the members of Fitzner Quartet (Rudolph Fitzner and Jaroslav Czerny, violins; Otto Zert, viola; and Friedrich Buxbaum, cello), which later premiered many of Dohnányi's works. Czerny and Buxbaum had participated in November 1895 performance of the Quintet.

By April Dohnányi had made a tour of fifteen concerts in Hungary. The whole country wanted to hear the young musician who had become the pride of his motherland. Dohnányi was one of those few artists who were lucky enough to enjoy popularity in their native land in their prime of life. After this trip he returned to Pozsony.

Meanwhile, Ludwig Bösendorfer, the piano-maker, had announced a competition to commemorate the seventieth anniversary of his factory in Vienna in 1899. There would be three prizes for piano concertos. Dohnányi wanted to submit his Piano Concerto, but he had not started the third movement. After paying a visit to the Kunwald family's summer home in Upper Hungary, at which time he became engaged to Elsa Kunwald, Dohnányi retired to a quiet, small health resort near Pozsony called Vaskutacska (Eisenbrunnell). Here, in solitude and surrounded by beautiful scenery, he worked to finish his Concerto. As the deadline rapidly approached, Dohnányi realized that he would not he able to complete the work in time without compromising its quality. He preferred to give his compositions time to evolve. He was conscientious and precise and did not hesitate to tear up several pages, even whole movements, if he was not convinced that they were in complete accordance with his intentions. After much thought, Dohnányi decided that his only choice was to arrange the first movement so that it could stand alone as a single-movement concerto. He altered the Adagio at the end of the movement, added a cadenza that he had initially intended for the third movement, and ended the Concerto with a short presto. After Dohnányi sent the Concerto to the competition, he began to complete the third movement according to his original intentions.

※

In the autumn of 1898 Dohnányi set out by train to follow Hans Richter to England. Before his departure he visited his parents in Pozsony, and he interrupted his journey for two days at Cologne to see his old friend and schoolmate Emil Lichtenberg, who was now conductor at the City Theater. Dohnányi joined Hans Richter at four in the morning on the Express Train to Calais. They had breakfast together and then talked until their arrival. Richter anxiously observed the gathering clouds. He was very susceptible to seasickness and was hoping that the Channel would be calm when they crossed it.

Unfortunately, the crossing turned out to be very rough. Dohnányi took his seat in the open air of the deck, but became nauseated when the boat began to rock dangerously. The people around him started to groan and vomit, and the sight made Dohnányi sick. He wanted to withdraw into a corner, but then he became annoyed with himself for this weakness. As he had done at the sight of the slaughtering of animals in Benried, he now decided to force himself to observe the seasick passengers. By doing so he cured himself forever of seasickness. Dohnányi found satisfaction in being able to fight any challenge. "As long as I am alive, I will keep on fighting," he would say. "Life is an eternal struggle, a permanent challenge. It is only in abhorrent death that one has peace and tranquility." Richter did not fare as well as Dohnányi. He crouched in a corner, struggling with seasickness. When Dohnányi went to inquire how he felt, Richter looked up with a deadly pale face. Suddenly he smelled the smoke of Dohnányi's cigarette, and snorted furiously at him, "Get away with that cigarette!" He seemed to forget that he himself used to be a habitual pipe-smoker. Dohnányi quickly cleared away and did not see Richter again until they had both arrived in London.

Upon arriving in London Dohnányi was met at Victoria Station by his former schoolmate Ludwig Lebell. The two young men climbed into a hansom cab, with which Dohnányi was very amused, and began to chat happily. Although Lebell had only been in London for two years, he had already quit his job as member of an orchestra because he was experiencing problems with his vision. He was now working as a teacher in a music school.

The hansom stopped at a house on Inverness Terrace, near Kensington Gardens, where Dohnányi was to be the houseguest of Caroline Geisler-Schubert. Miss Geisler-Schubert, called "Linchi" by her friends, was the granddaughter of Ferdinand Schubert, Franz Schubert's brother. She was a very gifted pianist herself and had been a pupil of Clara Schumann in Frankfurt am Main. Linchi was originally from Pozsony and, as a friend of the Dohnányis, had invited Ernst to stay with her and Mrs. Marguerite Oliverson, with whom she shared her home. Linchi had met the wealthy Mrs. Oliverson, who was also very musical, in Vienna. Mrs. Oliverson was an insatiable traveler. After she took Linchi with her on her trips, the two became inseparable friends.

Although Mrs. Oliverson had never met Dohnányi before, she received him as though they were old friends. "She became a second mother to me," Dohnányi recalled. "Next to my mother, she had the greatest effect upon my character, and I admired and worshipped her. She was a lady in every sense of the word: she had distinguished manners, delicate feelings, and noble thoughts. She was quiet, sometimes even reserved, toward strangers, but warm at the depths of her heart and reliable in her sentiments. Like my mother, she possessed marvelous self-control." Mrs. Oliverson's house became a second home to Dohnányi, who liked the fact that formal evening clothes were worn at dinner. This formality gave solemnity to the meal, to the conversation, and to the temperament of the diners. Mrs. Oliverson would relate their travel experiences, but she never touched on private affairs, nor did Dohnányi ever ask or inquire about them. Soon both of the women treated their young guest as though he was their own son. It became his privilege to carve the meat at the table. In the evening they made music; sometimes Linchi and Dohnányi played pieces for four hands on Linchi's two pianos.

While in London, Dohnányi tried to experience all the cultural pleasures that the city could offer. Linchi and Lebell never grew tired of taking him to museums, picture galleries, and places of historical interest.

On 24 October 1898 a sedate audience gathered in the Queen's Hall to listen to a Richter Concert that was to introduce a young man who came from Hungary. When Dohnányi was asked how he felt as he walked onto the stage in front of this formidable and reserved audience, he answered, "This was the third time I was to play the Beethoven G Major Piano Concerto with Hans Richter. I had done my job well on the first two occasions. How could I fail now? I simply tried to do my best." Nevertheless, he confessed that, in spite of his self-assurance, he was overwhelmed by the emotional applause with which the reserved audience rewarded him.[2]

Although Dohnányi had come to England for the sake of one concert, this successful evening led to engagements for twenty more performances in England, including five recitals in London. In the same season, he played Beethoven's G Major Concerto in Birmingham, Edinburgh, and Glasgow. It was said that he was as unsurpassable in playing this piece as d'Albert was in performing Beethoven's E-flat Major Concerto. Dohnányi's first solo recital in England took place on 10 November in St. James's Hall, which was acoustically one of the finest halls in Europe.[3]

Whenever Dohnányi walked out onto a concert stage his every movement was dignified, from his serene smile to his graceful bows. His spirit captured and dominated the whole audience. People would watch him unpretentiously take his place at the piano, almost breathless with excitement.

---

2. A review of this performance appeared in *The Times* on 25 October 1898; see Appendix C.
3. See Appendix C for a review of this recital that appeared in *The Times* on 11 November 1898.

Instead of starting to play immediately, Dohnányi would sit there for a few moments, looking down at the keyboard. He would throw slight side-glances at the audience, patiently waiting for perfect silence. Only then did he touch the keys. Dohnányi's audiences were dazzled by his playing. His fortissimo was a thundering force that made the walls tremble, and his pianissimo was like a breath or a sigh; one could feel it more than hear it. "It is certainly through a kind of hypnotic power that a performing artist can hold his audience," Dohnányi said. "When an artist appears on a stage, he has to find contact with those who are listening to him and get them under his spell. If he succeeds, he can be sure of the success of his performance." It often happened that after a dramatic performance the audience was so spellbound by Dohnányi's playing they forgot to applaud. Gripped by the power of his interpretation, they sat there, breathlessly staring at the stage with tears in their eyes.

Dohnányi became so popular in England that newspapers published not only articles about his art, but also amusing episodes about his stay in England. One weekly London paper included a humorous story about Dohnányi, the young Hungarian pianist who had come to England with no more knowledge of the English language than the two words "So sorry." The paper related how Dohnányi, when getting off the boat in Dover, accidentally gave a porter a half-crown instead of a half-shilling. He then told the porter the only words he knew, "So sorry." The porter quickly answered, "Don't mention it, sir." From this time on, according to the paper, Dohnányi's vocabulary was enlarged to include this new expression. Of course, this did not really happen. It was, however, a cute little story, and Dohnányi was much amused by it. In reality, Dohnányi tried hard to learn English, which was not even necessary because Linchi and Mrs. Oliverson both spoke fluent German. Although Dohnányi never formally studied English, he did absorb it by listening to people talk and by visiting theaters frequently.

Among other activities, Dohnányi appeared in chamber music concerts, especially in the "Hampstead Chamber Concerts," "Mr. Halford's Concerts," and the "Popular Concerts" founded and organized by Thomas and Arthur Chappell, who were music publishers and piano manufacturers.[4] Starting with a performance on 26 November, Dohnányi played in several Popular Concerts with Lady Hallé, the widow of Sir Charles Hallé, who had founded the famous Hallé Concerts in Manchester. "She was one of the finest violinists I ever met," Dohnányi said. "She was born with an infallible

---

4. The Popular Concerts, which took place each Saturday during the concert season, featured many outstanding artists.

instinct for musical interpretation and was equipped with stupendous technique. She played with a temperament that made her age of sixty years appear to be false. It was a pleasure to play with her." He had heard much about her in his childhood, when she was known as Wilma Neruda. Through the Popular Concerts, Dohnányi also became acquainted with Hugo Becker, the famous cellist.[5]

On 17 December 1898 the first London performance of Dohnányi's Quintet took place with the cooperation of Lady Hallé and the Pops Quartet. The success was so great that a second performance was demanded during the same season. This performance, which took place on 4 March 1899, was Dohnányi's last appearance that season at a Popular Concert. It was at this concert that he premiered his new piano composition, the Passacaglia, op. 6, which he dedicated to Mrs. Oliverson.[6] Years earlier in Budapest, Dohnányi had finished his Quintet only four days before its performance at the Budapest Academy. The Passacaglia, however, was completed only on the stage; Dohnányi had to improvise the last bars, because he was so busy with his concert obligations and social activities that he could not find time to compose. Dohnányi would frequently program pieces on which he was still at work. Although he always believed that he would get them ready in time without having to rush them, his compositions were often not finished until the last minute, or, as in the case of the Passacaglia, their endings were improvised. He cheerfully admitted he could work better by being forced rather than urged to complete something by a certain date.

Dohnányi interrupted his concert tour of England to spend Christmas with his parents in Pozsony. Although his children were now adults, Frederick von Dohnányi still decorated a Christmas tree that reached from floor to ceiling. Both Professor Dohnányi and Mitzi were filled with awe upon hearing about Dohnányi's accomplishments. Professor Dohnányi, who had continued to collect the reviews of his son's concerts, took much pride in Dohnányi's success, even if the principles of his strict education prevented him from saying so openly.

On 11 January 1899, Dohnányi was again soloist at a Philharmonic Concert in Budapest conducted by Hans Richter. This time he played his own Piano Concerto, op. 5. Although he had submitted the single-movement version of this very work a year earlier to the Bösendorfer Competition, he was able to perform it now because he had already been announced as one

---

5. Hugo Becker (1863–1941) was an excellent cellist and pedagogue. He was professor at the Conservatory in Frankfurt am Main and later the Königliche Hochschule in Berlin.

6. The Passacaglia shows Dohnányi's strong sense of form. In addition to forming a regular passacaglia, it has also the form of a rondo, using the passacaglia theme in a slightly varied form as a contrasting theme.

of the three finalists. For this concert, Dohnányi played the work in its intended three-movement form.

Soon afterwards Dohnányi returned to Pozsony to play Beethoven's G Major Concerto, which was quickly becoming his trademark piece. The concert took place on 19 January 1899 with a military orchestra whose pitch was a half-step higher than the normal pitch. Because of this, the piano technicians had tuned the piano one month prior to the concert and had made special preparations so that it would stay in tune. When the Fitzner Quartet came from Vienna on the day of the performance to play Dohnányi's Piano Quintet with the composer, it turned out that their instruments could not safely be tuned a half-step higher. To compensate, Dohnányi struck an A-flat on the piano to enable the quartet to tune to their usual pitch of A natural. He then calmly proceeded to play the piano part half a step lower, in B Minor instead of C Minor. On the orchestra concert, the orchestra also played Dohnányi's *Zrínyi* Overture, which had won the Millennium prize but remained in manuscript.

On 11 March 1899 Dohnányi played some of his piano pieces in a concert of the Glee Club in Gotha. After the concert the performers, as well as a great part of the audience, went to a restaurant in the same building. Dohnányi sat at a long table, surrounded by a group of gentlemen who started to talk about spiritualism. They boasted about some of the wonderful materializations they had personally witnessed. Dohnányi remarked, perhaps somewhat too frankly, that he did not believe in superstitions.

"What do you mean by 'superstitions'? We are talking about facts!" the gentlemen ardently insisted.

"I don't believe in that sort of 'facts,'" the young artist replied stubbornly.

"What would you give us if we succeeded in convincing you this very night?" they demanded.

Dohnányi shrugged a shoulder and adventurously answered, "I'd offer you the proceeds from tonight's concert!"

The spiritualists began to organize a séance and hastily summoned a medium. They all gathered in a small, gloomy room illuminated only by an oil lamp. In the center of this chamber stood a heavy pedestal, around which they sat, resting their hands on the table top. After a time their hands began to tremble, even to shake, and the so-called table-turning began. Although Dohnányi did not believe anything they tried to prove, he had to admit that the heavy table rose and moved about so rapidly that they almost raced to keep up with it. Dohnányi's paycheck was almost in danger when the spirits themselves came to his aid. The spirit who had been conjured strictly refused to answer. The faces of the spiritualists darkened with disappointment, and the medium asked the spirit whether perhaps some unbeliever's presence was disturbing the séance. A determined "yes" was the answer. Dohnányi, on his part, did not need much persuasion to leave with the money safe in his pocket. An hour later, the spiritualists emerged from the ghostly room, boasting about the successful conjuring they had experienced after his departure.

❧

The final round of the Bösendorfer contest took place on 26 March 1899. There were two other concertos that had been chosen from about seventy entries by a jury of five outstanding musicians in Vienna. The three works were to be publicly performed, with the audience voting on which would receive the first prize. The concert took place on a Sunday afternoon with the cooperation of the Orchestra of the Vienna Opera, conducted by Johann Nepomuk Fuchs. According to the conditions of the competition, the composers could either conduct their concertos or play the piano parts. The three prize-winning works were placed on the program in the order in which they had been sent to the competition.

The hall was crowded with people. The audience had been given ballots with their tickets, and everyone was filled with excited anticipation. The first number was the concerto by Edward Behm, who conducted his work himself and had brought a pianist from Berlin. Dohnányi followed. From the moment he touched the keys, the audience made its decision. The third composer, Jan Brandts-Buys, realized with resignation that he would have to content himself with second or third place. When the result of the voting was announced, no one was surprised that the Grand Prize of 2,000 crowns was given to Dohnányi, who had received 706 votes. Brandts-Buys was awarded 1,200 crowns for receiving 607 votes. Behm came in third, the prize for which was 800 crowns, by only nine votes. Brandts-Buys congratulated Dohnányi with warm admiration, and from that day on the two musicians became close friends.

Ludwig Bösendorfer, the owner of the piano factory that had sponsored the competition, was one of the most respected figures in Vienna. He appeared not only at all significant concerts, but also at popular events, such as horse races. He was so popular that musicians would call him "Uncle Bösendorfer" and come to see him whenever they visited Vienna. He insisted that he was not a piano manufacturer but a "piano maker" because every part of his pianos was handmade. No instrument ever left his factory without having been thoroughly examined by him. Important recitals and chamber music concerts in Vienna usually took place in the Bösendorfer Hall. In this way, "Uncle Bösendorfer" came in close touch with Liszt, Rubinstein, von Bülow, Brahms, Joachim, and other great musicians of the time. Whenever a musical event occurred, his hall was jammed with music lovers. Bösendorfer himself sat in a benchlike chair in a hidden corner, withdrawing into the background while keeping an eye on every detail. In spite of all his activities, Bösendorfer was a modest man. In his attempts to remain in the background, he called his competition prizes "von Bülow Prizes" instead of using his own name. He was nevertheless closely involved in all musical affairs, and many musicians sought his advice or assistance.

Bösendorfer was able to solve a rather delicate problem for Dohnányi, whose recitals in Vienna had been arranged by the leading Viennese concert agency. Because this agency had tried to capitalize on Dohnányi's naïveté, Dohnányi had fired his agent and in his bitterness decided to not give any more concerts in Vienna. On hearing the details, Bösendorfer arranged Dohnányi's recitals himself. When the former agent heard what was happening, he became hostile and tried to jeopardize Dohnányi's success by arranging a recital for the more famous d'Albert in the huge Musik-Vereinsaal on the same date as Dohnányi's first independent recital. Fortunately, both halls were crowded, and both artists had their audiences. The hostile agent nevertheless continued to arrange performances for the biggest names on the evenings of Dohnányi's recitals. Although this was nerve-wracking at first, Dohnányi's concerts were always sold out. He became reassured that he had already built up his own following. Years later, after the death of the hostile agent, Dohnányi made peace with his son and even worked with him.

During World War I the building containing Bösendorfer's Hall and piano showrooms was sold. The new owner decided to demolish it in order to build a splendid palace in its place. Although Bösendorfer moved with his pianos into the Musik-Verein Building, he was never able to emotionally recover from this blow. He became melancholy, sold his factory, and soon died, as people said, from a broken heart. Dohnányi often saw him standing there, in his last year of life, on the empty lot, with a faraway look in his eyes. Dohnányi grieved for him, for he liked and respected the old man and regarded his pianos as the best in Europe.

Another concert of great importance this season was a 28 March 1899 performance of the pieces that had won the Millennium competition, including Dohnányi's F Major Symphony and his *Zrínyi* Overture, in Budapest.

After the concert Dohnányi remained in Budapest, where he rented two rooms near the Kunwalds' home. He worked busily on his String Quartet in A Major, op. 7, which he completed within two months. Antal Kunwald, to whom Dohnányi dedicated the piece, copied the parts. The work was first performed in the Kunwalds' home before a small group of musicians and amateurs, most of whom found the third movement, the adagio, incomprehensible.[7]

Dohnányi spent part of the summer with the Kunwald family in Körmöcbánya, in the mountains of northern Hungary. One day, while wandering alone through the woods, he heard something rustling in the bushes, and a poisonous snake slid toward him. Dohnányi was not afraid; all his life he considered cowardice to be shameful. He was instead rather amused by the snake. He liked all animals, and, even though he felt no inclination whatever for snakes, he considered it to be a precious living being. He approached the snake and almost instinctively started to whistle a little tune to please the reptile. The effect was so striking that Dohnányi himself was astonished to see the body of the snake straighten upwards. The snake raised his head and listened motionlessly to the tune. When Dohnányi stopped whistling, the snake turned and glided away into the thicket.

When Dohnányi returned to Pozsony to visit his parents, he started to compose his Cello Sonata, op. 8, and completed its first movement. He also took this opportunity to practice, which he rarely did. He possessed a gift, which he had inherited from his father, of being able to maintain a remarkable technique with very little practice. This time, however, he faced the formidable task of having to enlarge as well as perfect his repertoire. His English manager, Mr. Vert, had arranged a number of concerts in England for the following autumn, which Dohnányi had gladly accepted. The prospect of returning to Great Britain filled him with joyous excitement. Having formed such a close friendship with Mrs. Oliverson and Miss Geisler-Schubert, and being on such good terms with the English audiences, Dohnányi felt as though he were going home. He used to say, "People in Europe think that the English are cold. In my opinion, this coldness is only a certain kind of reserve. In reality English people have warm hearts. It may be difficult to get close to them and gain their confidence, but once this occurs, one can build upon their friendship as upon a rock."

Dohnányi reached England in September 1899. He arrived well in advance of his first engagement so that he could spend a month in Eastbourne with the two women. He also continued to work on his Cello Sonata, which he completed later during his England tour, working in trains and hotel rooms. Dohnányi was able to do creative work in spite of distractions that some composers would have found intolerable. He needed solitude only at the start of a composition. Once the general character of a

---

7. The first public performance of Dohnányi's String Quartet in A Major was given in London on 18 December 1899.

work was developed in his mind, he could put it on paper in the most un-favorable places.

The concert tour started in October. People still wanted to hear the Beethoven Piano Concerto in G Major, so Dohnányi played it in Liver-pool, Manchester, and other places. Over the next two months he played thirty-two concerts in England, Scotland, and Ireland. On 23 October he gave the first English performance of his own Piano Concerto at a Richter Concert in London. The Concerto was very successful and was received with equal enthusiasm in Manchester and Bradford.

Dohnányi welcomed the opportunity to have further discussions with Hans Richter, and they again talked about Wagner. Once Richter related a little episode that, in his view, had caused the deep break in the friendship between Wagner and Nietzsche. Everyone who knew that Nietzsche had been an enthusiastic admirer of Wagner was greatly shocked when he turned against Wagner in his book *Der Fall Wagner* (The Wagner Case). According to Richter, this break happened one day when Nietzsche, who frequently visited the Wagners in their home, came with a musical compo-sition of his own. Everyone was surprised to find that Nietzsche had been composing. Richter and Cosima Wagner played the work, which was writ-ten for piano, four hands, from the manuscript. Wagner leaned back in his armchair, listening. His face became more and more gloomy; finally his fea-tures distorted into an expression of absolute weariness. Then his servant, either noticing the annoyance of his master or having a good ear for music, approached Wagner and whispered in a Bavarian accent, "Herr Wagner, dees scheint mer net guat!" (Mr. Wagner, this doesn't seem good to me!). Upon these words Wagner broke out into a fit of laughter. Nietzsche left the room, stung and wounded, never to return again.

When Wilhelm Jahn retired from the Directorship of the Vienna Court Opera in 1899, Richter rejoiced and remarked that whoever suc-ceeded Jahn could not possibly be any worse. Nevertheless, Richter was annoyed, even hurt, when Mahler was appointed Director instead of him. Richter's resentment was so deep that he left Vienna without even giving a farewell concert. He settled in England in 1900 to become the conductor of the Hallé Concerts in Manchester.

On 4 December 1899 the first performance of Dohnányi's Cello Sonata took place in London. The cellist was Ludwig Lebell, to whom Dohnányi had dedicated the Sonata. As was becoming characteristic of Dohnányi, two days before the performance the composition was still in-complete. When Lebell visited Dohnányi to ask him for the last movement, he found the composer still busily copying the cello part. Lebell must have had to work hard to prepare himself properly at such short notice. He nevertheless did a fine job; the concert was a success, and the two friends enjoyed playing together. On 18 December Lebell participated in the premiere of Dohnányi's String Quartet during a concert of the London Chamber Music Union.

That year Dohnányi again spent the Christmas holidays in Pozsony with his parents before resuming his busy concert schedule. On 3 January 1900 the Fitzner Quartet performed Dohnányi's String Quartet in Vienna. The composer appeared in the same concert, playing the piano part of the Beethoven Trio, op. 70. On 7 January Dohnányi joined the Fitzner Quarter for a performance of Beethoven's Piano Quartet in E-flat Major. Later that month in Budapest Dohnányi performed Beethoven's E-flat Major Concerto with Richter. On 29 January 1900 he appeared in Munich, playing his own Piano Concerto with Felix Weingartner and the Kaim Orchestra. On 2 February in Pozsony the Fitzner Quartet performed Dohnányi's A Major Quartet and his Sextet, a work from his student years that he had revised yet left in manuscript. Dohnányi never cared whether his works were published. "An artist should not write for the publisher," he used to say. "He shouldn't care if he is paid or not. He should create by an inward need, a necessity."

On 3 February Dohnányi performed in a Philharmonic Concert in Berlin in which he played his Piano Concerto under the baton of Arthur Nikisch. Dohnányi considered Nikisch to be as good a conductor as Richter, even though they were musicians with different personalities. Perhaps Nikisch's greatest merit was that he accompanied the soloist with such tact and sensitivity that he seemed to know in advance what the soloist was going to do. Dohnányi never met a finer accompanist among conductors. Nikisch did not belong to the type who, partly out of arrogance or partly out of lack of accompanying skill, want the soloist to play just as they conduct. Nikisch wanted to please the soloist and let him play at his ease. After all, it was the soloist who was responsible for the success of the performance.[8]

This was also Dohnányi's opinion. When later he himself became conductor of the Budapest Philharmonic, he always tried to let the soloist freely develop his interpretation. On one occasion Dohnányi conducted the performance of a famous pianist. Although the pianist played contrary to Dohnányi's taste, Dohnányi let him have his way. At the end of the performance, the pianist cried out with enthusiasm, "How delighted I am to see that your interpretation of the work is just like mine!"

---

8. Arthur Nikisch (1855–1922) was also an excellent accompanist at the piano; he often accompanied Elena Gerhardt, the famous Lieder singer.

The Philharmonic Concerts took place on Mondays. They were preceded by a matinee, which was actually a public dress rehearsal, on Sundays. These matinees were far more important than the concerts because they were visited by music lovers, musicians, and the press, who criticized, praised, or blamed the performers freely. When Dohnányi played his Concerto at the matinee, the performance had a mixed reception. Part of the audience applauded most heartily, but a rather considerable part broke into a furious whistling, which in Europe signals disapproval. Dohnányi was not upset by this. Smiling and perfectly composed, he bowed to those who made such a moving effort to reward him with their appreciation. The others he simply ignored. After the matinee several outstanding musicians, among them the well-known French pianist Eduard Riesler, came into the artist's room to express their appreciation. "Congratulations on the whistling," Riesler said. "This shows that your composition was considered important. Nobody would bother to oppose a mediocre work!"

Nikisch and the concert agent, Hermann Wolff, were perturbed by this incident. They asked Dohnányi to make a cut in the third movement for the Monday evening concert, but he refused. "I am sure you will change your mind," said Wolff. On Monday morning Nikisch called a special rehearsal. When Dohnányi appeared Nikisch and Wolff again tried to persuade him to make the cut. Dohnányi stuck to the opinion he had already expressed the day before. Nikisch then flicked over the pages of the third movement, and proposed a cut from one B major chord to another B major chord that had no regard for the form of the movement. Dohnányi finally agreed, but only to please Nikisch, whom he highly respected. When Dohnányi performed the abridged piece that evening, however, he was not pleased. Although there was no whistling this time, Dohnányi knew very well that this different reception was not a result of the cut. The Monday audience was simply much colder and less interested than the audience of the day before.

The next time Dohnányi performed his concerto was on 20 February at one of the famous Gürzenich Concerts in Cologne. The score and parts had been forwarded to the conductor, Franz Wüllner. Wüllner was nearly seventy but was still respected as a musician of fine qualities. Although he belonged to the "old Classical school," he was one of the first to recognize the genius of Richard Strauss and perform his works. When Dohnányi arrived in Cologne and called on Wüllner, the conductor made a few polite remarks and then suddenly asked, "Who made this cut in the last movement?" When Dohnányi explained what had happened, Wüllner shook his head in disapproval and remarked: "Der Satz ist zwar lang, der Strich ist aber brutal!" (The movement may be long, but the cut is brutal!). Without hesitation he restored the cut, and the movement was performed as it was originally written.

After playing the concerto in Leipzig on 26 February, Dohnányi rushed to England to see Linchi and Mrs. Oliverson again. There was much to discuss now, for the young artist was preparing himself for his first trip to the United States. He had an invitation from Wilhelm Gericke, the conductor of the Boston Symphony Orchestra, to play Beethoven's G Major Concerto during a tour that was to include concerts in Cambridge, Boston, Philadelphia, Baltimore, New York, Brooklyn, and Providence.

The young Dohnányi smoked his cigarette with his usual composure when he boarded the *Oceanic* in Liverpool. As usual, Dohnányi departed at the last moment and arrived in New York only one day before the performance in Cambridge, Massachusetts. He was enchanted and spellbound, yet puzzled at the same time, by the fascinating city. During this first visit he could spend only a few hours to get acquainted with this most overwhelming town. Dohnányi had to continue his journey by train to Boston, accompanied by his American manager, a brother of his London agent, Mr. Vert.

Dohnányi's performance with the Boston Symphony Orchestra in New York took place in Carnegie Hall on 22 March 1900. This concert was a glorious success, and Dohnányi immediately gained a following in the New World. Even after the tour for which he had been engaged came to an end, he remained in the United States for further hastily booked concerts.[9] His New York recitals took place on 3, 9, and 14 April 1900 in Mendelssohn Hall, which at that time was more centrally located than Carnegie Hall.

During his visit in New York, Dohnányi stayed in a German hotel with many other world-famous artists. In the corridors one could hear music filtering from most of the rooms; the whole building resembled a conservatory of music. Each apartment had a bedroom, a bathroom, and a sitting room in which the musicians could practice, rest, and entertain friends. Dohnányi became closely acquainted with some of the other artists, including Hugo Becker, Arthur Friedheim, who had been one of Liszt's last piano students, and Josef Weiss, another pupil of Liszt. In Dohnányi's opinion, Weiss was extremely gifted and could have easily been the best pianist in the world, if he had learned to control his nerves. If Weiss did not care about a concert, he played his best. When he found that much depended on a performance, however, his playing became exaggerated and distorted. Dohnányi also developed a great admiration for Ernestine Schumann-Heink, the famous Wagner singer from Dresden. He deeply appre-

---

9. Dohnányi gave two recitals in Boston, two in New York, and two appearances with the Kneisel Quartet, which years ago had performed his Quintet for Brahms in Ischl. Now they performed it publicly in New York and Boston with the composer at the piano.

ciated her art, but it was her serene, natural disposition that truly aroused his admiration. She was never fussy or whimsical but always her sweet self.

During his stay in the hotel Dohnányi also became acquainted with Vladimir de Pachmann, the Polish pianist. Dohnányi had heard Pachmann play during his student days at the Budapest Academy and considered his art to be delicate, especially in his interpretations of Chopin and Schumann. Pachmann had an interesting personality and was sometimes very amusing. He was present at Dohnányi's recital in Mendelssohn Hall, and after the performance he exclaimed, "He plays excellently, but sits too high." Although Dohnányi always sat with his back straight, he was nevertheless relaxed; there was nothing artificial or forced about him and not the slightest sign of effort could be discovered in his poise. "I relax when I play; this is why I am never tired after a performance," he would say. Pachmann also disapproved of Dohnányi's decision to play Brahms's *Handel* Variations on the recital. Pachmann hated Brahms's music so much that during this piece he left the hall and paced up and down in the foyer. Witnesses related that he even covered his ears with his hands to block out the sounds that filtered out from the hall. In the artist's room he remarked to Dohnányi, "You play Brahms beautifully. He doesn't deserve to be played this way!"

In New York Dohnányi met several other personalities of importance. He was invited to private homes and enjoyed the city with all its peculiarities and vigor. As he became more familiar with Americans, their musical life, and their characters and habits, he became quite fond of them.

After his last concert, which took place on 14 April, Dohnányi left on the steamer *Etruria*. Although this was a rather small ship, it made the crossing to Liverpool in six days. Dohnányi stayed in London until June. He was now convinced that England was the place to which he wanted to return after his trips to relax and gather strength for further work.

Arriving back in Hungary, Dohnányi rejoiced to see his old friends, especially Béla Bartók. Bartók was a student at the Academy of Music in Budapest and a pupil of Koessler and Thomán, as Dohnányi had been not long ago. Bartók, a pale young man of delicate health but strong will, was in a rather gloomy mood. When Dohnányi asked about his studies, Bartók declared that he had stopped composing because he felt that everything in music had already been written. Since there was nothing new left for him to create, he had decided to limit his activity to playing the piano. Dohnányi then remembered *Also sprach Zarathustra*, the new symphonic poem in which Richard Strauss had given expression to his modern musical ideas. Gericke had performed this work in Boston on the evening when Dohnányi had played the Beethoven Concerto. Dohnányi told Bartók about this composition, and the two friends played the work from the piano score for four hands. Bartók became deeply interested and examined it attentively over and over. Suddenly he pronounced that he had found the solution to his problem and was now determined to follow the new ways of modern art.

Dohnányi spent that summer with his family in Pozsony, where he joined his father every day as he went to drink beer in a restaurant, proudly introducing his son to his friends. Dohnányi also started his D Minor Symphony, op. 9. He spent the second part of the summer with the Kunwald family in Fenyöháza in the Tatra Mountains. Dohnányi's relationship with Elsa Kunwald deepened even more during these days. It was no longer a secret that the twenty-three-year old artist was going to marry Elsa, and the two tried to set a date for their wedding. First they chose 12 October, but this was a Friday, and the superstitious Mrs. Kunwald protested. The thirteenth was again a date of bad omen. The fourteenth was too late, because Dohnányi wanted to spend a few days in England before his next trip to the United States. The eleventh was the only day left, but on this day Dohnányi, subject to military service, had to appear in Pozsony before the Draft Board. The only way to carry out the wedding ceremony was for him to hurry back from Pozsony on 11 October.

Dohnányi and his bride-to-be entered the Registrar's Office at ten o'clock at night. The clerk was angry, of course, when he had to open his office just for this occasion. After grumbling about "queer, modern youngsters," he did his duty, and the young couple was united in marriage. They rushed straight from the Registrar's Office to the train for England.

❧

Dohnányi and his new bride sailed from Liverpool to New York in October 1900. He appeared as a soloist with the Boston Symphony Orchestra conducted by Gericke, in Pittsburgh under Victor Herbert, and with the New York Philharmonic under Emil Pauer. He performed his own Concerto in Boston, Philadelphia, Baltimore, New York, and St. Louis, played with the Kneisel Quartet, and gave several solo recitals in various cities throughout the United States and Canada.

On 24 November 1900 Dohnányi performed his Concerto in Chicago with the veteran conductor Theodore Thomas. Thomas was an excellent musician who had been active in American music for over fifty years. Although he was now an elderly man, he still took a lively interest in contemporary art and programmed the American premieres of many of the works of Richard Strauss. Besides their enthusiasm for the arts, Dohnányi and Thomas shared a great appreciation for good food and drink. When Thomas, who had an excellent wine cellar, learned that Dohnányi also valued good wine, he invited the young couple into his home for an intimate dinner. Mrs. Thomas served them a delicious meal of five or six courses, each of which had been chosen to match the wine served with each. This dinner was always one of Dohnányi's most cherished memories.

In Troy, New York, on 6 December 1900, Dohnányi performed Beethoven's *Kreutzer* Sonata in a joint recital with Fritz Kreisler. Kreisler had recently resumed his musical career after devoting ten years to medicine and military service. There were no rehearsals, as both artists arrived in town late. Dohnányi met Kreisler for the first time in the artists' room a few minutes before the performance. Kreisler's first question was, "Do you have the music for the piano part?" Kreisler had only the violin part, and Dohnányi did not have the piano part; he never carried music with him. Although the situation was most disturbing, the concert started on time. Dohnányi performed a solo number by memory, and Kreisler followed with his own solo. When it came time for the Beethoven Sonata, however, the situation was still unresolved. Finally, the resourceful agent noticed a young audience member, probably a student, attentively examining the piano score he had thoughtfully brought with him. It was snatched from his hands with apologetic words and carried to the artists. Despite the difficult situation, the performance was brilliant, and the enthusiastic audience never knew what had preceded it.

On this tour Dohnányi met William Mason, a fine American musician who was then in his seventies. Mason, who had once been a pupil of Liszt, invited the Dohnányis to his home. The young composer played his Symphony in D Minor, which he had just finished, on Mason's piano. Mason described this event in his *Memories of a Musical Life:*

> Early in March of the present year [1901] Von Dohnányi, his wife, and a few other friends among them Emil Pauer, dined at my house, and during the evening Von Dohnányi played his symphony on the pianoforte. This instrument is naturally quite inadequate to the interpretation of such a work, but Von Dohnányi's technic [*sic*] is so complete, his tone so massive while intensely musical, and his enthusiasm so contagious, that we became conscious of an ever-increasing interest, steadily growing in intensity. The occasion and its experience will not be forgotten by any of those present.[10]

This successful tour came to an end in March 1901, and the Dohnányis spent a few pleasant weeks resting in England in the home of Mrs. Oliverson. From London they traveled to Gmunden, in Upper Austria, which was a popular and fashionable summer residence on Lake Traunsee in the Salzkammergut. Dohnányi rented an apartment in Gmunden for the summer

---

10. William Mason, *Memories of a Musical Life* (New York: Century, 1901), pp. 264–65.

and hired a cook and a chambermaid from Linz. It was a joyful summer, for Dohnányi's parents and his sister Mitzi came to stay with them. Frederick von Dohnányi, who had busily continued to collect articles about his son's triumphs, had many questions about Dohnányi's experiences. Unfortunately, they did not spend too much time together, for Gmunden was crowded with interesting people whom Dohnányi wanted to meet.

One day while Dohnányi was working on the scoring of his Symphony, he was interrupted by Victor von Miller zu Aichholz, a wealthy Viennese patrician who owned several lovely villas in Gmunden. Although he was not a musician, he was a most enthusiastic music lover and a great admirer of Brahms, who had frequently been his guest in Gmunden and in Vienna. After Brahms's death, Miller-Aichholz had built an exact replica of Brahms's house in the park of his own villa. He had equipped it with the furniture from the three rooms in which Brahms had spent the last ten summers of his life. Everything was in its original place: the coffee grinder, Brahms's favorite books, and music; even Brahms's nightshirt lay on a chair next to his bed. Miller-Aichholz used the third room, in which Brahms had kept only his piano, as a Brahms Museum. He collected every object he could find that had any connection with his beloved friend.

Miller-Aichholz frequently invited the Dohnányis to his villa. Mrs. Miller was a charming woman who was delighted to have guests. The Dohnányis had dinner there every Sunday along with many other well-known artists. Karl Goldmark, who customarily spent his summers in Gmunden, was a frequent visitor. He and Brahms had often been guests of the Millers. On those occasions Goldmark's place at the table had been at the left side of the hostess; the seat of honor on the right side had been reserved for Brahms. Now, for some superstitious reason, Goldmark sat in his old place, and it was the young Dohnányi who had to take the seat of honor. Dohnányi had met Goldmark in Budapest during his student days, and the two artists were happy to see each other again.

In the Miller house Dohnányi also met the violinist Joseph Joachim, who spent every summer as a guest of the former Queen of Hanover.[11] Dohnányi and Joachim, who was Director of the Königliche Preussische Hochschule für Musik (Royal Prussian Academy of Music) in Berlin, often played chamber music together. Dohnányi also met Eduard Hanslick, who had once been a critic for the *Neue Freie Presse* and an author of books on musical aesthetics. Although he criticized Wagner and wrote most enthusiastically about Brahms, he was far from understanding Brahms's real value.

11. When Prussia annexed the Kingdom of Hanover in 1866, the Queen went into exile and took up residence in Gmunden. She lived with her two daughters, whom Dohnányi met when they visited the Millers, and her son, the Duke of Cumberland.

The composer who stood much nearer to Hanslick's heart was Antonín Dvořák. Once, at the Miller's house, Dohnányi and Hanslick played a four-hand version of Dvořák's Piano Quintet. Dohnányi was surprised to find how well his partner played, and it gave him amusement to quicken the tempo in the last movement until poor Hanslick was sweating and panting. Nevertheless, Hanslick kept up with Dohnányi to the last chord.

Hanslick's wife loved to sing, but people did not have a very high opinion of her ability. Hanslick, who was so severe in his judgment of other musicians, was nevertheless enchanted by the artistic activities of his wife. One long-suffering friend impiously wrote in Hanslick's guest book, "Liebe macht nicht nur blind aber auch taub" (Love makes one not only blind but also deaf).

After the serene and sunny days of Gmunden, the Dohnányis left for Vienna, where they rented an apartment on Theobald Gasse. It was in this home that on 1 January 1902 their son Hans was born. It was here also that Dohnányi completed his op. 10, a Serenade for String Trio.

Dohnányi had to leave his wife and their infant son to fulfill his concert obligations. On 11 January 1902 he played at a Pope Concert in London, followed by four solo recitals in the same city. On 30 January, in Manchester, Hans Richter gave Dohnányi's D Minor Symphony its world premiere. Dohnányi had played this Symphony for Richter one year earlier, before he had completed the scoring. Upon this first hearing, Richter had waved his hand, and said mockingly, "This is probably your first symphony, and such should be handled like first puppy dogs: drowned!" Dohnányi had smiled. "But this is not my first symphony, sir!" he had said. "It's my second. Although the first won a prize years ago, I have 'drowned' it. I have put it aside and have not let it be performed since, for I am not satisfied with it."

Dohnányi had to depart quickly to arrive in time for a concert in Vienna. He took the Dover–Calais route. At the port in Dover, the sea was so stormy that the boat was being tossed about like a toy by the waves. Most of the passengers decided to abandon the journey, but Dohnányi felt it was his duty to take the chance. He often said that an artist was like a soldier: his concerts were his duty. He went determinedly on board, but his courage was to be tested further. The ship had hardly left the port when it turned around and struggled desperately back to the harbor. The paddle wheels had been damaged by the raging sea and needed repair. Now even those who had initially decided to brave the crossing withdrew. Even Dohnányi hesitated for a second, wondering whether it would be more prudent to take another boat to Ostende. Then he decided to stick to his original plan. It was the worst trip he had ever experienced. Nevertheless, he was lucky; he arrived the same night at Boulogne instead of Calais, while the ship that sailed to Ostende plunged about for three days on the stormy waves.

Dohnányi arrived in Vienna at the last moment for his recital on 3 February 1902. This was followed by solo performances on the eleventh and the twenty-seventh. On 12 February Dohnányi played Brahms's Second Piano Concerto with the newly organized Concertverein Orchestra. Until then symphonic music had been performed in Vienna only by the Opera Orchestra, and this was the first Viennese orchestra that played exclusively at concerts. The conductor at this concert was Ferdinand Löwe, a pupil of Bruckner. On the same concert Dohnányi conducted his own *Zrínyi* Overture. This was his first appearance as a conductor. When people asked him how he learned to conduct in such a short time, he answered with a smile, "It is not difficult to conduct. With talent, one can easily learn it through expert guidance; without talent, one will never become a good conductor, not even after having studied for decades!"

Dohnányi expressed the following opinion about conducting:

> In the list of performing artists and interpreters, the conductor now occupies one of the most distinguished places. His aim may be achieved in various ways, but the goal is always the same: to convey his intentions and his conception of the work through the orchestra. He may be more or less skillful, but above all he must possess a suggestive force to make himself understandable to his orchestra. Conductors also differ in rehearsing. Some need many rehearsals to carry out their intentions and produce a technically faultless performance, as far as this is possible; some need fewer. But there are also conductors, who in an effort to get this effect vainly torture the orchestra, the capacity of which is limited. The result is that the orchestra gets reluctant and does not give its best. Most people like it when the conductor makes eccentric gymnastic movements on the platform. There are, of course, others who don't care for his gestures and are most interested in the result of his production. The latter are correct. The value of a conductor should not depend on his neck-breaking movements or bodily contortions. Sometimes a slight, almost insignificant gesture suffices and can say more to the musicians in the orchestra than the most energetic waving and shaking of the baton.

As for the necessity for a conductor to appear at all, Dohnányi maintained:

> There have been many debates about this. There were attempts in Heidelberg to conceal the orchestra with the conductor. But the experiment was a failure; it turned out that people do want to see the orchestra with its conductor. They want to participate in his efforts and in his endeavor to achievement, just as in recitals they want to see the hands of the pianist. An invisible orchestra and conductor is only adequate in the opera, where the attention of the audience is focused upon the stage.

After one more recital in London, Dohnányi spent another summer in Gmunden with his family. This time they stayed in a villa belonging to the Millers. Their neighbor was Max Kalbeck, author of the first extensive Brahms biography. Kalbeck was working on the last part of his book. Dohnányi, who had learned much about Liszt through his discussions with William Mason, was even able to persuade Kalbeck to change one passage based on Mason's version of facts. Kalbeck had originally alleged that Liszt's inspiration for his B Minor Sonata had come from Brahms's F-sharp Minor Sonata, op. 2. According to Mason, however, when Brahms was accompanying the Hungarian violinist Eduard Reményi, the two artists came to Weimar and paid a visit to Liszt. Brahms showed Liszt some of his compositions, including the Sonata in F-sharp Minor. Liszt listened attentively and afterwards sat at the piano to play his B Minor Sonata. It was evident that this work had been written before Liszt knew Brahms's composition. Unfortunately Brahms, exhausted from the journey, began to doze in his chair while Liszt was playing and actually fell into a slumber. Liszt made no remark, but—according to Mason—never forgave Brahms and never supported Brahms's music.

During the summer of 1902, Paul Heyse, the famous German poet and writer, was a guest of the Kalbecks. He was in his seventies and was passionately fond of drawing. He made a drawing of Dohnányi and one of Dohnányi's father.

Béla Bartók, who had completed his studies at the Budapest Academy, came to Gmunden to study with Dohnányi. As Dohnányi had once received his final training from d'Albert, Bartók came to Dohnányi to receive similar finishing before starting his career. He also showed Dohnányi his compositions, which were mostly programmatic, written under the influence of Richard Strauss. The two artists were united in a deep friendship. Dohnányi always appreciated Bartók; he admired his talent and was very fond of him. "Even if there might be something I disapproved of in Bartók's music," he used to say, "and even if in some ways he acted somewhat strangely, I always acknowledged that he had the most sympathetic character and that he was the most honest and sincere man I have ever known."

That autumn Dohnányi had a concert in Frankfurt on 24 October 1902, where he performed his Cello Sonata with Hugo Becker. This occasion was of great importance to him, for it was then that he became even more closely acquainted with Becker. There were three cellists at that time who were acknowledged to be the best in the world: Becker, Pablo Casals, and Julius Klengel. The friendship between Dohnányi and Becker lasted for the rest of their lives.

Another concert tour followed in England. In December Dohnányi attended the premiere of *Der Münzenfranz* (The French Coin), an opera by his former teacher, Koessler, in Strassburg. That winter the Dohnányis rented an apartment in Budapest at 88 Andrássy Avenue, in the same house in which Dohnányi's uncle Ernő Szlabey and the Kunwald family lived. Dohnányi's young wife was expecting another baby and wanted to be near her mother. For the first time, Dohnányi did not spend Christmas in Pozsony.

❧

On 7 January 1903 Dohnányi was again on the concert stage, conducting his D Minor Symphony with the Budapest Philharmonic. This performance had a success that surpassed all other triumphs. People were so fascinated that for several moments after the last bar had resounded they sat stupefied. They then burst out into enthusiastic applause. Dohnányi also conducted his Symphony a few weeks later in Vienna. In the meantime, he had other concerts and recitals in Budapest, Vienna, and various German cities. Among these was his performance of Beethoven's E-flat Major Piano Concerto on 4 March in Karlsruhe. The permanent Music Director there was Felix Mottl, who was also a famous conductor of Wagner's music.

This concert, however, was conducted by Siegfried Wagner, Wagner's son. This gave Dohnányi an opportunity to get more closely acquainted with the Wagner family. There were pieces on the program by Richard Wagner, and the whole family came to take part in the event, including Richard Wagner's widow, Cosima, and his daughters. They were staying in the same hotel as Dohnányi and usually ate meals with him. At the rehearsal Dohnányi realized that Siegfried Wagner was not a skillful accompanist. Nevertheless, Dohnányi remained patient when they rehearsed the same things over and over again. When the rehearsal finally came to an end, one of the musicians whispered into Dohnányi's ear, "Don't worry! You can rely on us. We shall do our best to accompany you as you play." The musicians kept their promise, and the performance turned out to be a success with which not only the conductor but also his family was pleased.

On 7 March 1903 Dohnányi had a concert with the Mannheim Orchestra in which he played Beethoven's G Major Concerto. During his stay in Mannheim he was a guest of the Kahn family, along with the famous singer Julia Culp. On the morning of the concert, Dohnányi came down into the drawing room where his hosts and their other guests were chatting. With a triumphant smile, he showed them a telegram that he had just received from Budapest. "I am informed that my little daughter was born," he announced. Everybody looked at him with surprise. Women remarked that they had no idea until now that he was married, because he made the impression of an elegant young bon vivant. When they grasped the situation, they congratulated him warmly. The little girl was christened Grete. Perhaps, thinking of the popular fable of the Brothers Grimm, they wanted to have a "Hansel and Gretel."

In Prague on 11 March 1903 Dohnányi played Brahms's B-flat Major Concerto, conducted by Leo Blech, whom he deeply respected. A Museum Concert in Frankfurt on 13 March, however, greatly annoyed Dohnányi. The conductor, Gustav Friedrich Kogel, was one of those who paid no attention to the wishes of the soloist. When Dohnányi asked him to take a passage in an orchestral *tutti* section according to his own interpretation, Kogel answered briskly and firmly, "Play the *solo* passages as you prefer, but I'm going to conduct the *tutti* after my own liking."

After a short visit in England the Dohnányis came to Gmunden for the third summer in a row. Once more Dohnányi's family came to stay with them, to celebrate their two grandchildren. Even though the vacation villa was becoming crowded, there were no arguments; Dohnányi's mother, with her usual tactfulness and delicacy, ensured that everyone was perfectly at ease. This time they had one more visitor: Jan Brandts-Buys, the Dutch composer who had competed with Dohnányi for the Bösendorfer Prize and had since become a close friend. The villa had a tower that contained a cozy room, and Brandts-Buys stayed there for five weeks, dedicating himself to his compositions. Although it rained most of the time, the Dutch artist kept a calm disposition and regarded it with indifference. Whenever people complained about the continual drizzle, he only shrugged his shoulders and said, "Well, at least what is down is down; it won't come down again!"

This summer Dohnányi allowed himself to enjoy a true vacation. Instead of making music, he played tennis and took boat trips on the Traunsee. He also made his first excursion into the mountains of the Tyrol. Dohnányi was accompanied by his former teacher, Koessler, who had come to visit him. During this three-week trip Dohnányi fell in love with the mountains. The beauty of the sinister rocks, magnificent glaciers, and enchanting slopes covered with green forests filled him with ecstasy. From then on, he spent all his free summer time in the mountains. Dohnányi and Koessler's trip was far from comfortable. Because they had to carry their belongings in backpacks, they had tried to reduce their weight as much as possible. Dohnányi took only three shirts and used up the third one during the first half of their excursion. What else could he do but pick out a less soiled shirt and change into it? "Everything in life is relative," he used to say when people complained about something. In spite of the grubby shirts and the homely fare, the tourists were cheerful and content. It was a joy for the young artist to share his delight with his former teacher, who, since having become godfather of little Hans von Dohnányi, was tied with a new link to the family.

Although Dohnányi traveled quite a bit and adapted himself to the habits and traditions of various countries, he remained strictly Hungarian at heart.

In time, the F-sharp Minor and the C Major Rhapsodies became the most popular. When Dohnányi was asked why people preferred these two, he only smiled and shrugged his shoulders. "The taste of the public is unaccountable," he said. "Usually it not the favorite works of an author which become popular." When asked what his favorite work was, Dohnányi responded, "I have no favorite composition, nor do I have a favorite composer. I seek and appreciate in everything the beauty that can also be found in contrasting elements."

Fifty years later his protégé Edward Kilenyi, Jr., the renowned American pianist, characterized the Rhapsodies as follows:

> At the present time there is certainly no twentieth-century music for the piano in larger form as popular as Dohnányi's Four Rhapsodies, op. 11, composed in 1902. Their fascination for the listener and performer might be explained by an almost unique combination of divergent qualities. The rhapsodic character of each is balanced by the perfection of the four individual forms, which in turn are part of a grandiose cyclical form culminating in the last piece. Melodic and harmonic wealth still allow play for some superior polyphonic passages, and the piano's great orchestral effects are controlled by the fastidious part-writing of an unsurpassed master of chamber music.
>
> The first Rhapsody, in G Minor, is built up on three contrasting themes—one powerful and impassioned, an agitated transition, and a deeply touching sustained melody. The second, in F-sharp Minor, strongly Hungarian in character and a favorite of aspiring pianists, is saved from the fate of Rachmaninoff's C-sharp Minor Prelude by its nobility and certain technical demands. The third, in C Major, is a sardonic Scherzo in 3/4 time with a soaring melody for contrast. This may well be called the most popular of Dohnányi's pieces. The fourth, in A-flat Minor, beginning with a tolling of bells, and the medieval "Dies Irae" passing through longing reminiscences of the previous rhapsodies, ends the cycle with an apotheosis of plainchant, and of the opening theme of the G Minor Rhapsody. A veritable "Death and Transfiguration."[14]

Dohnányi premiered the Rhapsodies in a Vienna recital on 29 November 1904. The press praised them, and the audience was thrilled. From then on, they were performed all over the world.

---

14. Edward Kilenyi, Jr. (1910–2000), a student of Dohnányi and later a fellow Professor of Music at the Florida State University, wrote this specifically for this biography in 1955. "Death and Transfiguration" is a sly reference to the well-known tone poem by Richard Strauss.

A chamber music concert followed in Vienna with the Böhmische Streichquartett (Bohemian String Quartet). This was followed by another recital in Vienna and recitals in Berlin on 13 and 20 December 1904. One of the recitals in Berlin was attended by Ernst Rudorff, who was a composer, pianist, and the head of the Piano Department at the Hochschule für Musik in Berlin. While the ovations were still resounding in the hall, Rudorff visited Dohnányi in the artist's room and offered him a teaching position at the Hochschule. This institution, of which Joachim was Director, was very prestigious. Dohnányi answered that if their terms were acceptable, he would gladly agree. The offer, with the terms on paper, reached Dohnányi in February 1905, while he was on his annual tour in England. It promised a respectable, comfortable position. Dohnányi would have almost half a year's vacation, would work six hours weekly, and would receive for his work the highest possible fee.

After leaving England, Dohnányi returned to the continent to give concerts in Hungary, Germany, and Denmark. On 18 March 1905 he played Beethoven's G Major Concerto with Felix Weingartner in Copenhagen. This performance was so successful that he was engaged for recitals on 22, 27, and 31 March in the same city. Denmark was a country to which Dohnányi always came with pleasure. He liked her beautiful capital, and he liked the Danish audiences. He had friends there and often spoke about the lovely blonde women of that country—seemingly silent, shy, and quiet, yet ardently passionate. Dohnányi always believed that women in southern countries were rather cold and strict in morals, while northern women were easily carried away by their emotions.

Being a young man at the height of the glory of an artist, he was surrounded everywhere by the tempting attentions of lovely women. Being so responsive to the beauties of life, he did not always remain aloof. He did not, however, communicate even a whisper about any interest he displayed or any attention he ever paid to any particular woman. While he was reserved, even in the company of his friends, about ordinary private concerns, he was completely silent about romantic relationships. He considered it the greatest infamy for a man to even hint at the name of a woman in connection with some secret affair. The names of those women who must have had an influence upon the young artist's feelings will remain unknown forever.

In May 1905 Dohnányi was engaged to take part in the Beethoven Festival in Bonn, Beethoven's birthplace. The most outstanding musicians of Germany assembled here on such occasions, and the event drew music lovers from all over the world. The festival lasted four days, from 28 to 31 May, and Dohnányi performed daily in chamber music concerts and solo recitals.

Ferruccio Busoni, the well-known pianist, played in one of the concerts, and Dohnányi had an opportunity to become acquainted with him.

As they were both en route to Berlin, they took the same train. When they had to change at Cologne, they went into the Dom Hotel and had dinner together. This gave Dohnányi a chance to exchange ideas with Busoni about music and musicians. He was shocked to find that in many essential questions they differed greatly. The debate between them started when Busoni expressed his regrets over the fact that Dohnányi had accepted a position as teacher at the Hochschule. "Don't you teach?" Dohnányi countered.

"This is a different matter," Busoni argued. "I teach without accepting a fee. So I do it only when I am in the mood for it. To teach for money damages one's art." Dohnányi could not see the difference. He did not accept money from private pupils, but was engaged by the German State. Nevertheless, he preferred to remain silent, because there were so many other points on which the two artists could not agree.

Busoni had several unusual and extreme ideas about music and musicians that were incompatible with Dohnányi's opinions. For instance, he was a great admirer of Wagner. Dohnányi might have readily joined him in this enthusiasm, if Busoni had not stated that on one single page of a Wagner score there were more ideas than in the works of Beethoven up to his op. 80. Busoni also did not have an appreciation for Haydn, but he did acknowledge Mozart's importance. Naturally, Busoni had no sympathy for Romantic composers such as Schumann, Schubert, and Brahms. He was, however, enthusiastic about Liszt, whom Dohnányi also admired but could not agree in placing above the other great Romantics. Busoni was also amazingly insensitive to the beauties of nature; he usually spent his summers in dusty Berlin. The two musicians, so different in their characters and feelings, never sought another opportunity to meet.

Dohnányi rented an apartment in Grunewald in Berlin, where he planned to settle with his family. In Düsseldorf, at another Music Festival on 12 and 13 June 1905, he played Brahms's B-flat Concerto and Beethoven's *Choral* Fantasia. When he returned to Vienna, he dedicated himself to completing his Cello Concerto.

He spent a part of August in Madonna di Campiglio, in the Brenta Dolomites, with Viennese friends. Dohnányi, again among his beloved mountains, ventured many dangerous climbs and gazed with delight across the green valleys at the snow-covered glaciers, which, in their sinister beauty, seemed to speak a language that he could understand. He spent several summers at the Madonna di Campiglio. Once, he undertook one of the very difficult climbs, the "Castelletta," with friends and a guide. Descending via a perilous route, he injured his hand on the sharp rocks and wrapped it in his handkerchief. This was observed by tourists from the Berliner Hütte (Berlin Lodge). Passing a Viennese couple, Dohnányi overheard the man saying in indignation to his wife, "What irresponsibility! Such an eminent artist shouldn't be allowed to squander his hands in this way!"

At the end of the month Mrs. Dohnányi arrived in the Dolomites, and together they made a trip to Trento. Because Venice was not far away—one could see its blue lagoons from the top of the mountains—it was only natural that they visited this ancient city.

Before taking leave from Vienna, Dohnányi wanted to say farewell to his friends. Since he was accustomed to expressing his feelings in music, he started composing *Winterreigen* (Winter Round Dances), Ten Bagatelles for Piano, op. 13, which he dedicated to them.

THREE

1905–1919

Dohnányi started his work at the Königliche Preussische Hochschule für Musik in Berlin in October 1905. Although he was the youngest teacher, he was paid the highest salary at the Hochschule. After just three years, he would receive the prestigious title "Professor." Upon swearing an oath as a State employee, Dohnányi was told that he had also automatically become a Prussian citizen. This came as a surprise to Dohnányi; in Hungary one could be employed by the State without being a citizen. His teacher Koessler, for example, had remained a German citizen. Nevertheless, Dohnányi refused to give up his own nationality and maintained his citizenship in Hungary as well.

Dohnányi was very happy in Berlin because he was able to find everything he wanted: comfort, art, culture, and civilization. He could also find privacy whenever he wanted to be alone. The Dohnányis rented an apartment, for which they paid 5,000 marks a year. It was a spacious house in the fashionable suburb of Grunewald. When their furniture arrived from Vienna, they decorated their comfortable new home together.

Although the music life at the Hochschule was rather conservative, the opera featured a repertoire influenced by the newer style of Richard Strauss, who had become its conductor in 1898. Dohnányi's workload was relatively small. In addition to receiving an annual vacation of three months, he taught just six students, dedicating one hour a week to each. He refused to teach more pupils, so that he could dedicate himself to composing and performing, as well as teaching, without neglecting any of his endeavors. Of the three, teaching interested him least, but he did enjoy several distinguished pupils, including Mischa Levitzki, Max Trapp, Astrid Berwald, Imre Stefaniai, and Erwin Nyiregyházi.

Once, when Dohnányi was asked how he defined "teaching music," he shook his head and replied,

> This term generally does not cover its real meaning, because the teacher who only "teaches" music does not fulfill his calling. Teaching signifies much more; it means

the exploitation of the possibilities that are lurking within a pupil, with the object of eventually allowing him to stand on his own two feet. Of course, there are various means and methods of teaching, but the aim is the same. A teacher is surely to be condemned who requires a talented pupil to imitate exactly what he is telling or demonstrating. Such a method is acceptable only for pupils who have no individuality at all and should therefore not even be in the music profession.

To the question of how much a student can gain from his teacher, Dohnányi said, "This varies with the individual. Sometimes he gains even more than he is given. After all, Liszt, Mozart, Haydn, and the other greats were also once pupils." As for how long a pupil should study, Dohnányi believed that "There comes a time when a gifted pupil has to be dismissed. If the pedagogue does not honor this moment and instead continues to pester his student, he might hinder his artistic development. On the other hand, it would be wrong to send the student away too early, for then he would be helpless and uncertain, and would lack the foundation upon which to build." When asked how one can recognize when the appropriate time has come, Dohnányi responded, "One must have the right senses to feel it. It is like painting a portrait, when an artist has to know when to stop. Often one extra stroke of the brush can spoil the picture." Once he was asked how his pupils, who were surely under the influence of his great art and personality, were able to free themselves afterwards from this influence and become individuals. "In the beginning, every pupil tries to imitate his teacher, and is under his influence," Dohnányi would answer. "But I do my best to develop their personality and make them stand on their own feet as quickly as possible."

In October, Dohnányi's work at the Hochschule was interrupted by a trip to Denmark, where he performed in sonata recitals with Lady Hallé in Copenhagen and other cities. Lady Hallé's age did not hamper her art; she was in splendid form. During one visit to Copenhagen, Dohnányi stayed in the same hotel as Edvard Grieg and his wife, with whom he often dined. During one of these meetings Grieg recommended that Dohnányi hear a young Norwegian pianist, Fridtjof Backer-Grøndahl. Dohnányi later accepted Backer-Grøndahl as his pupil and taught him for several years in Berlin. Upon completing his studies, Backer-Grøndahl played Grieg's Piano Concerto, with Grieg conducting, in several cities. In November, Dohnányi performed several recitals and concerts in Vienna, including the 22 November 1905 Viennese premiere of the three-movement version of his Piano Concerto.

On 12 January 1906 in Dresden, Dohnányi played Beethoven's *Emperor* Concerto with Ernst von Schuch on a concert that also included Dohnányi's D Minor Symphony. This was Dohnányi's first contact with this famous conductor, and it led to a lasting friendship. Dohnányi found

Schuch to have a charming personality with naive but very sympathetic traits, such as being superstitious. Throughout his career, Schuch received numerous honors. Once, after Schuch received a new decoration, the members of his orchestra hurried to congratulate him. Only the orchestra manager did not move. When they urged him to express his best wishes, he shrugged his shoulders. "By the time I reached the stage to congratulate him," he said, "he might have already obtained another award."

On 7 March 1906 in Budapest, Dohnányi conducted the Budapest Philharmonic for the world premiere of his new *Konzertstück* (Concert Piece) for cello and orchestra, op. 12, with Hugo Becker, to whom it was dedicated, as the soloist. At the end of May 1906 Dohnányi appeared in Bonn at a Schumann festival, playing solos and chamber music with the Joachim Quartet. He also played Schumann's Piano Concerto with Joachim conducting. On 23 and 24 May 1906, Dohnányi accompanied two famous Dutch singers: Johannes Messchaert in the *Dichterliebe* and Julia Culp in *Frauenliebe und Leben.* These works need a very delicate and expressive accompaniment, and participation in these performances gave Dohnányi much pleasure.

Since he lived in Berlin, Dohnányi had many opportunities to meet with Joachim, who was the director of the Hochschule. The Dohnányis were frequently invited to his home, and Dohnányi and Joachim often played music together in the house of Franz and Robert Mendelssohn. They also judged the graduate examinations together. During one examination a pupil sang a song that Joachim, who had a remarkably wide knowledge of music literature, did not recognize. He asked a professor who sat next to him who had composed the song. The professor glanced in surprise at Joachim, and then said with a broad grin, "If I'm not mistaken, it's a composition by our faculty member," and he named a colleague whose works Joachim disliked.

"Well, this time he seems to have done better," Joachim remarked, grumbling. "I somehow cannot help liking this song." When the song was over, he asked the girl's teacher, Ms. Breiderhof, who the composer was.

"Don't you recognize it, Professor Joachim?" the woman answered with astonishment. "You yourself composed it! It's an early work of yours that has not been published. You gave it to a friend of mine. I found it among his music, and my pupil was delighted to learn and perform it."

The first composition Dohnányi completed in Berlin was a collection of ten bagatelles for the piano, *Winterreigen* (Winter Round Dances), which he wrote in memory of the happy days he had spent in Vienna.[1] Each piece

---

1. The *Winterreigen* were first performed by the composer on a recital on 29 November 1906, in Vienna.

is dedicated to a specific friend and makes reference to a personal experience. For example, "Sphären Musik" (Music of the Spheres) is written in remembrance of a balloon flight Dohnányi took along with a Commander of the Austrian Air Force. The craft was not a dirigible but a free balloon at the mercy of the wind. The only thing the pilot could control was the rising and descending. They took off from Vienna and landed in a small village in Bohemia after floating in the air for three hours. Dohnányi enjoyed this flight tremendously. After crisscrossing the world with numerous flights on modern airplanes, he said, "On an airplane I never really had the sensation that I was flying in the way I felt it when we ascended in that balloon. I had a splendid view of all the earth below, and it was an unforgettable sensation to hear all noises from below in a mystical, faraway manner." He dedicated "Sphären Musik" to the Air Force Commander. "Freund Victors Mazurka" (Friend Victor's Mazurka) is an arrangement of a composition by Dr. Victor Heindl, who was one of Dohnányi's most intimate friends. Heindl wrote a prologue to *Winterreigen* that gives a humorous and touching introduction to the whole composition.

The year 1907 opened with ten concerts in Germany, followed by a short trip to Russia. Czarist Russia was a country with a totally different habits and traditions. It was the only country, except Turkey and Romania, where Dohnányi needed a passport. St. Petersburg seemed like a wonderful dream to Dohnányi. People of culture and rank lived in luxurious splendor. On 9 February 1907 Dohnányi played his Piano Concerto, and on the thirteenth he gave a piano recital. Both concerts were wonderful events, and the elegant audience responded enthusiastically.

As usual, many concerts followed. It is amazing how Dohnányi completed so many obligations, crossing and recrossing various countries with such speed, defying the difficulties and obstacles that travel presented at that time. Despite all this traveling, Dohnányi continued to compose. On 27 March 1907 in Vienna, Dohnányi and Dr. Alfred Hassler, a Swiss singer, premiered Dohnányi's *Sechs Gedichte* (Six Poems), op. 14, as well as his *Im Lebenslenz* (In the Prime of Life), op. 16.[2] The *Sechs Gedichte* took their texts from Victor Heindl, whose poetry Dohnányi had also used in his song *Waldelselein* (Little Elsa of the Woods), which he dedicated "To the naughty girl, to quiet her."[3] *Im Lebenslenz* is another cycle of six songs for voice and piano. Its texts were taken from poems by Wilhelm Conrad Gomoll.

2. Dr. Hassler also performed the *Sechs Gedichte* on 4 April in Berlin, again accompanied by the composer.

3. The title of *Waldelselein* is a play on the word "Waldelfelein" (the Spirit of the Woods), using the similarity between "f" and "s" in German Fraktur script.

On 15 May 1907 the National Hungarian Royal Academy of Music moved to a new building and was renamed the Liszt Ferenc Zeneművészeti Főiskola (Franz Liszt Academy of Music). The music school had originally been founded in a modest building in Budapest by Franz Liszt himself. It later moved to 66 Andrássy Avenue, the building in which Dohnányi had completed his studies. In this building Liszt had three rooms in which he resided when he was in Budapest. The Academy had now moved from Andrássy Avenue into a splendid new building on the square that is now named after Liszt. Dohnányi was naturally present on this occasion, and he played his own Piano Concerto.

In May 1907 Dohnányi participated in a five-day festival held in Bonn. In one of his daily performances he played a Brahms Violin Sonata with Joachim. This would be Dohnányi's last appearance with Joachim; during the Bach Festivals in Eisenach on 27 and 28 June 1907, Joachim caught a cold from which he never recovered. After Joachim's death on 15 August 1907, Henri Marteau took his place as the Violin Professor at the Hochschule für Musik in Berlin. He became Dohnányi's partner for chamber music, and they soon undertook concert trips together, giving sonata recitals. This association lasted for many years. Cellist Hugo Becker later joined them to form a trio.

Dohnányi devoted the rest of the summer to composition, except when he was mountain climbing in the Dolomites. He completed his Second String Quartet, op. 15, which he dedicated to Dr. Adalbert Lindner, his doctor and friend from Vienna. The Quartet was premiered by the Klingler Quartet in Berlin the following fall. Dohnányi could not be present at this performance, however, because he was on a concert tour.

Dohnányi's 1907 tour of about eighty concerts began in Norway. It also included performances in Sweden, France, Germany, Austria, Holland, Switzerland, Denmark, and Hungary. Dohnányi often performed Beethoven's Piano Concerto in B-flat. Remarkably, he frequently gave the Concerto its premiere in many cities, even in Germany. Although Dohnányi usually performed his own cadenzas, he used a cadenza by Beethoven for this concerto. Beethoven was young and still much under the influence of Mozart when he composed the concerto. The cadenza, however, was written in his last years, and there is a great difference between the compositional styles of the two. One critic in Berlin, in the belief that this cadenza was Dohnányi's, wrote in a review of the performance that the cadenza was in the wrong style.

"He was quite right," Dohnányi said, smiling. "But can a cadenza written by the composer himself ever be in the wrong style?"

A professor who was present at a performance of this concerto in Budapest remarked, "This cadenza cannot be Dohnányi's; he surely would have written one more within the style."

On 10 October 1907 Dohnányi performed a new piano composition called *Humoresken in Form einer Suite* (Humoresques in the Form of a Suite), op. 17, in Bergen. The first piece, which Dohnányi simply entitled "March," is now better known as "March Humoresque." This movement in particular became very popular. It is composed on a ground bass of four notes (E-flat, D, C, and B-flat).[4] The second piece is a toccata. In the third piece, entitled "Pavane aus dem XVI Jahrhundert mit Variationen" (Pavane from the Sixteenth Century with Variations), one of the variations of the theme appears together with the old student song "Gaudeamus Igitur." The fourth piece, "Pastorale," includes a canon in contrary motion. The final piece is a humorous introduction and fugue.

On 11 December in Mainz Dohnányi played his Piano Concerto with Emil Steinbach conducting. On 27 December 1907 the American composer and conductor Henry Handley made his first appearance in Germany. He conducted at the Stadttheater in Mainz and asked Dohnányi to play his Piano Concerto with him. Dohnányi also performed several concerts with the seventeen-year-old violinist Franz von Vecsey.[5]

The 1908–9 season was also busy; it included fifty-four concerts. In 1909 Dohnányi composed two of his most significant works: the three-act pantomime *Der Schleier der Pierrette* (The Veil of Pierrette), op. 18, and the Suite in F-sharp Minor for Orchestra, op. 19. He worked on both compositions simultaneously: he completed the first two tableaux of the Pantomime, then the first two movements of the Suite, then the third tableau of the Pantomime, and finally the two last movements of the Suite.[6]

Der Schleier der Pierrette was premiered on 22 January 1910 in Dresden at the Royal Opera. It was conducted by Ernst von Schuch, to whom it was dedicated. The three chief roles were performed by opera singers, the subordinate roles by the members of the ballet. The premiere was a brilliant success. The pantomime was staged in the following years in Germany, Austria, Hungary, and Moscow, where it was performed almost daily during World War I. The success of a performance of *Der Schleier der Pierrette* always depends on finding a suitable Pierrette. This is a rather difficult

---

4. When Dohnányi would perform this, he would often play just the bass line a few times before actually beginning the piece.

5. Franz von Vecsey (1893–1935) had been a child prodigy, appearing at the same time as Mischa Elman, who was about a year older. Dohnányi considered Vecsey's talent of a very high quality and lamented the fact that Vecsey died at such a young age.

6. Dohnányi used music from *Der Schleier der Pierrette*, op. 18, in an orchestral suite, *Stücke und Tanze* (Pieces and Dances), op. 18, no. 1. Dohnányi also arranged the *Hochzeitswalzer* (Wedding Waltzes) for solo piano and for piano, four hands, and the *Hochzeitsmarsch* (Wedding March) for violin and piano as well as string quartet and piano.

role; it requires a very expressive actress who is also skillful in dancing. One of the best Pierrettes was Elza Galafrés, who first appeared in this role on 16 March 1912 in Vienna and later performed it in Prague, Berlin, Budapest, and other places. The Vienna performance had a tremendous impact on Dohnányi. Although Galafrés was married to the famous violinist Bronislaw Huberman, Dohnányi found himself deeply attracted to the energetic vitality of the clever and resourceful actress. She also became a close friend of Mrs. Dohnányi, and she frequently stayed with the Dohnányis as their houseguest.

The plot of the pantomime, which was written by Arthur Schnitzler, tells a fascinating story. The unfaithful Pierrette deserts her lover Pierrot to marry Harlequin. On her wedding night, however, she regrets her decision and escapes to Pierrot to share death with him. She offers him poison, which he drinks. At the last moment, Pierrette realizes that she does not have the strength to do the same, leaving Pierrot to die alone. The unfaithful girl, half-insane with horror, runs back to rejoin Harlequin, who is in a rage over her absence. She tries to dance with him, but the image of the dying Pierrot appears before her, extending the cup of poison toward her. Harlequin notices that her veil is missing and drags her into Pierrot's chamber, where he finds her veil next to the corpse of the young lover. Harlequin forces Pierrette to drink to the health of her dead lover and locks her in the room. Left alone with the body, she becomes insane, and Pierrot's returning friends find them both dead.

The Suite in F-sharp Minor, which Dohnányi originally entitled "Suite Romantique," was first performed on 21 February 1910 in Budapest, conducted by the composer. It became quite popular, especially in England and the United States. It has been recorded several times with various conductors, and a transcription of one movement is often played by bands. The Suite quickly turned into one of Dohnányi's most played pieces.

On 10 November 1909 Frederick von Dohnányi died. He had kept vigil throughout the years over the career of his son. This vigil, however, had been only from a distance; he had always been careful to never interfere with any of his son's plans. He had made suggestions without ever giving advice. The entire student body and the staff of the Gymnasium, of which Professor Dohnányi had been recently made Director, gathered at his grave. The funeral was also attended by many former graduates who had continued to return to him for help. As Iván Vargha said in his funeral oration, "His noble, unselfish soul was seeking in his fellow men kindness and affection, and those in whom he found this kindness and affection became his friends. Besides his family, he cared deeply for his colleagues, his friends, and all humanity; he strove indefatigably to better people. Even though he labored within a restricted sphere of activity in which he could obtain only limited results, his artistic son, renowned throughout the world with the international idiom of art, was to realize the ideals of his father."[7]

❧

In July 1910 the first Mozart Festival took place in Salzburg. Although it became the foundation of the famous festivals of today, this festival was modestly organized by the famous soprano Lilly Lehman. Because there was no Festspielhaus (Festival Play House), the chamber music concerts, in which Dohnányi participated, took place in the Aula of the University. The operas were performed in the intimate little theater by famous singers and the Vienna Philharmonic Orchestra under Karl Muck. Lilly Lehman herself sang the parts of Donna Anna in *Don Giovanni* and the Queen of the Night in *Die Zauberflöte* (The Magic Flute) in a way that Dohnányi thought could not be surpassed. The festival also marked the *Grundsteinlegung,* the laying of the cornerstones of the Mozarteum.

The 1909–10 season contained seventy concerts, embracing the usual tours in Norway, Denmark, Germany, Austria, Italy, Spain, and, of course, Hungary. The next season, 1910–11, included fifty concerts, including trips to Poland and Rome, where among other performances Dohnányi conducted his F-sharp Minor Suite. A similar series of concerts followed in the next season.

In 1912 Dohnányi composed his Sonata for Piano and Violin, op. 21, which he dedicated to Victor von Herzfeld. Dohnányi premiered the Sonata with Rudolf Fitzner on 11 April in the home of the Hämmerle family in Vienna. Mr. and Mrs. Hämmerle, to whom Dohnányi had dedicated his Serenade, op. 10, had a lovely home where Vienna's outstanding musicians would frequently gather for evenings of chamber music. Dohnányi would often play with the Fitzner Quartet at the Hämmerle house. The first public performance of the Violin Sonata took place on 14 April 1912 in Berlin, again with Rudolf Fitzner. On 16 July 1912 Dohnányi played the Sonata in Berlin with Karl Klingler, with whose quartet he also often collaborated.

In July, Dohnányi composed *Drei Orchesterlieder* (Three Orchestral Songs), op. 22. Dohnányi used as his texts three poems by Gomoll, whose poems he had already used for *Im Lebenslenz.* The first piece, "Gott" (God), a pantheistic poem, was performed on 17 February 1914 in Berlin by Richard Mayr, conducted by Carl Panzner. Dohnányi had also composed

---

7. For Iván Vargha's full funeral ovation for Frederick von Dohnányi, see Kumlik, *Dohnányi Frigyes 1843–1909* (see the Prologue, n. 4), pp. 8–10.

another song, "Am Bach" (At the Brook), to a poem by Gomoll which he and his wife had premiered in Berlin on 14 February 1912.

On 30 November 1912 Dohnányi introduced in Szeged (Segedin), the second largest town in Hungary, his *Drei Stücke* (Three Pieces) for piano, op. 23. Although Dohnányi did not plan it, the theme of the third piece resembles an old Hungarian folk song. This movement became very popular in Hungary, where they called it "Szeretnék szántani," after the folk song.

Even though *Der Schleier der Pierrette* had been successful all over Europe, many found it to be too short. It did not take up a whole evening, so opera companies usually had to pair it with another opera that was usually unsuitable. In order to fill out an entire evening, Dohnányi composed a comic opera in one act with the title *Tante Simona* (Aunt Simona), for which his friend Victor Heindl wrote the libretto. This opera was premiered on 22 January 1913 in Dresden by the Dresden Hofoper (Court Opera), paired with a performance of *Der Schleier der Pierrette.* Both were conducted by Ernst von Schuch. The opera was repeated several times in Berlin, Budapest, Charlottenburg, and other cities. Although audiences were enthusiastic over *Tante Simona,* the critics reacted less favorably to it. They expected the work to be groundbreaking, while the composer's only aim was to write a work in an easy style that would not attract too much attention and would prepare the audience for *Der Schleier der Pierrette.*

The 1912–13 season contained another a long list of performances, forty in all. On 18 February Dohnányi performed a sonata with Pablo Casals, whom he had long recognized as one of the finest cellists in the world. Dohnányi, with a true artist's perception, saw Casals's greatness before the world became fully aware of it. At the end of March 1913 Dohnányi played in a trio recital with Casals and Georges Enesco in Budapest. This evening always ranked among Dohnányi's favorite performances, because it was a most amusing event. The three artists, who had never played together, arrived from various parts of Europe shortly before the recital, so no rehearsal was possible. All three artists felt a real enjoyment in the performance, and the audience, which applauded frantically, was obviously convinced that several rehearsals had preceded the inspired performance.

The concert season in 1913–14 included more concert trips all over Europe. In Berlin, Dohnányi composed his *Suite nach altem Styl* (Suite in Olden Style), op. 24. The Suite contains six piano pieces: "Prélude," "Allemande," "Courante," "Sarabande," "Menuet," and "Gigue." The style is, of course, not really "olden"; the whole set is called that only because it contains six types of dances that were commonly used in Baroque suites. Dohnányi premiered this piece in Berlin on 17 February 1914.

On the same concert, Dohnányi performed in the world premiere of his *Variationen über ein Kinderlied* (Variations on a Nursery Tune), op. 25. This work would procure Dohnányi his greatest renown, especially in England and North America. On the manuscript Dohnányi wrote, "Freunden des Humors zur Freude, den Anderen zum Ärger" (To the enjoyment of friends of humor, to the annoyance of the others). Feeling that this inscription might sound somewhat provocative, he published the work without it and omitted it from the program of the first performance. He later regretted this action, because he found that many of the "others" became annoyed by the composition and criticized each detail with open hostility.

The work starts with a dramatic introduction followed by a theme that is a popular nursery rhyme, known throughout the world as "Ah, vous dirai-je, Maman" or "Twinkle, Twinkle, Little Star." There are eleven variations, including a waltz, on this theme. The twelfth variation contains a passacaglia that makes the work serious again before the humor is restored. The *Variationen* were very successful in England, where the audience seemed to have a real sense of humor. The daily papers wrote about the work at length, discussing with great interest how humor can be expressed and applied in music.

For several years Dohnányi had spent his summers in the South Tyrol, spending many happy weeks with his Viennese friends and dedicating himself to his hobby of mountain climbing. He spent the summer of 1914, however, in Switzerland at the Vierwaldstätter See, where he also did some mountain climbing. Coming down from Zermatt, Dohnányi went to Pallanza on Lake Maggiore, where he received the shocking news of the outbreak of World War I. Within a few days all the foreigners had cleared the alpine playgrounds and rushed home. Dohnányi, with his usual tranquility, stayed. Because he was taking a much-needed vacation and was not needed at home, he decided to remain among these quiet mountains and enjoy the magnificence of nature.

Dohnányi enjoyed the beauties of nature even more this time, because he was in the company of the actress Elza Galafrés, her mother, and her little son Johannes. He had already made up his mind to spend the rest of his life with her, and they both planned to obtain divorces. At that time, Dohnányi had no premonition of the difficulties they would encounter with the passing years. He also did not realize how deeply he would miss his children, whom he was going to abandon with their faithful and loving mother. He would especially miss his little daughter Grete, who resembled him in appearance as well as in character. Although he would try to remain in touch with them, his efforts would be hampered by his new family life. Nevertheless, he plunged into his relationship with Elza Galafrés with all his artistic passion. Dohnányi, who had always liked children, became extremely fond of the little Huberman boy, who was to become his stepson.

After the other hotels closed, the tourists who remained in Brunnen moved into Dohnányi's hotel. People of various nationalities lived together peacefully, even though their countries were at war and they were officially "enemies." In spite of this peaceful attitude, at meals they all anxiously read the war news that appeared in the papers. Although these usually recorded German victories, the tide turned against Germany in September. Italy declared herself neutral, and so France, which had huge military forces on the Italian border that it could aim against the German Army, respected her neutrality. Even though the war still lasted for four years, in Dohnányi's opinion Germany's fate had been decided at the Battle of the Marne.

World War I completely changed cultural life in Europe. People had previously attended concerts in their best garments and afterwards joined lighthearted parties in restaurants or nightclubs. Now, however, they were burdened with grief. Dohnányi himself said, "The joyful, irresponsible, cheerful days are over, and they will never return. Not, at least, for a lifetime." Dohnányi composed very little during these years, and his concert trips, which had formerly crossed and recrossed the world, were now limited to the Central Powers of Austria, Hungary, and Germany, as well as neutral lands. It was rare for Dohnányi to perform in a concert with "enemy" artists, as he did on one occasion in Scheveningen, Holland, where he played under the French conductor Rhené-Baton.

In 1915 Dohnányi introduced his talented pupil Mischa Levitzki to the public. Dohnányi played two-piano performances with Levitzki in Berlin and Budapest and conducted several orchestra concerts with Levitzki at the piano. As a result of these performances, Levitzki was soon booked for solo recitals all over Europe.[8]

When Dohnányi visited Budapest for a recital on 27 November 1915, he discovered that he was still eligible for the Hungarian Draft. Although Dohnányi was already registered for the German Draft as a German citizen, he had never dropped his Hungarian citizenship. He now decided to break the ties that had bound him to Germany and stay in his own motherland through these grave times. Fortunately, he was not drafted by either coun-

---

8. Levitzki's early death in 1941 prevented him from enjoying this popularity for long.

try. On 1 December Dohnányi returned to Budapest to live and soon afterwards accepted an offer from Edmund von Michalovich, who was still the Director of the Franz Liszt Academy of Music, to become Professor of Piano there. Another reason that Dohnányi moved back to Budapest was that he had left his family to join Elza Galafrés, whom, as soon as he was able to obtain a divorce, he intended to marry.

Dohnányi was excited to return to the Franz Liszt Academy, which had a different approach from the Hochschule. In Berlin there was complete freedom in teaching, and the choice of material for each pupil was left to the teacher. In the Budapest Academy, however, the students all used the same predetermined materials. Both systems, Dohnányi found, had advantages and disadvantages. In Berlin instruction was much more individual; this worked well when excellent teachers were matched with talented pupils. In Budapest each student was educated in the same way as the others, and even the less talented pupils were able to accomplish a remarkable result. The general level reached by the students in Budapest was much higher than that in Berlin. Dohnányi, however, did not change his method. In Budapest he continued to teach his pupils individually, after his own system and belief, as he had done in Berlin. He never had many pupils, because he would agree only to teach the most talented ones. His pupils became attached to him as though they were his children. Although most of them became famous and settled in various parts of the world, they always remained in touch with him.

Upset to find that the war had reduced music to a secondary consideration, people anxiously asked Dohnányi what his opinion was about the new generation of musicians. "I am no prophet," Dohnányi smiled, shrugging his shoulders. "How could I possibly tell? There are fewer creative talents among the musicians today than there have been before. In these days, talents don't show up as much in art as in the technical field."

"Is this perhaps because of the war?" was the inquiry.

Dohnányi shook his head.

> No. War has nothing to do with the decline of art. There have always been and there always will be wars, as long as humanity exists. Technology serves war, but then war develops fresh technical resources. In this field there is more possibility to create, to develop something new, than in art. When culture has reached its peak, civilization starts, and civilization is always associated with the decline of art. We live in comfort and perhaps have easier lives because of many technical achievements, but we have less to say at the bottom of our hearts.

Dohnányi explained that although creative talents were fewer, performing talents were more numerous than in the past. More people learned music in these days, and more were interested in it. "When I studied at the Academy," he said, "we had three hundred students. Now we have double that. The number of conservatories and music schools has also increased."

Once, someone asked his opinion about talented women. "The real destiny of a woman should be to be a wife and mother," he said.

In former years, women were perhaps oppressed and lived under more strict conditions, but they enjoyed in recompense more respect, consideration, and protective tenderness. Now they are emancipated, but men feel no obligation to be protective or gallant to those who have become equal to them. The increasing role women play in the arts is in connection with their emancipation. Of course, independence has its advantages. The independent woman can create much in the spiritual field, especially in literature. Only a woman can truly know the feminine soul, and so it is only she who is able to represent it with complete fidelity. I really believe that in this field women have the right to compete with men. They are able to see certain problems from a different point of view, and can thus illuminate them in a different way. Women writers should write just as they feel, without trying to be "masculine," for thus they lose their individuality.

When asked about women in the field of music, Dohnányi had a similar answer. "Women," he said, "are numerous as interpreters of music. But a female pianist is only interesting to me as long as she is displaying her feminine personality instead of imitating a masculine one. In general, women are most successful in Romantic music, where they are able to display beauties and details that men cannot. As to composing, there are few women composers; creative work in music does not seem to suit the feminine spirit."

❧

During the war Dohnányi spent much of his time giving charity concerts. Although he had become accustomed to the rich cultural and artistic atmosphere of other countries, he had always preserved a deep love for his motherland. People often accused Dohnányi of not being a true patriot and criticized him for spending too much time away from Hungary. They did not realize that he had actually secretly guarded his patriotism. It was a subject that he considered almost sacred, one that he never discussed publicly or boasted about. Now that the time had come when he had to come to his country's aid, he volunteered to do everything he could. The concerts he gave were mostly for the benefit of soldiers fighting in the battlefield or wounded and suffering in hospitals. In his 1927 biography of Dohnányi, Viktor Papp wrote,

In the horrible years of war, when our souls were filled with complaints and tears, when we were awaiting the morrow depressed and trembling, when art was dying in the torrents of sighs of desperate orphans, Dohnányi mounted the stage. As his fingers ran across the keys, our tear-filled eyes were dried and our agitated moods were soothed. We gazed with grateful eyes at the miraculous physician who was able to console us.[9]

On 12 December 1916 Dohnányi premiered his *Sechs Konzertetuden* (Six Concert Etudes) for piano, op. 28, in Szeged. This performance was repeated a few days later in Budapest. Of the six etudes, the last one, the F Minor Capriccio, became the most popular. Several pianists, including Sergei Rachmaninoff, Leopold Godowski, Josef Lhévinne, and Vladimir Horowitz, made recordings of this etude.

Dohnányi's attempts to legalize his relationship with Elza Galafrés resulted in a struggle that dragged on for years. Since they both were already married, they had planned to obtain divorces. This turned out to be unfeasible; Mrs. Dohnányi, who awaited Dohnányi's return until her dying day, flatly refused to divorce him, and Bronislaw Huberman also refused to divorce his wife. Anyone else would have lost the hope of finding a solution. Dohnányi, however, was not the type of person who would give up an aim merely because it looked difficult or even hopeless. Difficulties and obstacles only aroused his obstinate perseverance; no prospects of defeat discouraged him. A challenge to him signified life itself. "He who has given up the will to fight is dead," he would say.

Nevertheless, their constant striving for a divorce was a great strain. The process became even more worrisome on 8 January 1917, when Elza Galafrés gave birth to Dohnányi's second son. They named him Matthew, after his maternal grandfather. Matthew always remained close to Dohnányi's heart. As a consequence of this illegitimate family life, there were many arguments regarding who would take care of Elza Galafrés's first son. The little Huberman boy, for whom Dohnányi had become a thoughtful and affectionate father, was seven years old at the time. He lived with his mother and maternal grandmother in Dohnányi's home on Trombitás Street in Budapest. It was in the child's best interest to stay with his mother, because Bronislaw Huberman, with his numerous concert trips, could not properly care for him. Dohnányi's mother later joined them, and there were two grandmothers in the same home.

The fact that he had two mothers-in-law in his house caused people to look upon Dohnányi with admiration that almost amounted to awe. Once, when the communist government was confiscating rooms in the houses of wealthy families, officials came and asked the concierge how

---

9. Viktor Papp, *Dohnányi Ernő* (Budapest: Stádium Sajtóvállalat, 1927), p. 5.

many rooms the Dohnányi family possessed. "They have seven rooms," was the response.

"And how many people live there?" the question continued.

"The Professor with his wife, two children, a governess, servants and two grandmothers."

"What? Two mothers-in-law in the same lodging?" the officials exclaimed incredulously. "Upon our souls, this lodging cannot be shared with others!"

While enduring the strain that his complicated private life was imposing on him, Dohnányi was relieved to turn to his numerous recitals and concerts. He gave mostly benefit concerts because, in addition to his domestic troubles, the grave disasters of his motherland weighed heavily on him. He also composed his *Variationen über ein ungarisches Volkslied* (Variations on a Hungarian Folksong) for piano, op. 29. Dohnányi's affair with Elza Galafrés caused a most distasteful scene during a 1 October 1917 recital in the Vienna Musik-Vereinsaal. After the receptive applause, a woman shrieked hysterically, "Pfui Dohnányi! Heil Huberman!" (Down with Dohnányi! Hail Huberman!). Dohnányi turned his head in the direction of the voice with the slight smile that he always used when greeting an audience. His smile did not waver; it instead deepened with indifference for this insolent remark. Then he sat down calmly and started to play. The way he mastered this most awkward situation must have impressed the quarrelsome woman; she uttered no further sound during the rest of the performance.

Life had been rather chaotic in Hungary for a long time. In November 1916 Emperor Francis Joseph had died, and Charles IV had succeeded him. Although the new emperor wanted peace, the shortage of food, the misery and deprivation brought about by the years of war, and above all the conviction that this struggle must end in defeat, made people bitter. In April 1917 the Democratic Electoral Bloc, which had been founded by Count Michael Károlyi, the Radicals under Oscar Jászi, and the Socialists gained many followers. As Hungary drifted dangerously toward the Left, the population began to dread something worse than a military defeat. In September 1918, after the failure of the Piave Offensive, in which 46 percent of the fighting troops were Hungarians, the Government gave up the struggle.

On 25 October a National Council came into existence and elected as its President Count Károlyi, who also drifted toward the Left. An army of more than 200,000 soldiers, which stood near the border under the leadership of Field Marshall Mackensen, ready to defend Hungary, was disarmed by the Hungarian authorities. The October Revolution did not surprise most Hungarian patriots. Dohnányi, in spite of his optimism, had known that a disaster was imminent. Because there was no possibility of changing the situation, he tried to keep calm. On the morning of the revolution, a friend of Dohnányi's dashed into the room where he was sleeping and called out in alarm, "Get up! The revolution has broken out!"

Dohnányi only shrugged his shoulders. "Why should I get up? I cannot do anything about it, anyway," he said with his usual nonchalance.

Although the revolt was not particularly bloody, it had very grave consequences. The Emperor Charles abdicated. Every day a new, desperate change came about in political life. This depressed people and alarmed them; everybody could foresee the disaster toward which Hungary was rapidly drifting. Matters finally culminated in a dreadful explosion: the Proletarian Dictatorship took control on 21 March 1919. The Károlyi government made more and more concessions until it finally surrendered power into the hands of Béla Kun and his comrades. Béla Kun was in jail when they informed him that he had become the leader of the country. The reaction of the population was only a weary sigh. For days, even weeks, they had expected the disaster. It was far better to face the catastrophe, however destructive, than to live in constant fear of it. Revolt would have been useless, because any uprising was suppressed ruthlessly by the ruling party.

Before the communist regime came into power, the Károlyi government had, among other changes, reorganized the Budapest Academy. Michalovich had been dismissed from his position as Director, and the government had nominated Dohnányi in his place. Shortly after becoming the Director of the Academy on 17 February 1919, Dohnányi had succeeded István Kerner as the President and Director of the Budapest Philharmonic Society.[10] These appointments made Dohnányi many enemies, including Jenő Hubay, who himself aspired to be Director of the Academy. Dohnányi had accepted the distinction reluctantly, and when the communistic Proletarian Dictatorship came into power, he wanted to resign. He remained only at the request of his friends and other music lovers, who feared what might happen to the Academy without his support. Among those who persuaded him to stay was one of the People's Commissars.

There was one matter in which the Proletarian Dictatorship had unknowingly come to Dohnányi's aid. Under the new laws, Dohnányi could finally legally divorce his wife and marry Elza Galafrés. The civil marriage

---

10. The Budapest Philharmonic Society consisted of the members of the Royal Opera Orchestra, and their concerts were sponsored by the State and the City of Budapest. The Philharmonic Society elected its Conductor and President every three years. Through continuous reelections, Dohnányi remained in this position for twenty-five years.

took place on 2 June 1919. Although he had benefited from its laws, Dohnányi still wanted to demonstrate that he did not side with the principles of the regime. In addition to overthrowing almost everything that had once been the foundation of Hungarian laws, habits, and beliefs, the Proletarian Dictatorship had openly defied religion. Dohnányi decided that since his first marriage had only been confirmed in a registrar's office, this one should be solemnized in a church.

The church ceremony took place on 5 June in the Catholic Chapel of Matthew's Church and was performed by Father Dezső Demény. Immediately after the marriage ceremony, little Matthew was baptized. Among those who attended the service was the Archduke Joseph Francis, who, as a prisoner of the communists, could come only as a special favor, accompanied by armed guards. Dohnányi's witness was Count Andor Somsich, who had just been released from the jail cell that he had shared with the Archduke. After the ceremony, people leaving the church, fearing the agents of the hostile regime, tried to disperse as quickly as possible.

Dohnányi decided to leave Hungary as soon as he finished the school year at the Academy; he did not want to neglect his professional obligations. Meanwhile, the terror in Budapest grew worse and worse. About six hundred people were murdered by the terrorists, and many more were arrested. Dohnányi decided to flee to Norway.

❧

The trip to Norway was exhausting with immense difficulties. Because it was impossible to depart from the country legally, Dohnányi's only choice was to travel on an Austrian refugee train, which a kind Austrian consulate granted him permission to do. Dohnányi departed at the end of June with his wife, his mother-in-law, a governess, and the two children. Because there was no reliable way to transfer packages, Dohnányi had to carry the twenty-three pieces of luggage containing the family's belongings by himself. The train had no light or windows and was overcrowded. It traveled so slowly that it took twenty-four hours to reach Vienna from Budapest, a journey that usually would take no more than four hours.

They stayed in Vienna for a few days to arrange business affairs. These days were somewhat relaxing, especially for the children, after the starvation of so many months in Hungary. The Proletarian Dictatorship had not been able to furnish its citizens with food, firewood, clothing, or any other necessities. In Vienna, however, the stores were stocked with goods. The two little boys joyously stopped at the windows of the shops, where wonderful foods were temptingly displayed to their hungry gazes.

At Leipzig, the Dohnányis had to change trains, which would have been exhausting even without the twenty-three pieces of luggage. Because the women were busy with the children, Dohnányi had to drag the bags, one by one, to the other train. At some point, he dropped a huge bag filled with underwear. To make matters worse, the bag was not locked. Dohnányi quickly forgot about this loss, but his mother-in-law did not. When they arrived in Berlin, she took the trouble to go to the authorities about the lost bag. Dohnányi was greatly amused by her obstinacy. To him it seemed rather ridiculous to make such a fuss at a time when the whole country was in turmoil and the overcrowded trains were being stormed at every station. He was greatly surprised when a few months later, as they passed through Berlin again, the bag was restored to them undamaged. Not even a handkerchief was missing.

From Berlin the Dohnányis went to Copenhagen. Dohnányi had 30,000 crowns of Austro-Hungarian Blue Banknotes, which the Danish publisher Hansen exchanged for Scandinavian currency.[11] Mr. Hansen, who had formerly arranged concerts for Dohnányi, was so obliging that, although he delivered the Scandinavian money to Dohnányi, he did not make use of the Blue Banknotes. He instead carefully kept them, expecting their value to mount. This would allow Dohnányi to take advantage of a better rate of exchange. The Blue Banknotes eventually lost all their value, but Mr. Hansen never expected compensation.[12]

Dohnányi was greatly annoyed when he witnessed a demonstration in the street below his hotel in Christiania (now Oslo). Workmen were loudly cheering Béla Kun and his dictatorship. The explanation was simple: during the war many people had grown rich in Norway, and this caused much animosity among the poor. Conditions had worsened, and so had the political convictions of people. There was no longer any trace of that easy and pleasant life that Dohnányi had once enjoyed. Dohnányi had intended to settle in Christiania, but the city was now overcrowded with foreigners, and no apartments were available. Dohnányi and his wife hunted for a lodging from morning until night. Even when they found vacancies, they were flatly refused. "We don't rent rooms for children," was the customary response. Dohnányi endured this for a while, but when the search seemed quite hopeless, he became nervous. This nervousness burst into indignation when they had been refused at a building swarming with children. "But you have children here anyway, don't you?" he remarked. "They are allowed to stay?"

---

11. In Hungary the communist government produced White Banknotes, which were printed only on one side. This money was absolutely worthless; the soldiers of the Red Army wrote letters on the backsides. Only the Blue Banknotes printed by the old Austro-Hungarian Monarchy had any value.

12. Dohnányi nevertheless felt obliged to compensate Mr. Hansen for this loss and later composed a concert transcription of a Brahms waltz for him.

"Just because we already have children, we're not going to put up with more of them," was the landlady's brisk answer.

❦

The Romanians eventually defeated the Red troops and occupied Hungary. They were, however, unable to conquer the town of Szeged and the surrounding district, where the Hungarian counter-revolutionists had assembled under the leadership of Vice-Admiral Miklós Horthy. Béla Kun and the members of the communist dictatorship fled Hungary, leaving the country to the pillaging Romanians. Although Dohnányi in his optimistic, idealistic way tried to see in life only what was beautiful and agreeable, as a patriot he could not help being deeply grieved over the ruin of his country.

A desperate and helpless Hungary signed a devastating peace treaty with the Allies. From her original territory of 282,000 square kilometers, 189,000 square kilometers were taken. Hungary also lost 10.3 million people from her population of 18.2 million. The forfeited territories and their inhabitants were dispersed among neighboring countries. The Romanians and the Czechs expelled the Hungarian inhabitants from their land and confiscated all their possessions. Among the territories torn from Hungary was Pozsony, Dohnányi's native town. This was the greatest blow for Dohnányi. Pozsony was annexed by Czechoslovakia and renamed Bratislava, a tremendous injustice that Dohnányi never acknowledged. Whenever people asked about his birthplace, he always declared with obstinate pride, "I was born in the Hungarian Coronation City, Pozsony."

Dohnányi was relieved when he heard that the Proletarian Dictatorship had come to an end. Although he had finally found a home in Christiania, he said farewell to the country and started back to Hungary.

FOUR

1919–1936

O nce again Dohnányi was on a train with his family. The return trip
from Norway did not differ much from when they had traveled to
Norway as refugees. The trains were still slow and stopped at every station
for long periods of time. The travelers were jammed in cars that had no
light, painfully reminding them that their country had lost the war. When
the Dohnányis arrived in Wels, Austria, they were so exhausted that they
decided to interrupt their journey and stay for the night. They found
rooms in a hotel, which was difficult in the overcrowded cities. The next
day, however, when they tried to board the train to Vienna, the Dohnányis
saw with dismay that it was overcrowded; even the corridors were jammed.
It seemed unlikely that they would be able to join the crowd with their
twenty-three pieces of luggage.

"Maestro!" Dohnányi heard a deep voice calling out in German. "Are
you going to Vienna? Come . . . there's an empty compartment next to
mine!" The man who had come to their rescue was the famous singer Leo
Slezák, who was returning to Vienna from his summer vacation. He led
Dohnányi to a compartment that was indeed empty, but locked from inside
and marked *Courier Abteil* (Reserved for Diplomats). Without hesitation
Slezák broke a window and reached in to unlock the door from the inside.
He quickly ushered in the Dohnányis, who enjoyed their comfortable seats.
Later in the journey Dohnányi visited his friend and had an opportunity to
see for himself that Slezák actually did travel with all the animals he described in his book *Meine sämtliche Werke* (My Collected Works). Slezák,
along with his wife, daughter, and mother-in-law, was surrounded by little
cats, dogs, and birds that peeped out from the luggage nets above the seats.

When Dohnányi returned to Budapest, the Hungarian citizens were
still outraged over the Romanian occupation. Those who had been persecuted during the communist regime were now desperately trying to
avenge themselves. Those who had suffered nothing but only profited now
tried to take advantage of the new government. There are always clever

opportunists who sense the changes of the political wind and attach themselves to the new regime at the right moment.

The new political change also had an effect on the Franz Liszt Academy. Jenő Hubay quickly took advantage of this opportunity. Under the pretext that Dohnányi had been nominated by the ousted Károly regime, Hubay placed himself at the head of the institution in October 1919. In reaction, all of the professors—except one—refused to work to demonstrate sympathy for Dohnányi. Nevertheless, the one professor who did not share their opinion broke the strike and work had to start again.

After he became Director of the Academy, Hubay quickly started to make radical changes at the institution. He wanted to keep Dohnányi as Professor of Piano, but at the same time he instigated political persecution against Zoltán Kodály, who had been the Academy's Secretary under Dohnányi's directorship. This persecution went so far that Kodály was called before a statutory committee. Dohnányi raised his voice energetically in Kodály's defense and declared that he would return to the Academy only if the political accusations against Kodály were dropped and Kodály was allowed to return to work. The investigation of Kodály lasted for almost a whole year. The inquiry was very painful, and he and his wife suffered bitterly. Kodály nevertheless defended himself so boldly and wisely that after a year all accusations were dropped and Hubay had to consent to his return to the Academy. This constant strain and disillusionment inspired Kodály to start the composition that was later known as *Psalmus Hungaricus,* which is considered to be his most outstanding work.

The first of December 1919 marked the premiere of Dohnányi's Violin Concerto, op. 27. It was performed by Emil Telmányi in Budapest and conducted by the composer. Telmányi was an excellent violinist and a close friend to Dohnányi.

In the year 1920 a great national festival took place in Hungary. The Hungarian Army, which had assembled in Szeged under the leadership of Vice-Admiral Miklós Horthy during the Proletarian Dictatorship, now reentered the country. They were welcomed enthusiastically by the masses. The Romanians left Hungary on the decree of the Entente, and Horthy began to reestablish order.

Because traveling was difficult, Dohnányi chose to remain in Hungary and fulfill the demands that his own country was making. He became the sole provider of concert activity in Budapest, averaging 120 concerts a year. It was during this period that Bartók himself wrote, "Musical life in Budapest today may be summed up in one name—Dohnányi."[1] Dohnányi's

---

1. See Bartók, "Hungary in the Throes of Reaction," *Musical Courier* (29 April 1920), pp. 42–43.

concerts needed no advertising posters or newspaper articles. There was only one poster at the entrance to the office of the music publishers Rózsavölgyi & Co. that announced the dates of Dohnányi's performances. The Hungarian audience still bore the bitter scars of war. The concert hall was unheated, and Dohnányi wore a sweater under his tuxedo while the audience sat shivering in their overcoats. There were no taxis to take people home, and the trains ceased to run after ten o'clock at night. People, including the performers, had to walk home in the biting cold. Nevertheless, the hall was crowded every evening. People came not because it was fashionable to attend concerts and flaunt their evening clothes, but to gain comfort and consolation from music.

In 1920 the 150th anniversary of Beethoven's birth was celebrated, and Dohnányi gave sixty-five performances in Budapest to celebrate. Dohnányi played all thirty-two Beethoven sonatas in ten recitals, which were all repeated at the request of the audience. He conducted all nine of Beethoven's symphonies with the Budapest Philharmonic. Dohnányi also played Beethoven's five piano concertos with the Orchestra, all of his trios with Waldbauer and Kerpely, all the violin sonatas with Telmányi, and all the cello sonatas with Kerpely.

Although the persecution against Kodály had stopped, Dohnányi did not return to the Academy. He was so busy with his performances and compositions that he could not keep an eye on the affairs of the institution that had once been so dear to him. Dohnányi was nevertheless deeply hurt when he heard about the anniversary celebrations for the Academy. He was completely ignored in the festivities and was not even invited to them. Dohnányi, who had once been the pride of the institution and later its Professor and Director, was not even mentioned in its history. It was as if he had never existed.

There were, however, ample opportunities to see how deeply the rest of the country admired Dohnányi. On 27 December 1920 Dohnányi premiered his *Pastorale* on the Hungarian Christmas song "Mennyből az angyal" for piano in Budapest. On the same concert, Dohnányi conducted the premiere of his *Hitvallás* (Confession) for tenor soloist, chorus, and orchestra with Ferenc Székelyhidy and the Palestrina Chorus. Other nationalistic works composed around that time include a "Fanfare" and *Hiszekegy* (Hungarian Apostles' Creed) for brass and percussion, based on the musical material from Dohnányi's melodrama *Hitvallás—Nemzeti Ima* (Credo—National Prayer) for narrator, choir, and piano. Dohnányi also composed *Nemzeti Ima* (National Prayer) for chorus, *Magyar Jövő Himnusz* (Hungarian Future Hymn) for chorus, and *Magyar népdalok* (Hungarian Folksongs) for voice and piano.

When traveling became easier, Dohnányi booked concerts in Europe as well as in the United States for the 1920–21 concert season. This would be the first time Dohnányi had crossed the Atlantic in twenty years. He departed from Rotterdam on the Dutch liner *New Amsterdam*. The sea was rough, and the weather was very unfavorable; the sun did not appear for four days. When the weather finally improved, the cheerful passengers gathered on the deck for an evening of dancing. It was during this occasion that Dohnányi first heard jazz music. He listened, puzzled, to the trombones playing glissandos and the trumpets using mutes to create nasal sounds. Dohnányi thought that the musicians, rejoicing that the storm had finally ceased, were making a joke to amuse the audience. It was only upon his arrival in the United States that he was told that this was no joke but serious music called jazz.

When he later returned to Hungary, Dohnányi related to his friends with indignation what an odd and disgusting type of music had come in fashion overseas. They burst out laughing, "For Heaven's sake, where do you live? You could have heard jazz in Budapest, had you paid a visit to our nightclubs." Despite its popularity, Dohnányi always said, "I consider jazz to be a caricature of music. It is a product of the present era that absolutely lacks style."

❦

Dohnányi's tour in the United States started with a recital in Boston followed by two recitals in New York. Then he gave concerts with Pierre Monteux and the Boston Symphony Orchestra in Boston, New York City, Brooklyn, Philadelphia, Washington, and Baltimore. On 6 March 1921 in New York Dohnányi performed in the American premiere of the *Variationen über ein Kinderlied,* with Willem Mengelberg conducting. In Cincinnati, Dohnányi played a Beethoven concerto conducted by Eugene Ysaye; then he himself conducted his F-sharp Minor Suite. This performance was repeated in New York in Carnegie Hall. Dohnányi was very pleased to see how the number of first-rate orchestras had increased in America. The size of the music-loving public had also grown. Dohnányi valued the work of those who had achieved this progress in such a short amount of time. He was also delighted by the concerts for children given by the great orchestras, especially those organized by Walter Damrosch.

The 1921–22 season consisted mostly of concerts and recitals in Budapest and Hungarian cities. On 18 March 1922 the successful premiere of Dohnányi's opera *A vajda tornya* (The Magistrate's Tower), op. 30, one of his favorite works, took place in Budapest. Hans Heinz Ewers[2] had given

2. Ewers (1871–1943) was a well-known science fiction writer who is best remembered as the author of the "Frank Braun" trilogy: *Der Zauberlehring* (The Sorcerer's Apprentice, 1907), *Alraune* (Mandrake, 1911), and *Vampir* (Vampire, 1921).

the libretto, entitled *Ivas Turm* (Iva's Tower), to Dohnányi years before the war, in Berlin. Although Dohnányi was very interested in the plot, the Albanian legend on which it was based lay too far from his heart. When he discovered a similar legend in the history of the Transylvanian Székelys, Dohnányi asked Ewers to rewrite his story on this background.[3] Because Ewers was not acquainted with Hungarian history, he declared himself unable to do it. He did, however, consent to any changes Dohnányi wanted to make. Dohnányi decided to revise the entire text of the opera himself. Victor Lányi helped translate the libretto into Hungarian, and they had several assistants who contributed to the research work. The story was changed to depict the Székelys' fight against the Bessenyös, when the Hungarians had come to their aid. Many changes had to be made to render the work suitable for Hungarian characters and traditions. Even after it was pronounced ready for performance, the ending was altered three times, and a less poetical, but also less gloomy, ending was chosen.

A vajda tornya opens with the Székelys building a tower to defend themselves against the Bessenyös. The previous towers had all collapsed at the last moment. The desperate magistrate asks for help from the Spirit of the Mountain, who tells him that the tower will stand only if the first woman who arrives there the next morning is walled up inside it. The magistrate entrusts the secret to his two sons, Kund and Tarján, under threat of a curse. Kund, however, in his desperate love for his Hungarian wife Etelka, disobeys his father and tells her. When the Bessenyös attack, the Székelys are called back into battle. Tarján leaves his beloved Székely wife Eva, who loves him so devotedly that she wishes to join him in battle. Etelka, who secretly loves Tarján and wants to get rid of her sister-in-law, advises her to hurry to the tower early the next morning and ask the magistrate's permission to go into battle with her husband. Eva, unaware of the danger, hurries to the tower, and the magistrate is forced to wall up his own daughter-in-law. He leaves an opening through which she can see until she dies.

The Székelys are nearly defeated. Many of them are killed, including Kund, and there is no water. The dying magistrate entrusts the land to Tarján, forcing him to marry the widowed Etelka. Tarján is about to obey, when suddenly a warrior appears bringing him Kund's last message to his brother. This warns Tarján that Kund had betrayed the secret to his wife. Tarján realizes that Etelka had purposely sent Eva to her death. When she confesses to this, he stabs her in his desperate rage. The opera ends with a

3. Since the time of Attila the Hun, the Székelys had remained loyal to Hungary. When Hungary was occupied by the Turks from 1526 to 1686, the Székelys, who lived in independent Transylvania, still proudly called themselves Hungarians.

miracle: from the opening of the tower water suddenly pours, and triumphant shouts announce that the Hungarians have come to bring aid to
the Székelys.

The following season included many concerts. From 2 to 10 April
1922 Dohnányi took part in the Brahms Festival in Vienna. He conducted
Brahms's F Major Symphony and performed Brahms's piano concertos, as
well as trios and quartets with the Rosé Quartet. Dohnányi gave other
recitals in Munich and Berlin, including a performance of Mozart's G
Major Concerto, K. 453, with the Berlin Philharmonic Orchestra conducted by Bruno Walter on 30 October 1922. On 27 January 1923 he
performed in the London premiere of the *Variationen über ein Kinderlied*
with the Queen's Hall Orchestra under the baton of Sir Henry Wood.

On 16 February Count Szapáry, the Hungarian Ambassador in
London, threw a gala to which he invited diplomats from various nations.
The evening started with a concert of Dohnányi playing solo and chamber
music with the Waldbauer quartet. Dohnányi was deeply impressed by this
lavishly brilliant party, which, according to the estimate of an English businessman, must have cost the host at least 200 pounds. Ambassador Szapáry
had arranged the party in an attempt to arouse interest in his neglected and
humiliated motherland. Instead of a success, however, the party turned out
to be an utter failure. A small group of Czechs, Romanians, and Slavs, who
had already been spreading unfavorable rumors about Hungary, declared
that this lavish party proved that Hungary complained without reason if
she was rich enough to afford such luxurious events. People agreed, not
knowing that the expenses had been paid personally by Count Szapáry and
not by Hungary.

In 1923 the Chickering firm, whose pianos Dohnányi usually played
at his concerts, celebrated its hundredth birthday. Several recitals and concerts took place in connection with this event. On 26 March 1923 in
Chicago, Dohnányi played his Piano Concerto with Frederick Stock conducting. The concert was planned to demonstrate the technological ad-
vances that had been made by the American Piano Company, which
owned the Chickering firm. For this unique performance, Dohnányi
played only the first and third movements of the Concerto. The second
movement was performed by an Ampico player-piano roll that had been
placed in the piano Dohnányi was playing. He remained sitting at the
player piano, regulating it by means of a button that brought the roll into
action at the parts the soloist was to play, and stopping it for the orchestral parts. After the Concerto Dohnányi conducted his Suite in F-sharp
Minor for Orchestra. The highlight of the Chickering celebration was a
banquet in Boston that was attended by many famous musicians and a
number of eminent Americans, including Vice President Calvin Coolidge.
Because of Prohibition, no alcoholic drinks were served. Nevertheless, all

the guests were discreetly informed that in a certain room—Dohnányi even decades later recalled that it was No. 123—every possible drink, from whisky to champagne, was available. It was a most amusing night; the guests rose one by one to slip from the hall and refresh themselves in the mysterious room. At dawn, when many of the party, including Dohnányi, traveled by train to New York, their compartments resounded with merry songs.[4]

On 12 April 1923 Dohnányi played his Piano Concerto with the orchestra in Detroit. On 21 April, he performed his *Variationen über ein Kinderlied* in Boston with Pierre Monteux conducting. After a rather tiring schedule Dohnányi had to rush back to Hungary to resume his busy duties as head of the Budapest Philharmonic. He also performed several recitals, including sonata evenings with Emil Telmányi. The 1923–24 season started with a sonata recital with Karl Flesch in Budapest on 27 September 1923. That season included a festival to celebrate the Budapest Philharmonic's seventieth year of existence, and Dohnányi conducted Beethoven's *Missa Solemnis* on 7 and 8 October.

On 19 November 1923 Budapest celebrated a great national event, the fiftieth anniversary of the union of Buda and Pest. Until the middle of the nineteenth century, the mountainous, ancient Buda and the flat, more modern Pest were two separate cities, divided by the Danube River. The first permanent bridge connecting the two cities was the suspension bridge known as the Chain Bridge, built in 1848 by Count Stephen Széchenyi. All of Hungary looked forward to the completion of this bridge with joyful impatience and patriotic triumph. When the long-expected day finally came, however, it brought more tears than delight. After Emperor Francis Joseph enlisted the Russians' help to conquer his own subjects, the hostile troops of the Austrian Army became the first to cross the bridge. In the following peaceful years Buda and Pest quickly began to flourish, becoming united as the capital of the country.

For the anniversary celebration the city of Budapest commissioned Dohnányi, Bartók, and Kodály to write orchestral works. Dohnányi composed his *Ünnepi nyitány* (Festive Overture), op. 31, for double orchestra. The Overture comprises three themes: the principal subject is original, the second subject is an elaboration of Béni Egressy's popular Hungarian hymn "Szózat," and the development section includes Dohnányi's *Hiszekegy*. At the end of the Overture, a brass band plays Ferenc Erkel's Hungarian National Hymn, "Himnusz," while the other themes are repeated by the two orchestras. This work was premiered on 19 November, with Dohnányi

---

4. During this tour, Dohnányi conducted the American premiere of his Violin Concerto on 11 March, with Albert Spalding and the New York Symphony.

conducting the Budapest Philharmonic. The concert also included Bartók's *Tánc-szvitje* (Dance Suite) and Kodály's *Psalmus Hungaricus,* which was then known as "55. zsoltára" (55th Psalm). Dohnányi concluded the program with a performance of Liszt's *Hungarian Fantasia.*

That winter Dohnányi again visited England. In January 1924 he undertook his yearly tour to the United States. This time he traveled on the *Majestic,* and Wilhelm Backhaus and Fritz Kreisler were his fellow passengers. During the journey, the three musicians gave a concert for the crew in the ship's hall, which seated an audience of six hundred. The American trip was extremely busy. It started with a recital in New York in Carnegie Hall on 12 January. Dohnányi also played in various cities, including Chicago, St. Louis, and Cleveland, en route to San Francisco, where he participated in the American premiere of his Second Quintet.

In the autumn of 1924 Dohnányi limited his musical activities to Hungarian cities. The highlight of this tour was the premiere of his *Ruralia Hungarica,* op. 32, which he dedicated "To my dear mother." This composition is based on ancient Hungarian folk songs: real folk songs, sung by country people in the villages and on farms in the mountains. Dohnányi reworked and elaborated these songs according to his own musical style. The original version of *Ruralia Hungarica* was comprised of seven pieces for piano. These were premiered during a recital on 24 September 1924 in the Hungarian city of Pécs. Dohnányi also orchestrated five movements of *Ruralia Hungarica* for orchestra and premiered them with the Budapest Philharmonic on 16 November 1924.[5]

❧

In Hungary, Dohnányi was considered to be an authority on music. He was often bombarded with inquiries about music, some of which were almost unanswerable. When he was asked such questions, he usually smiled evasively. This characteristic smile, which gave a glimpse into his personality where secret passions were always kept in check by a marvelous self-control, won many lasting friends for him. "I would gladly describe music," he would often say, "if I could describe it in tunes and melodies instead of words."

Reporters always found it hard to conduct interviews with Dohnányi. In the end it was usually the journalist who did most of the talking, answering Dohnányi's questions. Nevertheless, eager writers sometimes succeeded in getting information from him. During one interview, Dohnányi

---

5. Dohnányi also composed a three-movement version of *Ruralia Hungarica* for violin and piano. Emil Telmányi premiered this piece on 15 November 1927, with Dohnányi at the piano. A final version of *Ruralia Hungarica* was an Andante rubato for cello, or violin, and piano, op. 32d.

was asked what it means to create. "I never reflect over what I am doing, or what happens to me while I compose," he answered.

> I do not know what happens in my head, in my soul, or even in my heart. But one fact is certain: one cannot *learn* how to create, for this is absolutely a matter of talent. Of course, there are conditions and factors that, in addition to talent, must be adopted for an artist to be able to compose. These constitute a special knowledge of music and the technical rules of the craft. The composer must possess these capacities and be able to handle them with ease and superiority. All this knowledge, of course, does not assure him that what he will produce is a real creation. A poet may know all the rules of meter and rhyme in vain; what he writes will not be a real poem unless he has the soul of a poet. Merely committing to paper the most exquisite expressions in rhyme will not always constitute poetry.

Dohnányi was also frequently asked if an artist has to be inspired to create. "The knowledge of craft and the possession of talent don't suffice to create a composition," Dohnányi affirmed.

> If anyone was to place paper before me and command me to compose, at any season of the year or any hour of the day, I would certainly be able to comply. It is questionable, however, whether a piece thus produced would be of real musical value and show the particular signs that distinguish the work of an artist from the work of a craftsman. A composition always depends on the composer's mood, the form of expression, and many other factors that are difficult to describe because one must feel them. Although some irresistible force inside inspires a composer to work, it often happens that this force urges him to work without any remarkable result. Sometimes the creator racks his brains for weeks over how to express a musical idea properly, without succeeding. Then, unexpectedly, there comes a lucky moment when he easily finds the way to develop his thoughts.

When asked how this moment comes, Dohnányi replied,

> In most cases unexpectedly; it would be difficult to explain. It might be brought forth by a beautiful summer morning as well as by the effect of a noisy street, or by an exciting lecture, or even by some agreeable surprise. But it would be a mistake to think that these so-called moments of inspiration are always the results of pleasant events; many a masterpiece of great creators sprang from the deepest chagrin. The artist himself does not feel the decisive moment of creation. It is also hard to draw a line where artistic creation really begins. As the painter, who puts down a color upon his canvas, and then steps back to decide whether it is right, so the musician should retire from his work to judge whether what he created is artistically worthy. It is only on the following day that one can clearly appraise the value of one's work.

Another question was how one begins a composition. "In various ways," Dohnányi said.

Amateurs usually believe that the composer hums a tune and then starts to compose the harmonies to it, but a real creation doesn't come about this way. The musical idea doesn't always reside in melody; it may be in harmony, in the orchestration, or tone colors. It often happens that the composer hasn't the slightest idea on what melody he will base his work. The melody is born later in his mind, perhaps only when his thoughts grow ripe enough to be expressed. Sometimes a composer has a musical idea and carries it for months, even for years, within himself before it is ripe enough to be put down upon paper. Even when a musical thought ripens to an expression, and the composer has found an appropriate form for it, the composition is not complete; the creator will polish it, make changes, and reduce it or add to it later. People usually think that a composer works sitting at a table, with the paper before him and a pen in his hand. This is a mistake. Compositions come to existence often when the composer walks, sits in a garden, or travels in a train or an airplane. Even in the midst of a crowd one can remain alone with one's thoughts.

This was the way Dohnányi's compositions came to life, and why he was able to create so much with so little free time. Whenever he heard people say that they were bored, he shook his head disapprovingly. "How can one be bored?" he would say. "There are plenty of books to read and keep one busy. And if one feels tired of reading, there are thoughts. I can never remember having ever been bored in my life, and I am sorry for those who are."

❧

Dohnányi's European tour in the autumn of 1924 consisted of two recitals in Berlin and concerts in England, including the first English performance of his Second Piano Quintet on 5 November in Manchester Memorial Hall.

Dohnányi's obligations with the Budapest Philharmonic recalled him to Hungary again. His compatriots profited from his presence, and he was asked to make tours in Hungarian provincial towns so that the people might have a chance to hear the music of "the Maestro," as they called him. This label had become Dohnányi's established title by popular impulse in Hungary. Even though his admirers attached no surname to the title, everyone knew that they were talking about Dohnányi. All other distinctions that were later bestowed upon him by various governments and authorities paled in comparison to this distinction given to him spontaneously by the people themselves.

In January 1925 Dohnányi made his annual tour in the United States. He played his Piano Concerto in Buffalo. On 17 February Dohnányi conducted the New York State Symphony for an "All-Dohnányi" concert, in which he conducted the American premieres of *Ruralia Hungarica* and

Ünnepi nyitány. He also conducted his Suite in F-sharp Minor and played his *Variationen über ein Kinderlied.* He had several other concerts all over the country, including a recital in Los Angeles. On his way back to Europe in May, Dohnányi again played recitals and concerts in London, including a performance of the *Variationen* with Wood and the Queen's Hall Orchestra.

After these tiring activities, Dohnányi needed a vacation. Although he had resumed his practice of spending his summers in the mountains of the Tyrol, he decided to spend the summer of 1925 with his family in Vulpera, Switzerland. Once more he rejoiced to see his beloved mountains, but he did not go on many mountain-climbing excursions. He was occupied with his sons, opting to go on easier walks with them.

In September 1925 Dohnányi made a tour with his Budapest Philharmonic. He always spoke of the Orchestra as "his very own," because the musicians were in soul and spirit so much in tune with their conductor that it seemed as though the Orchestra was actually one person. "When I conduct them, it seems to me like I am playing a big piano," he would say. His eyes were radiant with pride whenever he talked of his Orchestra, which had very few equals in Europe. After giving performances in Brünn and Prague, the orchestral musicians returned to their homes, but Dohnányi and his family traveled to New York. In addition to his usual engagements in the New World, Dohnányi stayed for five months as the conductor of the New York State Symphony Orchestra.[6]

Because his family was going to stay in America for such a long time, Dohnányi had to make arrangements for the education of his two sons. The Hungarian Minister of Education granted a leave of absence to Father Gáspár, a high school teacher who was also a Catholic priest, to instruct them. The Dohnányis were also accompanied by a nurse who acted as a chambermaid. People in Hungary had difficulty in comprehending how anyone could undertake such an expensive trip with such a luxurious entourage. Envious tongues maliciously suggested that Dohnányi was traveling in the company of his confessor, whose constant aid he needed.

In February 1926 the Dohnányis returned to Europe. On 2 March he was in Düsseldorf for the German premiere of *A vajda tornya.* In the spring of 1926 Dohnányi was busy in Hungary with a long tour of various provincial towns that included several concerts with the Budapest Philharmonic. On 11 and 12 March, Dohnányi and the Orchestra performed Béla Bartók's *Tánc-szvitje.*

---

6. Olin Downes reviewed Dohnányi's inaugural concert as the conductor of the New York State Symphony, which took place on 21 October 1925 in Carnegie Hall, in *The New York Times* (22 October 1925); see Appendix C.

The Dohnányis spent that summer in Pontresina, Switzerland. Dohnányi enjoyed spending time with his sons, who seemed to share his love for the mountains. Matthew was especially devoted to mountain climbing. His father took him on some of the less strenuous climbs, including Piz Languard, which is 3,200 meters high. The nine-year-old boy was enchanted by this adventure and enjoyed it tremendously at the beginning. As time dragged on, however, he became exhausted and somewhat bored by the expedition. He seemed unwilling to continue. "Whoever has said 'a' must also say 'b!'" his father rebuked him gently, but firmly. "What one starts, one must complete; things done by halves are never done right. So get up, and let's reach the top!" Matthew obeyed, as he always did, without complaint.

Dohnányi reared his sons according to his own beliefs about education. "One must not be severe with children," he would say, "only consistent. This consistency must be uncompromising; one must never waver. Children are very good observers and will notice immediately if their parents are unstable and give in, and they will consider it a weakness. Although you should be firm, you must never be rude or spank your children. They will understand what you expect them to do without threats and punishment."

Once Dohnányi went for a walk with his wife and his little stepson. The boy carried a jumping jack but really wanted his mother's umbrella. "I want the umbrella!" he insisted.

"You cannot have it!" his mother retorted severely. "You already have your jumping jack to play with!"

In anger, the boy flung the jumping jack to the ground and stomped on it.

"Pick up the jumping jack!" his mother commanded.

The boy refused. His mother hesitated for a while, then, trying to end the annoying scene, she told him, "Pick up the jumping jack, then you may have the umbrella!"

"Such yielding," said Dohnányi, "is the destruction of discipline and good education. What one doesn't allow today, one shouldn't allow tomorrow." Often parents worry that if they are strict, their children will not like them. When he heard this, Dohnányi smiled and said, "When I was a child, my mother slapped me on the cheek whenever I committed something wrong. There were no endless explanations, reproaches, sermons, or scolding; just these slaps, and I shall be grateful for them to the end of my life. Parents who show no weakness but are firm and logical are usually loved and respected by their children."

Dohnányi disliked the systems of education in which a child, in order to develop and preserve his individuality, is allowed to mature freely without being oppressed or influenced by parents. He felt that those brought up without discipline would drift into the wrong ways. On the other hand,

Dohnányi never tried to force his own opinions upon his children. "If I am asked, I will give my advice willingly," he would say, "whether they follow it or not. If they want to bang their heads against the wall, let them do so. They will profit from it and do better next time."

After recitals in Berlin in 1926 Dohnányi set off on his usual tour to the United States with his family. A recital in Carnegie Hall was followed by a performance in Detroit of Brahms's D Minor Piano Concerto with Ossip Gabrilowitsch conducting. Dohnányi also conducted his *Ruralia Hungarica* with the orchestra. The ensuing tour was composed of concerts, recitals, and chamber music performances extending all the way to California. In San Francisco Dohnányi played Beethoven's Fifth Piano Concerto with Alfred Hertz conducting, and conducted his own D Minor Symphony. He did not make preparations to return to Europe until late February.

In New York, before their departure, someone gave the Dohnányi boys a baby alligator that had been brought from Florida. Although Dohnányi was more annoyed than delighted by this unusual gift, he could not refuse it; his sons were enchanted by their new pet and were determined to take it home to Hungary. Dohnányi tried to devise a way of transporting the alligator, but was fortunately spared of further trouble. The boys left the window of the bathroom, where the little reptile was sleeping in the tub, open during the night. The weather turned icy cold and in the morning, to their horror, they found the alligator and the water frozen solid.

The homeward trip was most unpleasant. Except for Dohnányi, the whole family became seasick. This time the ship took the Mediterranean route, passing Gibraltar and landing in Genoa. Taking advantage of the opportunity to perform in Italy, Dohnányi gave recitals in Genoa, Milan, and Monza.

Upon returning to his homeland, Dohnányi was kept busy with concerts all over the country. The number of concerts was larger because he was celebrating his fiftieth birthday. Although Dohnányi hated public celebrations, the type of homage he received on this occasion was most gratifying to him. The Hungarian State honored him with a lavish birthday gift of 50,000 pengős.[7]

Although Budapest resounded with Dohnányi's praises, the number of envious enemies increased, which included the so-called modern composers. These were not the famous ones, like Bartók or Kodály, who under-

7. In 1926, Hungary had adopted the pengő as its monetary unit, replacing the old krone.

stood and appreciated Dohnányi in spite of his conservative style.[8] The adversaries included only obscure composers who felt that Dohnányi was neglecting them by not performing their mediocre works with the Budapest Philharmonic. Despite their accusations, Dohnányi never condemned modern composers. He appreciated music of every description, as long as it was good and showed talent. He only ignored those musicians who used their "modernity" as a screen to hide their lack of talent or knowledge.[9]

When Dohnányi was asked about modern music, he would say, "There is only good music and bad music. The distinction is difficult, because the followers of 'modern music' don't follow all contemporary music. But the so-called modern music has only a small group of enthusiastic admirers, and it seems like the same audience is at every concert of this type. Although the masses despise it, many of them don't dare to admit it openly; they rather say evasively that they don't understand it." When asked why modern music found such enthusiastic followers, Dohnányi responded, "Because the composers of 'modern music' have overthrown every rule, this kind of music gives ample opportunity for untalented composers in displaying their ideas." As to the question of how "modern music" arose, Dohnányi believed that

> We are now in a period when creating has great difficulties. It seems that almost everything has already been expressed. This is, of course, not quite so; geniuses can still find ways of showing originality without destroying all the rules of the past. The striving for originality at all costs, which may easily lead to many errors, is the refuge of the less talented composers. "Modern music" is desperately seeking originality, where really there is none. I am afraid that the time is not very far off when our whole culture will come to an end, if this lack of self-understanding spreads.

❧

In March 1927 festivals began in Hungary celebrating the hundredth anniversary of Beethoven's death. Dohnányi played a great part in these festivities, which lasted through the first days of April. Celebrations took place all over the country, and Dohnányi appeared in a dozen provincial

---

8. Bartók repeatedly performed Dohnányi's compositions and openly declared that at the start of his career he was quite under the influence of Dohnányi's music.

9. When Dohnányi would perform a work by a modern composer with the Orchestra, he would be bombarded with letters full of angry comments protesting against such music. Among the composers against whom the audience rebelled was one who became one of Dohnányi's most vocal opponents after World War II. Because Dohnányi had never told him how poorly his work had been received by the public, he believed that Dohnányi was purposely neglecting his compositions.

towns. He also conducted Beethoven's *Missa Solemnis* and Ninth Symphony in Budapest. As he had done in the 1920 Beethoven festival, Dohnányi played Beethoven's concertos, the trios with Waldbauer and Kerpely, and the violin sonatas with Telmányi.

During this period Dohnányi was able to pay more attention to his private life. After all of his world traveling, he had decided to settle down. He was now fifty years old and longed for the beauties of nature and a peaceful domestic life. When his mother-in-law had been in a hospital in Buda two years earlier, Dohnányi had frequently met with his friend Dr. Vilmos Manninger, who was supervising her treatment. The doctor had shown Dohnányi some land: a spacious private lot of 400 *hold* (568 English acres) that was for sale nearby. Although it lay within the boundary of Budapest, it had not been developed. The lot, which was on a mountain slope covered with ancient pines, offered an entrancingly picturesque view. "I intend to buy a part of this lot," Professor Manninger had told him, "and I advise you to do the same. You may later want to build a house on it."

Dohnányi was so enchanted by the superb beauty that he decided it would be a crime to cut this magnificent lot into pieces. Dohnányi and Dr. Manninger bought the whole lot and divided it in half. Because Dohnányi was not a good businessman and was always too polite to defend his own interest, he entered the negotiations at a disadvantage. The owner of the lot was a woman, and he could not help showing consideration toward her. The result was that Dohnányi made a rather poor deal. Nevertheless, he was content because he was already deeply attached to the enchanting place.

Dr. Manninger started to build his house immediately, but Dohnányi had decided to wait. He had planned a luxurious and unusual, but at the same time comfortable, building that he could not yet afford. Although he earned considerable salaries with his concerts as well as his work in the Academy and with the Philharmonic Society, he was very often in need of money; he liked to live comfortably and spend lavishly. He considered money a "means to obtain an agreeable way for living" and felt contempt for misers, who hoarded it without making use of it at all. When he combined the income from his recent American tour with the money given to him on his fiftieth birthday by the Hungarian State, however, he could finally afford to start building. Dohnányi had made some preparations for the new home in advance. Months before the construction of the house began, a tennis court and a swimming pool had been installed among the pines. Although the State had granted water to the Manningers, who had already built their house, it refused to provide water solely for a swimming pool. The State eventually conceded, but only on the condition that the water was to be used sparingly. The huge basin was filled, and the Dohnányis looked forward to getting much enjoyment from it.

During the summer, however, the swimming pool became infested with tiny frogs. Because it would have been a waste to drain the water, Dohnányi looked for some other means of getting rid of these unwanted visitors. His friend Count Andor Somsich sent him a quantity of sheatfish, which were to eat all the frogs and then in turn be eaten by the Dohnányis. Because the pool was lined with concrete, however, the fish were injured by the rough surface and mercilessly devoured by the frogs. Dohnányi, realizing that there was no other way to remove the intruders, had the pool emptied and refilled.

The planning of a home in this picturesque setting gave Dohnányi much pleasure, and his excitement increased when the builders started work. He himself had prepared the floor plan to suit the needs of the family. An architect had perfected the design without changing Dohnányi's suggestions. The address of the new home was 16 Szeher Street. It had a wide roof, which drooped low on both sides, prompting some people to call it "Attila's Tent." It contained three floors and twelve rooms. Since the house stood on a slope, the first floor extended back into a cavity in the side of the hill, and thus could be considered a basement. The living room, dining room, and Dohnányi's study were on this floor. Five bedrooms were on the second floor, while a large room and the servants' quarters were on the top floor.

❧

In August 1927 Dohnányi participated in an exhibition in Frankfurt am Main with the title "Musik im Leben der Völker" (Music in the Life of the People). He conducted the Budapest Philharmonic for "Zwei Tage Ungarischer Musik" (Two Days of Hungarian Music). These concerts featured works of Hungarian composers, including Dohnányi's own compositions as well as those by Bartók, Goldmark, Hubay, and Kodály.

In the autumn the Budapest Opera House celebrated Dohnányi's fiftieth birthday and thirtieth anniversary as a professional musician by performing *A vajda tornya*. On 24 October 1927 the Budapest Philharmonic marked this event with a special "all-Dohnányi" concert. On the following day the Waldbauer Quartet performed Dohnányi's chamber music, including the premiere of Dohnányi's Third String Quartet, op. 33, which Dohnányi had dedicated: "To my dear wife." Dohnányi said of this work, "The first movement is capricious and moody, the second religious, and the third a little dance-like." He believed this to be the best of his three string quartets, but this may have been merely because it was the most recent and the least known.

As Dohnányi himself remarked, "Authors often make favorites of their least popular works." He found it quite natural to see his more popular compositions favored over works that had gained his special approval. Nevertheless, Dohnányi looked upon all of his compositions as though they were his children. Although he was severe with them and often punished them with the most cruel cuts and drastic changes, he felt affection for them. Dohnányi's works were often prematurely rejected because they were somewhat complicated and far from easy. It sometimes takes the listener quite a bit of time to understand and appreciate a composition. When Dohnányi's works do become popular, however, they remain in the repertoire. For example, the *Variationen über ein Kinderlied* were initially received almost with hostility in Germany but after more than twenty years of constant performance were publicly acclaimed as immortal. Similarly, Dohnányi's new Quartet was not received favorably at first.

The highlight of the year was a visit from Albert Spalding, the famous American violinist. Dohnányi had met Spalding on 11 March 1923, when Spalding had performed Dohnányi's Violin Concerto at a Damrosch Concert in New York with Dohnányi conducting. When Spalding had visited Dohnányi in Budapest, they had played sonatas together on 24 April 1927. Spalding returned in December to play the Brahms Concerto with Dohnányi conducting the Budapest Philharmonic. The Dohnányis invited Spalding and his wife to lunch at their new home. That morning the chambermaid, setting the table in the dining room, noticed with horror that the silver had disappeared from the cupboard. The silver was hastily replaced, and the Spaldings were never aware of the panic that had seized their hosts. Soon after their guests left, the Dohnányis discussed matters with detectives and the insurance agency. The thief was traced when he tried to sell one of the silver bowls to a jeweler, and part of the stolen property was recovered.

Consenting to pressure and intervention from friends, Dohnányi reconciled with Hubay. This was not hard for Dohnányi, because he had not started or maintained the hostilities and had treated the whole affair coldly, without wasting too much emotion on it. In 1928, Dohnányi finally accepted Hubay's invitation to return to the Academy as Professor of Piano for advanced students, again selecting his pupils from the most talented young artists.

During the 1928 season Dohnányi gave more than seventy concerts. He reached his fifteen hundredth concert early in the year. Among the numerous concerts in which Dohnányi performed in 1928 was a two-piano concert with his pupil Mischa Levitzki. Dohnányi often played with his favorite pupils, including Edward Kilenyi, Jr., and Boris Goldovsky, who had both come to Budapest to study with Dohnányi at the Academy.

In May Dohnányi gave concerts with his Orchestra in Italy. They performed in Trieste, Treviso, Bologna, Milan, Cesena, Ancona, Parma, Modena, and Fiume, often playing more than one concert in each town.

Dohnányi enjoyed this trip; he was always enchanted by the beauty of Italy and of Italian art. "Italians," he used to say, "should never make war. They should only sing and create art. Art is their field and beauty." In June 1928 Dohnányi and his Orchestra visited London, giving three concerts there. In July they performed three times in Paris. These concerts consisted mainly of works by French and Hungarian composers, but one included Mozart's G Major Piano Concerto, which Dohnányi conducted from the keyboard. The Orchestra also performed in Scheveningen, Zurich, and several German cities, including Cologne, Heidelberg, and Munich.

In November 1928 Hungary commemorated the hundredth anniversary of Schubert's death. Dohnányi made an orchestral transcription of Schubert's F-minor Fantasia for piano, four hands, and conducted the Budapest Philharmonic in its premiere on 26 November 1928. He also made an orchestral arrangement of Schubert's *Moments musicaux,* for which his wife Elza Dohnányi-Galafrés created a one-act scenario with choreography. This work was premiered by the Hungarian State Opera House in Budapest as *A músza csókja* (The Muse's Kiss) on 6 January 1929. Dohnányi also gave recitals of Schubert's solo works, including his own arrangement of Schubert's *Valses nobles,* as well as some of Schubert's chamber music with the Waldbauer Quartet.

In January 1929 Dohnányi paid yet another visit to England, Scotland, Ireland, and the Netherlands. He arrived back just in time for the dual first performance of his comic opera *Der Tenor* (The Tenor), op. 34, which took place on 24 February in Budapest and Nuremberg. The opera was based on Karl Sternheim's play *Bürger Schippel* (Citizen Schippel), which Ernő Goth had transformed into an opera libretto. The opera caricatures the conventional German Glee Club and the petty, narrow-minded, philistine life of a small German principality.

At the beginning of the opera, a vocal quartet assembles in the house of Hicketier, their second bass, mourning the death of their first tenor. After some reminiscences of the deceased and the competitions they had won with him, including the Duke's Prize, they begin to wonder how they will win their next competition. Hicketier announces that he has found a tenor with a fine voice, named Schippel. Unfortunately, Schippel is not a respectable citizen; he is a vagabond who squanders away his life in taverns, making him unworthy of admission to their club. Because they desperately need a capable tenor, the quartet decides to accept him, but to avoid interacting with him socially. They quickly bring in Schippel, who proves to be a fine singer, but devoid of all manners. He agrees to join the quartet not to sing at the competition but to be accepted into society. The Duke then enters with an arm injury he sustained falling from a horse just outside the house. Hicketier's daughter Tekla dresses his wound. Before leaving, the Duke whispers to her that he will come back at night to see her again. Meanwhile, the singers' discussion ends in failure; Schippel declares that unless they accept him as their social equal, he will not sing with them. He insolently sticks out his tongue and walks out of the room. The quartet reluctantly decides to call him back and invite him to stay for dinner.

The second act starts with an evening rehearsal in the house. Tekla, to whom both the second tenor and Schippel are attracted, sneaks out for a stroll with the Duke. After the rehearsal ends, Schippel sees the ladder that Tekla used to climb out and is seized by an amorous impulse to climb up into the girl's room. At this moment the other quartet members discover him. Schippel declares that he will not sing unless he is given Tekla's hand in marriage. Meanwhile, the Duke and Tekla return. Despite the Duke's stammered claims of innocence, Schippel announces that he will not claim the girl anymore, because he considers her to be the Duke's mistress. Hicketier is outraged by this insult and challenges Schippel to a duel as soon as the competition is over.

The third act takes place one week later. The quartet has once more won the Duke's Prize, and the members meet in a forest to fulfill Hicketier's challenge. Both combatants tremble, dreading the duel. In his fear, Schippel shoots into the air, while Hicketier collapses before he even fires. Because their hostility has now come to an end, they make peace. The quartet leaves, triumphantly singing Mendelssohn's "Der Jäger Abschied" (The Hunter's Departure).

Despite the initial popularity of *Der Tenor* in Budapest and several German cities, it later became the subject of several scandals. In the postwar period, the play became disfigured by obscene jokes, even though *Der Tenor* was meant to be a subtle comedy. The opera was further desecrated by being staged in the gigantic Charlottenburg opera house, where its small-scale orchestration was almost lost. Finally, under Hitler's regime *Der Tenor* was censored because the librettist Ernő Goth was a Jew. During World War II, Clemens Krauss, the General Music Director of the Munich Opera, planned to revive *Der Tenor*. He sent his conductor to discuss matters with Dohnányi. "There is a problem with your opera," the conductor began.

"I know," Dohnányi replied, cutting him short. "You object because the author of the libretto is Jewish."

To Dohnányi's surprise the conductor answered, "This doesn't matter anymore. A law has recently been established in Germany according to which the librettist doesn't matter."

Dohnányi realized that the Germans had been forced to introduce such a regulation because almost all of the librettists of Richard Strauss's and Franz Lehár's works were Jewish. "What other problem could there be with my opera?" he wondered.

"At the end you use Mendelssohn's quartet, 'Der Jäger Abschied.' Mendelssohn cannot be performed. You must change this part, entirely omitting the song."

Dohnányi was indignant. "This is out of the question and I will never do it," he declared. "Mendelssohn's song perfectly exemplifies the Glee Club in my opera, and the whole work is based upon it. Besides, it is repeated several times, so I would have to rewrite the entire work, which I have absolutely no intention of doing." Both men stuck to their words; Dohnányi did not rewrite the opera, and the Germans did not perform it.

❦

In addition to the usual Philharmonic concerts and chamber music performances in Budapest, Dohnányi performed concerts with his Orchestra. On 14 March 1929 he played Schumann's Concerto, Liszt's E-flat Major Concerto, and Beethoven's G Major Concerto, all without a conductor. On 25 April, Dohnányi and Ossip Gabrilowitsch each played and conducted a Brahms Concerto. In August Dohnányi was again in Salzburg for the Mozart Festival, this time conducting the Vienna Philharmonic Orchestra as well as performing chamber music.

Dohnányi was thoroughly occupied with teaching at the Academy and presiding over the Budapest Philharmonic Society. As a result, his concert trips to foreign countries in the 1930–31 season were limited. He performed in Belgium and the Netherlands in April, and played in Athens on 16 November 1930 with Dimitri Mitropoulos conducting.

On 25 October 1930 the town of Szeged dedicated its Votive Cathedral with solemn festivities.[10] The consecration was a sacred event for all of Hungary. The Mass was celebrated by the Archbishop of Esztergom, several bishops, and Regent Horthy. The festivities included Dohnányi conducting the premiere of his *Missa in dedicatione ecclesiae*, op. 35, which became known as the *Szegedi mise* (Szeged Mass). This performance was the result of a competition organized by the State in which Dohnányi won the first prize of 10,000 pengős. Dohnányi composed the Mass for soloists, double choir, orchestra, and organ; the premiere involved three hundred performers, including the Budapest Philharmonic and the united choirs of Budapest and Szeged. After the solemn performance in the Cathedral, Dohnányi's Mass was given in several other churches, with smaller numbers of performers. Dohnányi also conducted the first concert performance of the Mass in Budapest on 24 November 1930.

---

10. In 1922, Dohnányi had received an honorary doctorate degree from the University of Szeged.

In 1931 Dohnányi was engaged as the General Music Director of the Hungarian Broadcasting Society, conducting the Magyar Rádió Szimfonikus Zenekara (Hungarian Radio Symphony Orchestra). It was a joint-stock company with sole broadcasting rights in Hungary, under the absolute control of the State. Everyone who possessed a radio had to make a monthly payment that was strictly collected by the Post Office. Anyone who used a broadcasting instrument without being a subscriber was severely punished. Despite its strong governmental ties, the Radio was forbidden to transmit advertisements or any kind of propaganda.

In spite of all his obligations in Hungary, Dohnányi visited England in February 1931, where he gave recitals in London, Oxford, and Liverpool. In June he returned to the Salzburg Mozart Festival, which had become a permanent obligation for him. This time he conducted concerts with his own Orchestra on 27 and 29 July 1931.

As time passed, Dohnányi began to spend more and more time in his home on Szeher Street. He had always had a great admiration for the beauties of nature, and he now became exceedingly attached to this place surrounded by a superb view of the faraway mountains. He hired a gardener to plant a vegetable garden, an orchard, and a lovely flower garden. The gardener ensured that flowers were blooming throughout the year. Dohnányi was especially fond of his roses and his rock garden on the slope of the hill.

Dohnányi was also fond of animals, especially dogs. Even during his stay in Vienna, he had always kept at least one dog in his home. Now that he had a permanent house, his friends gave him a huge komondor.[11] The superb dog had been bred by the late Hungarian poet Endre Ady. Because the dog, Zsofi, felt lonesome and strolled about at nights in search of company, the Dohnányis found her a worthy mate. Soon a puppy was born, named Bundás, which won the first prize at an exhibition. Eventually, the three enormous dogs outgrew Dohnányi's garden. Because he considered it a cruel torture to keep them on a chain, Dohnányi had special quarters built, surrounded by a wire fence. One komondor was given the privilege of being free while the other two took their turns in the enclosure. One day two children came to the house with a message. After they saw the komondors, they hurried back in alarm to their parents with the news, "We saw polar bears in the Dohnányis' garden! Real polar bears!" These "polar bears" were later joined by a small puli, a black shepherd dog, which became the favorite; Dohnányi found the Hungarian puli to be the cleverest and most intelligent of all breeds.

---

11. Komondors are a Hungarian breed of large, powerful dogs with long, white fur.

The tennis court and swimming pool provided Dohnányi with further diversions. He played tennis for an hour every day, and in the summer he enjoyed the cool water with his family and friends. Dohnányi's mother and mother-in-law got much pleasure from the garden but avoided the water, finding it too chilly.

The elder Mrs. Dohnányi lived with her son and his family, spreading her characteristic air of cheerful tranquility until the day of her death in 1933. She was eighty when she slipped on the stairs and broke her leg. It must have been very painful, but she uttered no word of complaint when the doctors came to help her. Although she never really recovered from this accident, she suffered peacefully. There was a smile on her lips when Mitzi, who slept at her side, woke up to find her dead one morning.

Because Dohnányi had become so attached to his home, he spent his summers there. He left only occasionally to visit his beloved mountains in the Tyrol or Switzerland. Dohnányi also repeatedly visited the magnificently luxurious home of Count Somsich. The Count was a bachelor, a fine pianist, and a very entertaining companion. His property of 400,000 Hungarian acres contained a lovely park with a lake where his guests could go boating. Dohnányi brought his wife here on several occasions and his little son Matthew once. In the evenings Dohnányi enjoyed long conversations with his host by candlelight, because the conservative Count never had electricity installed in his home. Count Somsich and Dohnányi exchanged the most frightening ghost stories. The Count thoroughly believed that the spirit of his Aunt Marie, from whom he had inherited the castle, visited her old home by night. During the night, the Dohnányis shuddered when they thought that Aunt Marie might pay them a visit on her haunting rounds.

On 1 April 1932 the Duke Paul Esterházy sponsored a solemn and ceremonial performance of Haydn's oratorio *Die Schöpfung* (The Creation) in Budapest. It was performed by the City Choir and the Budapest Philharmonic, with Dohnányi conducting. For months the Duke, a cultured, musical young prince, had contemplated organizing this festival in honor of Haydn, who had worked as Conductor and Music Director for most of his life at Eszterháza, the estate of the Duke's ancestors. Duke Esterházy was also planning to have many of Haydn's manuscripts, which were still lying there in heaps, published, but this plan was upset by World War II. Esterházy, probably the richest duke in Europe, was an able businessman who knew how to preserve his fortune. For many weeks his secretary discussed the financial side of the performance of *Die Schöpfung* and haggled over every expense. Finally he and Dohnányi agreed that the orchestra should get a fee of 3,000 pengős, the chorus and Dohnányi 1,000 each, and the soloists 500 pengős each. When the concert took place, however, the Duke was so impressed that with a truly aristocratic gesture he doubled the fee of the orchestra, chorus, and soloists, and tripled the fee of the conductor.

During the winter of 1932–33 Dohnányi organized the First International Liszt Competition for the Academy. This tremendous undertaking made more demands on Dohnányi's time and energy than any previous activity. Because the Hungarian State, the City of Budapest, and private individuals sponsored the competition, it was able to offer large prizes. The first prize was 5,000 pengős; the second 3,000; the third 2,000; and there were five prizes of 1,000 pengős. The competition lasted more than two weeks, and there were a hundred and fifty competitors.

With his usual precision Dohnányi worked out a plan to ensure complete impartiality. He himself was not a member of the jury, which he assembled out of the most outstanding musicians of the world, including Leonid Kreutzer from Germany, Alfred Cortot and Isidor Philipp from France, Józef Turczyński from Poland, Paul Weingartner and Emil Sauer from Austria, and Donald Francis Tovey from England. The voting was based on a well-thought-out system of awarding points. Although most members of the jury praised Dohnányi for his scheme, a painful conflict arose between him and Emil Sauer. The aged professor, once a student of Liszt, had brought with him a gifted pupil, who later became his wife. She was a fine pianist who had every chance of gaining the first prize. Unfortunately Sauer did not want to take chances; when he learned of the voting method, he declared with indignation, "This competition is not conducted in the spirit of Liszt!" Together with the young woman, he left in disgust. It deeply hurt Dohnányi to offend Sauer, but it could not be helped.

Eight candidates qualified for the final stage of the competition, which was spread over two evenings. They were to play a Liszt concerto of their choice with the Orchestra, conducted by Dohnányi. Since seven of the competitors chose the E-flat Major Concerto, and the rehearsal for both concerts took place on the morning of the first performance, Dohnányi conducted this concerto eleven times that day. The result, however, was a triumph for Dohnányi; the winner of the first prize was Annie Fischer, his own pupil. Her success also proved the impartiality of the competition, showing that the jury had no preferences in gender, religion, or race, for Annie Fischer was Jewish.

On 23 October 1933, Dohnányi conducted the premiere of his *Symphonischen Minuten* (Symphonic Minutes) for orchestra, op. 36, which he dedicated "To the members of the Budapest Philharmonic Society."

Although Dohnányi was fifty-six years old, he was more vigorous than many youngsters half his age. This was due to his good health and his spiritual vitality. He had adopted the demeanor of his mother, and it became the foundation of his whole mental and spiritual outlook on life. This helped him to be always balanced and content, even cheerful. Dohnányi was once asked whether his demeanor actually spared him suffering or if he just suppressed his feelings through self-control. "I am perhaps not entirely spared from suffering," he answered. "But as soon as I feel pain over an insult or offense, I quickly remind myself that I must eradicate this feeling. And with an effort I soon succeed." There was something that greatly helped him to do so: his pride, which did not allow him to feel concerned about base and vile actions. He could easily forgive an offense, if it could be explained with an acceptable reason. Nevertheless, he could never forgive grave insults; the offending person simply ceased to exist for him. The one thing that Dohnányi could never forgive was hypocrisy. Perhaps very few have followed Christ's principles so intensively as he did, but he rarely went to church. He felt contempt for those who knelt there during every Mass, but as soon as they left God's house forgot to act like Christians. He also felt contempt for the excessively religious people who made shows of their faith; he called them *Crucifix-beissers* (Cross biters).

In July 1934, Dohnányi returned to the post of Director of the Budapest Academy. Shortly afterwards, he developed a thrombosis, which left him immobilized for several months. It was during this illness that he composed his Sextet, op. 37, for piano, violin, viola, cello, clarinet, and horn. Dohnányi's first performance after being bedridden with the thrombosis was a recital with the violinist Emil Telmányi on 14 June 1935. Three days later Dohnányi participated in the premiere of his Sextet. Other important chamber music recitals from around this time included a 5 March 1936 performance with violinist Jacques Thibaud and cellist Jenő Kerpely and a 16 December 1936 recital with Imre Waldbauer and Kerpely. In addition Dohnányi continued to appear with the Budapest Philharmonic, including a 3 April 1936 performance of Beethoven's Triple Concerto in which violinist Erica Morini and cellist Gregor Piatigorsky joined Dohnányi, who conducted from the piano, as well as a concert of Hungarian and Italian music in Rome on 7 May 1936 that was attended by Benito Mussolini.

An etching of Pozsony made in 1921 by A. Steger. The first house on the right is 12 Clarissa Street, the house in which Dohnányi was born and in which he spent his entire childhood. Courtesy of Dr. Seán McGlynn.

Dohnányi (left) with his sister Mitzi, ca. 1880. Courtesy of Dr. Seán McGlynn.

The program from Dohnányi's first public performance, during which he premiered two of his *6 Fantasiestücke* (6 Fantasy Pieces) and premiered his Scherzo in A Major as an encore. This was a concert of the Pozsonyi dalegylet (Pozsony Singing Society) on 28 December 1890. Courtesy of the Ernst von Dohnányi Collection, Warren D. Allen Music Library, Florida State University.

Pages 52 and 53 of a manuscript of Dohnányi's String Sextet in B-flat Major (1893; revised in 1896), showing revisions he made to the work. Courtesy of the Ernst von Dohnányi Collection, Warren D. Allen Music Library, Florida State University.

Dohnányi in 1897, the year he graduated from the National Hungarian Royal Academy of Music (now the Franz Liszt Academy of Music) in Budapest. Courtesy of Dr. Seán McGlynn.

The Dohnányi family in their home in 1900 (from left to right: Frederick, Ernst, Ottilia, and Mitzi). Courtesy of Dr. Seán McGlynn.

This playful tintype was taken ca. 1900 at a carnival in Budapest (from left to right: Dohnányi, Béla Bartók, and Zoltán Kodály). Courtesy of Dr. Seán McGlynn.

TOWN HALL

113-23 W. 43rd ST.   NEW YORK

SUNDAY AFTERNOON
MARCH 13th
At Three o'clock

*A SECOND
CONCERT OF PIANO
COMPOSITIONS PLAYED*
BY

ERNO
Dohnányi

COMPOSER-PIANIST

Programme :

I.

a) Passacaglia Op. 6 . . .	Dohnanyi
b) Sonata E flat Op. 31 No. 3 . . .	Beethoven
c) Sonata quasi una fantasia op. 27 No. 2 (Moonlight)	"

II

a) Klagegesang . . .	Bela Bartok
b) Baerentanz	" "
c) Abend am Lande. . . .	" "
d) Allegro Barbaro . . .	" "
e) Intermezzo of E Major Op. 116, No. 4 .	Brahms
f) Rhapsodie of G minor- Op. 79, No. 2 .	"

III.

Carneval Op. 9.	Schumann

Chickering Piano Used

A program from Dohnányi's 1920–21 United States tour, which was his first trip to America in twenty years. Dohnányi specialized in performing the works of Romantic composers such as Beethoven, Brahms, and Schubert, but he also championed Bartók's compositions. Courtesy of the Ernst von Dohnányi Collection, Warren D. Allen Music Library, Florida State University.

Dohnányi, ca. 1927. Courtesy of Dr. Seán McGlynn.

An etching by Ernő Koch titled "Konzert az Operában"
(Concert in the Opera House), depicting Dohnányi conducting the
Budapest Philharmonic during their 100th anniversary season in 1943.
Courtesy of Dr. Seán McGlynn.

FRIDAY
JULY 6, 1945

The *65th Division SSO*
presents

Linz

ERNST von DOHNANYI

Conductor and Guest Pianist

with the

Philharmonic Broadcasting Orchestra

(Bruckner Orchester)

PROGRAMME

FRANZ SCHUBERT'S Symphony No 8 in B Minor (Unfinished Symphony)

> *1st Movement* . . . . *Allegro Moderato*
> *2nd Movement* . . . . *Andante Con Moto*

BEETHOVEN'S Concerto No 5 for Piano (Emperor Concerto)

> *1st Movement* . . . . *Allegro*
> *2nd Movement* . . . . *Adagio Un Poco Mosso*
> *3rd Movement* . . . . *Rondo Allegro*

Three Selections from ERNST von DOHNANYI'S "Ruralia Hungarica"

> *1. Presto Ma Mon Tanto*
> *2. Adagio Non Troppo*
> *3. Molto Vivace*

The program for Dohnányi's first appearance after World War II.
The handwriting on this copy is Dohnányi's. Courtesy of the
Ernst von Dohnányi Collection, Warren D. Allen Music Library,
Florida State University.

The Dohnányi family at their Tallahassee home in 1952
(clockwise from bottom right: Ernst, Ilona, Christoph, Helen,
and Julius). Courtesy of Dr. Seán McGlynn.

Dohnányi (right) with
Edward Kilenyi, Jr., ca.
1955. Courtesy of
Dr. Seán McGlynn.

Dohnányi in his
Tallahassee home, ca.
1955, revising his
Symphony in E Major,
op. 40. Courtesy of
Dr. Seán McGlynn.

Dohnányi conducting the Ohio University Symphony Orchestra,
ca. 1955. Courtesy of Dr. Seán McGlynn.

Ernst and Ilona von Dohnányi on the *Queen Mary,* returning to America from his critically acclaimed performances at the 1956 Edinburgh Festival. Courtesy of Dr. Seán McGlynn.

Ilona von Dohnányi in 1943. Courtesy of Dr. Seán McGlynn.

FIVE

1937–1944

I n 1937 Hubay died, and Dohnányi succeeded him in the Upper House of the Hungarian Senate.

From 2 to 10 April 1937 Dohnányi undertook an exhausting but successful concert tour with his Budapest Philharmonic. He conducted the music of German and Hungarian composers over a period of nine days in as many cities: Breslau, Berlin, Hamburg, Mülheim, Cologne, Frankfurt, Mannheim, Baden-Baden, and Munich. Everywhere they went, the Orchestra and its Conductor were guests of the city, and they were granted every luxury and hospitality imaginable. Dohnányi, however, became fatigued. He conducted most of the concert in Munich with a fever, and then practically collapsed. The final piece on the program was conducted by his concertmaster Carl Melles. Dohnányi subsequently committed himself for two weeks to a hospital in Garmisch-Partenkirchen.

In July 1937 festivals celebrating Dohnányi's sixtieth birthday were arranged all over the world, especially in Budapest.[1] The main celebration, a huge banquet of a thousand people, had been held in the winter with Dohnányi present. In July, when it actually was his birthday, Dohnányi fled into the Austrian Mountains. He spent two weeks in Styria and two weeks in the Tyrol on the high peak called the "Ehrenbach-höhe" to escape the celebrations and be alone to relax. To his surprise, when he turned on the radio, he heard his own music. Radio Vienna was celebrating the birthday of the Hungarian Maestro by playing his *Variationen über ein Kinderlied.*

That winter my parents gave a dinner party to which they invited Dohnányi and his wife.[2] I happened to be in Budapest and was present on

---

1. Hungary's feelings were best expressed in an article of the *Pesti Napló* written on 28 July 1937; see Appendix C.
2. My father, Julius Zachár, was Dohnányi's friend from Breznóbánya and Budapest. Dohnányi's grandmother and my father's grandmother were cousins.

this occasion. I was very excited about this evening because I had never met Dohnányi before. Nevertheless, I could not get close to him in the crowd of guests who were swarming in the room. After supper, I felt two palms being gently pressed against my eyes from behind me. A man's voice I had never heard before asked mockingly, "Guess who I am?" Puzzled, I wheeled around to find myself face to face with Ernst von Dohnányi. There was a smile on his lips and in his bright blue eyes as he looked at me. He gently took both of my hands and, patting my flushed cheek, murmured, "You resemble your father, my dear . . . I recognized you immediately."

I congratulated him on having been so widely celebrated on his sixtieth birthday, but he waved away my compliments with a shrug of his shoulders. "I would be happy to have such a birthday," I remarked awkwardly.

"Not if it were your sixtieth," he said smiling. He asked how old I was.

"Twenty-seven," I said, almost ashamed. In spite of my few years, I realized that I felt older than him. In appearance, as well as in spirit, he was full of vitality.

"That reminds me," he said, "how a friend of mine felt when he was over eighty. 'If I only could be seventy again!' he would say longingly."

A few minutes later Mrs. Dohnányi came to tell him that they had to leave. She reminded him that he was recovering from his thrombosis as well as a pleural inflammation and that he should not wear himself out. By the way she commandingly spoke and the look of reproach and annoyance he secretly threw her, I realized that there was little understanding between them and that he was probably just as unhappy and lonesome as I was in my marriage.[3] He awoke in me such a deep sympathy and an infinite admiration that I would have given anything to make him as happy as he deserved to be. The Dohnányis left abruptly; Dohnányi was not the type of man to protest or say even one offensive word to a woman, especially his wife. When they were gone, people began to whisper about the way Mrs. Dohnányi was keeping her husband perfectly under her thumb. In her jealousy she would energetically interfere whenever he tried to speak to another woman, even in company.

A few days later, I anxiously dialed the number of the Franz Liszt Academy of Music and asked to speak with Dohnányi. This displayed tremendous audacity, because it was well known that Dohnányi came to the phone only for the most important affairs. Nevertheless, I felt that my case was urgent, even if only to myself. I also felt a secret longing to find out whether he still remembered me and would be as nice to me as he had been at my parents' party.

---

3. I had been in an unfulfilling marriage for nine years. Because my husband was a landowner, I lived on his estate with our eight-year-old daughter Helen and six-year-old son Julius.

Dohnányi arranged an appointment with me at the Academy, where I was received by his Secretary, Kálmán Isoz. Isoz, who was called Uncle Kálmán by the students, was a very kind, elderly gentleman and a loyal friend to Dohnányi. He ushered me into the spacious, although somewhat gloomy room that was his own office. After offering me a seat, he informed me that Dohnányi was busy in a meeting and would see me afterwards. While I waited, my eyes fell upon a huge piano that occupied almost a quarter of the room. It was an impressive instrument, with magnificently carved legs. Mr. Isoz noticed my interest. "It once belonged to Franz Liszt," he explained. "Two pianos were given to him by the Chickering firm, and he bequeathed them both to the Academy. The other is in the office of the General Director, as you will soon see." I became increasingly excited and embarrassed. My plans now seemed childish and naive, and I had an impulse to run home without accomplishing anything. Suddenly, the door flew open, and Mr. Isoz announced that General Director Dohnányi would now see me.

I entered the study. It was a spacious room enveloped in the mist of a foggy day, which further emphasized the dignified and solemn atmosphere. In the foreground stood a table surrounded by comfortable armchairs, beyond which stood Liszt's second Chickering piano. Next to the window was a writing table covered with papers, where Dohnányi was sitting. He rose to greet me and offered a seat in an armchair. Dohnányi then occupied the chair opposite me. "Is there anything I can do for you?" he asked in a rather casual, reserved manner. He was strict and stiff, as a Director should be when hosting someone in his office. He must have been tired and probably wanted me to immediately get to the point of my visit.

I desperately searched for a familiar smile on his face, but his features were now earnest and cold. His blue eyes, which were expectantly fixed on me, were almost indifferent. In my confusion I fumbled with my handbag. Realizing that I was wasting his time, I braced myself and explained in a shaking voice that I was seeking employment.

"Why do you want a job?" he asked quietly, still keeping his steady gaze on me, as though he was trying to penetrate my soul. Then he added with a frown, "Is it your intention to abandon your life on the estate?"

I became even more flustered. Then, on an involuntary impulse, I opened my heart to him. I told him about the failure of my marriage, which had become so full of suffering that I could not bear it any longer, and my need for independence. He listened attentively. First he was almost shocked by my confession. Then the frown slowly disappeared from his forehead and his features softened. When I rose to leave, I could again detect the familiar smile in his bright blue eyes. "I shall do what I can to help you," he said warmly, "although it will not be easy. There are no openings at the Academy, and as to the Radio, although I am the Director of Music, I do not have the power to hire personnel. This much I can tell you: you should learn typing and stenography. Although you can speak five languages, that knowledge is of no use if you cannot make practical use of it." I promised to start my studies immediately. When we parted, he touched my cheek lightly with his lips. Although it was only a casual kiss from a respectable uncle to his niece, my heart warmed and I knew that he liked me.

I could not find a job in typing or stenography. I did, however, obtain a full-time job with a high salary. I worked as a secretary in the airplane department of the Manfred Weiss factory. Nevertheless, Dohnányi continued to give me useful advice, and we often met.

During my intimate talks with Dohnányi, I found out that he, too, was unhappy. For years he had known that his second marriage could not fulfill him, and he missed the freedom that was indispensable to his very existence as well as to his creative ability. He felt lonesome and depressed, and was tired of the loud arguments with his wife. It was only natural that his wife wanted to put an end to our meetings, but this time Dohnányi refused. He continued to visit my parents' home, where my children and I had been staying since I had left my husband's estate. Dohnányi did not seek a divorce for the sake of his beloved son Matthew, who had become a lieutenant in the Hungarian Army. Dohnányi nevertheless made it clear that he must at least have the freedom to see his relatives as frequently as he wanted.

His visits to us were not too frequent, because I worked at the factory all day. He did, however, usually spend Sundays with my children, their nurse—Fräulein Hermine Lorenz, who had once been my governess—and me. He would take us to the park, to a restaurant for dinner, or to the zoo. Dohnányi seemed to be happy in my company. This was no momentary, passing infatuation, but a lasting affection. Although there was a difference of thirty years between us, no one has ever understood me as he did. With his vitality and his limitless love for nature and humanity, he always completely understood my children and me. He once told my daughter, "Perhaps it is through your little joys and sorrows that I feel young."

❧

With political tensions in Europe mounting, Hungary, because she was located between Russia and Germany, had no choice but to abandon her hopes of remaining neutral and ally herself with Germany. In return, Germany and Italy helped Hungary recover some of the territories that had been taken by the Treaty of Trianon. Hungary regained land from Czechoslovakia in 1938 and from the Carpatho-Ukraine in 1939. The nation rejoiced over the re-annexation. Horthy rode into the newly restored cities on his white horse, followed by his warriors. He was received with hysterical enthusiasm by people who had suffered separation from their motherland and relatives. With loud sobs of joy they threw themselves on the soldiers, covering them with flowers. In Budapest, church bells rang and Masses were held in which sermons were preached in gratitude to God. In the streets University students and patriots carried huge boards with the names of the cities still under enemy occupation. "Restore everything!" they shouted. "Restore all of Hungary!"

On one occasion, Dohnányi traveled to Berlin by train for three performances. When he left the Hungarian border town of Komárom on 2 November 1938, the part of the city situated on the other side of the Danube still belonged to Czechoslovakia. When Dohnányi returned five days later, the entire town was decorated with red, white, and green Hungarian flags; the restoration of the territory had taken place during his absence. Every day Dohnányi hoped that the city of his birth, the ancient Hungarian coronation town of Pozsony, would also be returned to the motherland. This never happened, however, because Hitler declared Bohemia and Slovakia to be free countries and agreed that Pozsony should become the capital of Slovakia.

On the morning of 1 September 1939 we heard the radio play military marches, and there was tension in the air. It was announced that hostilities had started between Germany and Poland. This was followed by a declaration of war by England and France. In May 1939 Dohnányi had been sent by the Hungarian Government to Warsaw to conduct the Budapest Philharmonic in a performance of works by Hungarian composers. While he was there, Dohnányi had witnessed a magnificent parade of Polish troops, who were full of pride and self-assurance. The Polish Foreign Minister had declared in a thundering speech that the Polish Army was ready to face the German forces at any moment. Dohnányi, who had traveled through Germany and had seen the tanks and airplanes, was upset by the blind audacity with which the Poles threw themselves into the war. When he returned to Budapest, Dohnányi had met the German Ambassador, who had said to him with a shrug of his shoulders, "If the Poles want to commit suicide, we cannot stop them." When the war broke out in September, Dohnányi grieved for Poland; in addition to being Hungary's neighbor, Poland had been a close ally for centuries.

With the start of war, my work in the factory became more difficult. I became fatigued, and Dohnányi and my family persuaded me to quit. This was not a problem, because I had found my real calling: I was translating Lucio d'Ambra's *Italian Trilogy* and was also working on a collection of letters written by Clara Wieck to Robert Schumann, with which Dohnányi was gladly helping me. Dohnányi, meanwhile, had fallen ill with nicotine poisoning. Up to this time he had been a passionate smoker, but on the advice of his doctors he immediately stopped smoking.

Because I was still in poor health, I spent the summer of 1940 by the seaside with my children and Fräulein Hermine. We stayed in Cirkvenica, Yugoslavia, an enchanting little town bordered by rocky mountains. On 3 September we listened to the broadcast of a recital that Dohnányi gave in Belgrade. Because Dohnányi was already in Yugoslavia, he visited us at the coast and we enjoyed each other's company in the radiant sunshine. I was busily working on my second book, *Én terjesztem a Szent tüzet,* which is a biography of Ferenc Kazinczy.[4] Dohnányi occupied himself by suntanning, walking, and playing with my children.

Upon returning to Budapest Dohnányi was visited by his son, Hans von Dohnányi. When Dohnányi had divorced his former wife, he had been a citizen of both Hungary and Germany. Elsa Kunwald had kept her German citizenship and remained in Berlin, where she reared her two children. Now Grete had four children, and Hans had three.[5] Whenever Dohnányi had a trip in Germany, he would visit his grandchildren and bring them little gifts. Dohnányi was very proud of Hans, who was an extremely brilliant man and in an eminent position as a jurist. Dohnányi became depressed, however, when he heard Hans speak about political affairs in Germany. Despite his important position, Hans bitterly and openly criticized the regime that he was supposed to serve. He told his father that he took advantage of every opportunity to hamper the government or oppose its cruel regulations.

One morning in the autumn, Dohnányi informed me by telephone that he was suffering from a thrombosis in his right arm and had to stay in bed for three months. This was very bad news; this was the second time he had contracted a thrombosis, and his friends were worried. Dohnányi, however, accepted the unwelcome situation with his usual calmness. "Three months may be long," he said, "but there are many who are bound for all their lives to a wheelchair or even a bed." He tried to console me, for he, on his part, needed no consolation; he was always resigned to his destiny. I was especially upset by this news because the illness would separate us entirely, and I had already not entered Dohnányi's home for more than a year. I was relieved when he informed me by telephone, "I have moved into the hospital of the Hotel Gellert, where anyone may visit me." As he spoke, I could almost hear the smile on his face.

4. Ferenc Kazinczy, who lived in the eighteenth century, was an ancestor of mine. In addition to being the founder of Hungarian literature, he became a national hero after he was imprisoned for fighting for his country's freedom.

5. Hans's sons Klaus (b. 1928) and Christoph (b. 1929) became a distinguished German politician and a famous conductor, respectively.

In the hotel, he lay in his bed patiently, with his right arm propped up on a pillow as the doctors had ordered. "Since I have to go through this ordeal anyway," he said, "it is far better for me to face it calmly than make it worse by rebelling against it. Besides, against whom could I rebel? Against Fate? That would be as useful as banging my head against a rock." Everyone admired Dohnányi's composure and had to admit that he was an artist not only in music, but also in the "Art of Living." He was never bored, not even now, for he was busy with his thoughts or with the melodies that he would either scribble with his left hand into a tiny notebook or let drift away with the liberality with which he handled his material belongings.

In addition to revisiting the music of Bach, Mozart, Beethoven, and other great composers, Dohnányi occupied himself by reading books from his personal library of two thousand books. This included the complete works of the great Hungarian poets and other writers, such as Shakespeare, Goethe, and Schiller. There were many books in Dohnányi's library that he did not open twice; he favored only important books on music or philosophy. Although his favorite serious writers were Kant, Schopenhauer, Nietzsche, and Spengler, Dohnányi also enjoyed Dickens. "I like Dickens," he would say, "because his humor is pure and filled with goodwill, without malice or irony. This type of humor is also what I value in Haydn's music. Unfortunately, very few people understand it, and therefore few can perform his works well."

Most of Dohnányi's time, however, was taken up by his *Cantus vitae,* op. 38, on which he had been working for many years. This symphonic cantata, which could be called the work of a lifetime, was already complete, and he was now scoring it. Since his right hand had to remain motionless, he had to scribble with his left, and so most of the notes were somewhat blurred. I begged him to allow me to help him, and I was overjoyed when he agreed. Although my job was simply to make the indistinct notes clearer, I was extremely proud of this task. Usually his notes were tiny, but delicate and clear, reflecting his character: precise and exact to the slightest detail.

After the bitterly long three months, Dohnányi recovered entirely from his illness. This marked a new beginning in his life; to preserve his independence he decided to stay at the Hotel Gellert even after his recovery. He gave up everything that he had loved and possessed before, including the house on Szeher Street with the garden that was his pride, and surrendered his entire salary from the Academy and the Radio. He gave it all to his wife and family, keeping only the fees from his concerts, which, because of the war, were not numerous. He chose a modest hotel room as his new home. This tremendous sacrifice shocked me deeply, especially when on our walks I saw him admire gardens, resting his gaze with tenderness and longing upon roses or rock plants, comparing them with those he had in his garden. Nevertheless, I never heard him utter one single word of regret. He seemed perfectly content in that hotel room, visiting his house on Szeher Street only when he needed a book or some other object, or when he would give a party for his friends. Dohnányi spent his free time visiting me in my home.[6]

❧

On 30 August 1940 Germany and Italy forced Romania to return a part of Transylvania to Hungary. Once more, the country broke out into hysterical joy over a partial compensation for the unjust injuries she had suffered with the dismemberment of her territories.

In March 1941 the Philharmonic Orchestra of Belgrade gave a concert in Budapest. Although Hungary received the musicians amiably and afterwards gave a reception in their honor, everyone could feel the political tension between the two nations. Everyone guessed that sooner or later Hungary, under German pressure, would get involved in hostilities with Yugoslavia.

Hungary's alliance with Nazi Germany brought anti-Semitic laws. Although most of the Hungarian authorities tried to ignore these regulations, eventually they had to enforce them. One of the new laws reduced the number of Jews who could be employed at the Academy of Music. Dohnányi, with his characteristic fairness, refused to implement the regulations and openly opposed the Government. He protested against the dismissal of György Faragó, a fine artist and a former pupil of his. Dohnányi insisted that it was in the best interest of culture that such a man be allowed to teach at the Academy.

"We are in a war where culture is unimportant," answered a high Government official.

Dohnányi indignantly declared that if culture was not important, then he could not continue to serve such a regime. He then resigned from his position at the Academy. The State accepted his resignation, but asked him to stay until a successor could be found.

Horthy continued to try to maintain political stability, but his task became increasingly difficult as the Germans grew more and more suspicious. Everyone already feared that hostilities would break out any moment between Hungary and Germany. This would condemn us to a much worse fate than that of Holland or Belgium, because under the Treaty of Trianon we had been deprived of our army and had no forces other than those

6. Between my translations of books from Italian to Hungarian and my own books, I was able to make a comfortable living for my children, Fräulein Hermine, a chambermaid, and myself.

equipped by the Germans. Within a few hours we would be annihilated by German bombs and tanks. Meanwhile Count Pál Teleki, our Prime Minister, had been protesting a German order requiring Hungary to send troops against Yugoslavia. After it was discovered that Count Teleki had shot himself, everyone guessed that Teleki had publicly accepted the blame for Horthy's reluctance to appease the Germans. Teleki's suicide saved Hungary from the consequences of German revenge.

Dohnányi was busy at that time with the rehearsals of *Cantus vitae*. At the premiere, which had been postponed from 4 April to 28 April 1941 because of Teleki's funeral, a cloud of depression filled the Budapest Opera House. This quickly dissolved when the Budapest Philharmonic, with its President-Conductor, appeared on the stage, surrounded by the chorus, to start the performance.

The text for *Cantus vitae* is from Imre Madách's *Az ember tragédiája* (The Tragedy of Man), a dramatic poem that spans the history of humanity. Lucifer, who wants to ruin mankind, shows Adam visions of eleven tragic periods from ancient Egypt to the final days of the human race. Adam realizes that every great idea born in the human spirit eventually becomes worn out and has to die. This discovery fills him with such disgust that when he awakens from his dream he wants to commit suicide. At the last minute Eve enters and tells Adam that she is pregnant. Adam lifts his head once more to the Lord and decides to continue life, which, although a bitter struggle, can be fought through by faith. While the original poem was a gloomy and pessimistic drama, *Cantus vitae* is based on Dohnányi's optimistic philosophy. Dohnányi stripped *Az ember tragédiája* of all its historical references and made it apply wholly to the present. Although he adopted some of Madách's ideas, Dohnányi placed them in a different order and adapted them to his own optimistic view. Dohnányi agreed with Madách's assertion that life is a struggle, but he considered struggles and challenges to be not disasters, but necessities.

Cantus vitae is a five-part symphonic cantata for solos, mixed chorus, and orchestra. The first part asserts that great ideas wear out only to make room for new ones. The movement ends with a prayer to God to bring new ideas to the world. The second part is a "Bacchanalia," which proves how the rapture and ecstasy of orgies lead to disillusionment. The third part is called "Funeralia" and starts with a chorus of gravediggers, who chant:

> The cradle and the coffin are all one;
> What ends today, begins tomorrow,
> Always hungry, always full.
> Lo, the evening bell has sounded;
> Let those whom morning calls to a new life
> Begin the great work anew.

The soprano soloist, who defies the gloomy atmosphere of death and rises above the grave, represents the whole meaning of the work:

> Abyss, you do not terrify me at all.
> My laughter echoes from your deep chasm,
> For through it only scattering dust shall fall.
> Fair Poesy, Love, and Youth's unwasted might
> Shall bear me safe across the frightful pit.
> My smile brings to earth joy and light.
> When kindled by its warmth, another's face is lit.

In the fourth part the tenor, representing the fighting man and idealist, finally asks what the real meaning of life is:

> Spread out, oh spread, unbounded Heaven
> Your holy and mystical book before me!
> You are eternal, everything else is transient;
> You raise me, everything else presses me down.

The off-stage "Chorus mysticus" behind the scene gives answer: "Life is an eternal struggle." In this answer lies the real significance and meaning of the cantata:

> Family pride and sense of ownership
> Are the moving forces of the world.
> Life without struggle and without love
> Has no value.

The soprano warns man not to search further for the secret that God has so wisely hidden from human eyes, and a children's chorus of angels responds. The final movement, based on the text with which Madách started his work, ends with three solos praising God:

> Tenor: "Hosanna to Thee, All-Knowing One!"
> Bass: "Hosanna to Thee, All-Powerful One!"
> Soprano: "Hosanna to Thee, All-Righteous One!"

When the premiere of *Cantus vitae* ended, there was complete silence in the opera house. People were so gripped, so deeply shaken that they sat motionless. It was only after several moments that they burst out into thunderous applause.

In April 1941 war broke out between Yugoslavia and Germany, and Hungary was forced to take an active part in the campaign. Although this gave the country the possibility to regain her lost territories, it filled most

Hungarians with resentment. A worse blow fell in June, when Germany attacked her former ally, Russia. Among the Hungarian troops sent to fight against Russia was the young Captain Matthew von Dohnányi. Although he had recently married, he left cheerfully and courageously; he had inherited his father's optimism. The first reports from the East were encouraging: the army advanced rapidly, sweeping through the Russian territories. Everyday we heard the glorious reports of the blitzkrieg. All went brilliantly, until the assault on Stalingrad. Nobody knew why, but suddenly everything changed. From then on, the young Dohnányi wrote depressing letters to his father. When he came home after the defeat at Voronej, he had lost all his weapons and belongings. He was extremely pessimistic and saw no hope for victory.

Because Dohnányi had enjoyed the past summer in Cirkvenica, Croatia, he wanted to return there again for a few weeks. The papers constantly wrote that Croatia, having joined Germany, was now peaceful. In response to Dohnányi's inquiries, the Croatian Ambassador graciously invited us to visit his country. When we arrived, however, the country was still in such turmoil that we feared for our lives. Because it was impossible to return immediately, we spent several days there. Dohnányi was not worried and could enjoy the sunshine, the sea, and our company as though everything was peaceful. We were nevertheless relieved when we returned to Budapest.

The Hungarian territories that had recently been returned to the motherland had not heard Hungarian artists during their Romanian, Czech, or Yugoslavian occupation and were most eager to hear Dohnányi. On 22 January 1942 Dohnányi left for Transylvania to give concerts in Kolozsvár (Cluj), which had been under Romanian occupation. Those who have a feeling of patriotism will know how Dohnányi felt as he strolled about the streets of the magnificent, ancient city of Kolozsvár, admiring its glorious buildings and statues. It would be difficult to describe the enthusiasm of the people when Dohnányi appeared in front of the Orchestra; they cheered and hailed him for several minutes. Finally he sat down at the piano, and the audience became so silent that one could hear a sigh. Then Dohnányi signaled for the orchestra to begin his *Variationen über ein Kinderlied*.

In 1942 the Viennese Philharmonic Society celebrated its centennial. For this occasion the Budapest Philharmonic was invited with its President-Conductor to give a concert on 13 April. For this trip Dohnányi and the Orchestra packed not only musical instruments, but also various food provisions. Although Vienna had not yet been bombed, it had already suffered great hardships because of the war. The members of the Orchestra brought huge bags of sausage, bread, butter, and other delicacies. Because the concert consisted of works of Hungarian composers, it was very suitably followed by a Hungarian meal. At the banquet arranged by the mayor of Vienna in the Rathaus-Keller, the guests were served their own food. The mayor tried to save the situation by offering exquisite wines that cheered up everyone.

Because of the threatening war, Dohnányi spent the summer of 1942 in Hungary at Lake Balaton with my family. Many of our friends were also there, and we became very fond of the place. I bought some land there, and we decided to build a villa. Because Dohnányi had given up his home, we planned to plant another garden.

Dohnányi intended to also spend the summer of 1943 at Lake Balaton. He had already scheduled our trip when he suddenly fell ill with thrombophlebitis in his leg. The doctor advised him to stay in bed for at least six weeks. Because he needed no special medical treatment and it would have broken my heart to leave him in Budapest when he longed to be by the lake, I undertook the responsibility of nursing him. The doctor allowed me to place a couch in the garden, which was only a few steps from his room. Dohnányi was able to spend a few peaceful weeks at the lake, busily working in the shade of a huge oak tree on his *Suite en valse* (Waltz Suite), op. 39. He dedicated this suite to me because I had begged him to write such a work. It consisted of four movements: "Valse symphonique" (Symphonic Waltz), "Valse sentimentale" (Sentimental Waltz), "Valse boiteuse" (Limping Waltz), and "Valse de fête" (Festival Waltz). Dohnányi's leg improved so rapidly that he could walk by the last days of our vacation.

We had to hurry back to Budapest, because Dohnányi had a concert tour with the Budapest Philharmonic in several towns of Transylvania. This time we brought along my daughter Helen so that she, too, could see our lovely country. The ovation for the Orchestra's first performance, which was in Kolozsvár, was unforgettable. As we went from town to town, including Marosvásárhely and Nagyvárad, the performances turned into a march of triumph.

Although the German Army, with its Hungarian contingent, was withdrawing from Russia, people did not suspect any approaching disasters. I seemed to be alone with my premonition that something horrible was about to happen. "I do not think that we will keep the territories we have just regained for long," I complained.

"You're always a pessimist," Dohnányi scolded. "These territories have belonged to Hungary for a thousand years! It is only fair that we should have them back again for good."

In August 1943 the Government finally accepted Dohnányi's resignation from his Directorship of the Academy of Music. It was a relief that Dohnányi was no longer in a position of responsibility. Although Ede Zathureczky became the new Director, Dohnányi remained the Professor of Piano.

On 10 November 1943 the *Suite en valse* premiered in Budapest with Dohnányi conducting the Budapest Philharmonic. Although the audience was obviously aware of the approaching war, their faces lit up when the first bars of the "Valse symphonique" resounded. The "Valse sentimentale" followed with music that was soft and heart-gripping. The audience, with heavy tension in their hearts, broke into tears. "This is a most unusual waltz," someone murmured. "First it cheered us up, and then it made us cry."

Dohnányi spent Christmas Eve 1943 with my family, including my parents and my grandmother. Ede Zathureczky, who had recently lost his mother, joined us. We lit the candles on our Christmas tree, and Dohnányi sat at the piano to play "Silent Night" and his *Pastorale* on the Hungarian Christmas song "Mennyből az angyal." We all sang, unaware that this was to be our last Christmas in Hungary.

❧

The Russian Army was rapidly advancing, and the Axis nations were starting to distance themselves from Germany. Italy was the first to cut free from the alliance, and Romania was preparing to do the same. Hungary, however, lacked the ability to commit treachery; she continued to fight with the Germans against the masses of Russians who flooded toward her border. When Horthy tried to protest against certain orders and regulations, Hitler became irritated, and a threatening tension filled the air around us. Although it was not a surprise, it was nevertheless a shock when people awoke one morning in March 1944 and realized that during the night the German Army had occupied Hungary. With speed, the Gestapo arrested all those who were politically unreliable. These investigations and arrests were made according to their own sources of information. The Gestapo paid no attention to the accusatory letters sent to them by Hungarians, who shamefully tried to create trouble for their own countrymen by accusing them of anti-Nazism and other political crimes. It was said that these letters were so numerous that they provided the Gestapo's office with fuel for several days.

On 11 May 1944, two months after the Nazi occupation, Dohnányi disbanded the Budapest Philharmonic instead of following the orders to fire the Jewish members of the Orchestra.

Since Budapest was now exposed to bomb attacks, we moved into the country. My parents had a house in Gödöllő, thirty kilometers from Budapest, and I asked Dohnányi to join our family.[7] While in Gödöllő, we

---

7. By that time my fifth book was published and I was the editor of a fashion magazine called *Párisi Divat*. I was independent enough to disregard social conventions and invite Dohnányi to join me with my children, my grandmother, Fräulein Hermine, my chambermaid, and my housekeeper.

continued to receive news of the war. Dohnányi felt a bitter pain each time we heard Radio Budapest warn the citizens about bomb attacks. He saw the sky darken with smoke from the burning factories, hospitals, and private homes in Budapest. The first attack destroyed a children's hospital. It was horrible to be assaulted by nations against whom Hungary had never directed even one gunshot; Hungarian soldiers had not fought against the Americans or English. In spite of the sad circumstances, our stay in Gödöllő was pleasant. Dohnányi helped us plant vegetables in the garden. He also played with the tiny chickens, baby ducks, and rabbits I had bought for the hard times that were to come. The children took care of the rabbits, spending much money to keep and feed them. Whenever we wanted to eat one, however, they both rebelled. The rabbits all survived to await the Russians, who were surely not as scrupulous about rabbit stew.

Although Dohnányi had come to Gödöllő for peace and solitude, people often visited our home to ask his help or protection. Without hesitation he signed every petition and application that was handed to him. He saved hundreds of people whose names he never even cared to know. To act in this way required not only generosity but also immense courage and even audacity. To express any contrary opinion could easily cost someone his life. Dohnányi's principle, however, was to never be afraid; the greater the danger, the less one should withdraw from it. Dohnányi loved standing up to people and telling them his opinion frankly and openly. He especially enjoyed protecting those who were oppressed or persecuted unjustly. Dohnányi tirelessly continued to spare people from labor camps, including my editor Jenő Sugár, who succeeded in hiding and later escaped to Italy.

"I belong to no political party and never shall," Dohnányi often said.

> For I have my own opinion and my own party to belong to. A musician should never participate in politics. At the same time, a musician should never be persecuted for his beliefs. A musician is making music to give delight to his audience, under whatever political system, and *has* to make music, not only because this is how he earns money for himself and his family, but because this is a necessity for him, regardless of the listener's political party. Besides, if a great artist is forbidden to perform, it is not only he who is punished. His audience and the whole music world is deprived of the pleasure of hearing him.

Unfortunately, Dohnányi's apolitical beliefs turned out to be rather impractical; they exposed him to the crossfire of all parties, and he was protected by none. He did not mind, however, because he felt a thrill to face the whole world alone, if he needed to.

Despite his success in saving lives, Dohnányi was unable to help his own son Hans. Someone secretly brought the news that Hans had been arrested and incarcerated for months without a trial. Dohnányi wanted to find out why this had happened and went to see the German Ambassador. Although the Ambassador had often been Dohnányi's guest in his home on Szeher Street, he refused to see Dohnányi. Years later, after Hans's execution, Dohnányi found out that Hans had been arrested for his involvement in the 20 July 1944 bomb plot against Hitler in his field headquarters in Rastenburg, Germany.

In spite of all the shocks we had to undergo, Dohnányi continued to work on a symphony in four movements, which he dedicated to the memory of his deceased parents. In the summer Dohnányi decided to take the children and me to Lake Balaton for one month. He spent his mornings by the shore, watching the long, regular lines of American bombers, which glittered in the sunshine as they streamed toward Budapest.

Romania betrayed Germany, and the Russian Army concentrated its attacks on Hungary. Panic spread, and everyone rushed back to Budapest. The radio still assured victory, promising that nothing was lost, even if the troops were in retreat, and that the apparently unfavorable turn of the war was only a trick. This was all the information Dohnányi received; he did not listen to the English and Russian radio broadcasts, not because it was forbidden under the penalty of death, but because he was compelled by his own conscience and honor to be a good citizen and obey the laws of his country. It is unfortunate that it is always loyal citizens who have to pay the penalty for wars, while scoundrels and traitors adjust themselves to each change of regime. After World War II, when one Hungarian general returned to Hungary and was accused by the Russian-Hungarian authorities of not having deserted his army in time to join the Russian forces, he answered with superb irony, "At that time I didn't know that a soldier has to be a traitor, instead of obeying orders. But I certainly will do so in future."

❧

In October 1944 the radio declared that Horthy had asked the Russians for an armistice, and that Hungarians were to lay down their weapons. The announcer stifled a sob as he revealed the news of unconditional surrender, and we were all stunned. The surrender, however, could not be carried out because Hungary was occupied by the Germans and not free to act on her own. Meanwhile, the conflict and turmoil caused by the declaration had opened the way for the approaching Russian troops. After a brief fight, the Germans seized supreme power in the part of Hungary that they still possessed. They placed at the head of the Hungarian Government Ferenc Szálasi, who was the leader of the Arrow Cross Party. He was just a figurehead, a helpless puppet, with no freedom to act; Hungary was now ruled by Hitler.

After sending Fräulein Hermine back to Germany, Dohnányi hurried with the children and me to Budapest. Grave days followed as the Russian Army occupied our capital. Because of Max Yalta's promise to make Hungary part of Russia, bombs showered the city without interruption. Dohnányi was determined to flee to the West, perhaps not so much for his own sake than out of a desire to spare us from the Red Army. We had, however, made our decision too late. There was no possibility of getting out of Hungary; only those belonging to the Arrow Cross Party were granted transportation. No one found it important to worry about Dohnányi, who had formerly been considered Hungary's pride and glory.

Dohnányi met Szálasi on two occasions. He first met him in October 1944 when the Upper House of the Hungarian Senate invited Szálasi to their meeting. They wanted him to explain why he had taken over for Horthy, who was now a prisoner of Hitler's. The second time Dohnányi met Szálasi was in November, when the Arrow Cross leader asked Hungarian musicians to come to a "Kulturális konfericiá" (cultural conference) to discuss the future of Hungarian music. Over one hundred people attended; everybody wanted to know what attitude Szálasi would adopt toward music. On both occasions it was not curiosity but rather a sense of duty that compelled Dohnányi to go. He wanted to find out what projects this man had in mind. Although Dohnányi heard Szálasi speak only in public, he felt that Szálasi was insane.

Dohnányi concentrated on getting out of Budapest, but he still could not find transportation. Had he turned to Szálasi, or some other high political official, he could have easily been granted an available transport, but Dohnányi stubbornly insisted on managing his plans himself. Finally, when he had almost given up hope, the friendly German soldiers who had commandeered rooms in our house planned a trip with their empty truck to Vienna. They offered to take us and a few of our belongings. On the morning of 24 November 1944, Dohnányi, my children, my chambermaid, and I mounted the truck. After a stop at the home of Dohnányi's sister Mitzi and her husband, Dr. Ferenc Kováts, to say goodbye, we bid farewell to our beloved Budapest.

SIX

1944–1946

The trip to Vienna was an agonizing nightmare. The truck carried the few pieces of luggage that we were able to bring with us from Hungary. Dohnányi had packed only a small suitcase, into which he had placed nothing but his tuxedo, a suit, one or two of his manuscripts including his most recent symphony, and some other small items. He had also carefully placed his favorite book, Casanova's memoirs of his travels through Hungary, into the suitcase. This book, which was the only keepsake that Dohnányi had intended to save, mysteriously disappeared at some point in our journey. It was probably thrown out by German soldiers who, in their anxiousness to help us, replaced it with food. Later in the journey, German military guards stopped the truck at every corner and tried to make us get off to make room for their troops. It took all our courage to defend ourselves against them.

When the truck finally reached Vienna, Dohnányi received two rooms at the Collegium Hungaricum.[1] It was decided that Dohnányi and Julius would stay in one room while I would share the other with Helen, our chambermaid Bözsi, and our dwarf spitz Csöppi, which we had saved from Hungary. Fräulein Hermine would leave her sister's home near Karlsbad to join us two days later. The German soldiers carried our suitcases into the Collegium and put them in a corner. After they unloaded a box of bread, milk, and other provisions that had been packed at home by my mother, Dohnányi invited them to eat with us.

The German soldiers just stood there, hesitantly waiting in the doorway to tell us goodbye. "No, sir," one of the soldiers said roughly, to hide his emotion. "You and your family were most hospitable to us in Budapest, even though we were forcibly quartered in your home. Now you're no

---

1. This building had once housed the bodyguards of the Empress Maria Theresa. After World War I the Collegium Hungaricum had become the home of Hungarian artists and students who were engaged in research or studies in Vienna.

longer rich, your country is reduced to misery, and you're here in German-occupied Austria at our mercy. We are poor, sir, but we're still able to return at least a little part of your hospitality." He beckoned to his friend and they rapidly unpacked a huge ham, a loaf of bread, and a bottle of wine, placing them on the table. "This time you're our guests, sir. Bon appétit—and farewell." Without waiting for our thanks, they hurried away.

The loss of Dohnányi's book broke my heart. Although he was obviously upset that he would not be able to finish the book, he still tried to console me. "Let's not groan over what we have lost," he said. "The important thing is that we are alive and together. We must start a new life. Let's not look back any more, only forward. Always forward." Dohnányi continued, "Wars always have been, and always will be. This one is the worst because humanity has developed so much technology and is using all its knowledge for murder. Perhaps the greatest crime of all mankind was to invent gunpowder. All these horrors are consequences of that."

Dohnányi buried himself in the manuscript of his Second Symphony in E Major, op. 40. He had completed the first and fourth movements in Hungary in full score. Now he was going to finish the two inner movements. He was so absorbed in his composition that he seemed absolutely unmindful of the thunderstorm raging around him. While composing the Symphony, he also had very little chance to make use of a piano. There was one in the room of a former pupil of his who also happened to be staying in the Collegium, but Dohnányi hardly ever used it.

We spent our mornings in the cellar, where we were sheltered from the continual air attacks. Fortunately, these attacks consistently took place in the mornings, leaving our afternoons relatively safe. Dohnányi spent most of his free time in my room because my stove miraculously stayed warm for at least half the day, even though we were granted only a handful of coal each day. My room was also warmer because so many people, along with our little dog, lived in it.

Taking advantage of the afternoon lull on Christmas Eve 1944, the Maestro and I wandered through the streets, which were thick with the smoke from the burning buildings. We were shopping for gifts for the children, because in the turmoil we had forgotten to bring any toys for them from Hungary. All efforts were in vain, however; the stores were all empty, as though they had been plundered. Nevertheless, the Viennese people around us were chatting cheerfully, as though nothing had happened and they lived in the happiest of times. "I admire these people," Dohnányi said. "With their loyalty and strong will, they can control their desires and do without all of the things that used to be precious to them. They are heroically suffering all sorts of hardships without complaint, because they know it cannot be helped or changed."

a washstand, and a chest of drawers. This suite, which seemed almost luxurious to us, was completed by a worn rug and a tiny stove, which proved to be most useful on cold days. He shared the room with Julius, who slept on a straw pallet covered with a carpet. In the afternoons, those who dropped in to see Dohnányi would use Julius's bed as a couch. In the mornings, the makeshift couch was occupied by a cat, which most obstinately insisted on being, at least for a few hours, the third roommate.

Dohnányi's most frequent visitor was the priest of the village. He was kind-hearted, amusing, and had a sense of humor. Each time he visited, he brought a bag containing butter, eggs, or even a bottle of wine. The priest had long and intimate chats with Dohnányi and was delighted that Dohnányi could speak the Austrian dialect like a native.[2] On one occasion, the priest complained that the organist of the church had been wounded in the war and there was no one to play the organ.

"Would you like me to play the organ for you?" Dohnányi asked.

The priest's eyes flared up with joy, but then he sighed. "You are a great musician who used to receive fortunes for your performances. How could we pay you such a fee, in a village where only peasants live?"

Dohnányi assured him with a smile that he would not accept payment for a service to God. It was agreed that he would play on Sundays and on other solemn occasions without any remuneration. This duty became a pleasure to him. He organized a choir of Hungarian refugee officers, their wives, and local singers, who were amazingly skilled in music. It seems that the village had once had a musical schoolteacher. Dohnányi rehearsed them, and on Sundays and other festivals Neukirchen enjoyed beautiful Masses. Dohnányi became a popular and respected figure in the village. People never passed him without greeting him humbly. When they spoke of him, they would always say with deep reverence, "Der Herr Graf" (the Sir Count). They were told in vain that Dohnányi was not a Count, but they would just smile and continue believing that such a great man must be a Count.

The hostile attitude of the peasants changed, and they became willing to exchange food with our family. They would even go so far as give Dohnányi gifts of chicken, butter, milk, and fruit, without expecting anything in return. This made our lives easier, almost pleasant, because poverty was rapidly becoming a bitter problem in Austria. Even though black-market transactions were severely punished, people had to make them to survive. Black marketers maneuvered in the most curious ways to avoid being caught. Once the police discovered a suspicious wedding procession

2. Because Dohnányi had been brought up speaking Hungarian and German, he considered either to be his native tongue.

On Christmas Eve, Dohnányi sat at an empty table on which a small boxwood bush stood. Our chambermaid Bözsi, who hated the Germans, had stolen the bush from in front of the statue of Mozart in the square below. She had torn it from the ground with the excuse that Hitler had stolen enough from Hungary to give her the right to deprive him of this bit of property. We decorated this pitiful imitation of a Christmas tree with a few candles, which were very scarce in German-occupied territories, and a paper chain that the children had made. Dohnányi tried to force upon himself and us a Christmas mood by singing the Hungarian Christmas song "Mennyből az angyal." There was, however, no joy in our hearts, only dark and bitter despair.

As if all of these hardships were not enough, Julius suddenly became sick with the measles and a high fever. When we heard the call of the cuckoo, which the Viennese used as a radio warning of an approaching bomb attack, the Maestro and I carried Julius down into the coal cellar instead of the bomb shelter. Although it was evident that Julius had picked up this contagious disease in the bomb shelter, we refused to violate the strict regulation requiring those who suffered with infectious diseases to be quarantined. This included measles, which had become an epidemic.

Julius miraculously recovered, but in turn Helen and I caught the disease. Dohnányi decided that when a bomb attack came, we would stay upstairs in our room on the third floor. A four-hour stay in the coal cellar would have certainly killed us. Dohnányi stayed with us and our little dog, which kept moving around us excitedly, whining and wincing as though he knew what was happening. This raid, which took place on the anniversary of the Anschluss, was one of the worst bomb attacks on Vienna. Numerous private houses and public buildings were struck, including the Opera House, the Burgtheater, and even a wing of the Collegium. It was dreadful to hear the roaring engines of the attacking planes and the deafening explosions, followed by the clattering of windowpanes shooting out from their frames and shattering on the pavement below. Dohnányi sat calmly and a slight, ironical smile played over his face. The little dog howled with horror. I am ashamed to admit that I lost consciousness.

❀

As Easter approached, the Russians began their assault on Vienna. We had known for weeks that they were approaching, but I was ill and Dohnányi had been occupied with his Symphony. There had been little time to consider our personal safety. Now that danger was imminent, Vienna was seized by the same panic that had struck Budapest. Everyone who had the means fled in terror toward the West, but our family was trapped again. Because of constant bombing, trains were so scarce that one had to secure permission for rail travel weeks in advance. In addition, another permit was needed to enter the city to which one proposed to move. Even if Dohnányi had a specific destination in mind, the cities were already overcrowded with refugees and were giving no entrance permits. Of course, before the panic struck, it would have been easy for Dohnányi to acquire such documents. Now, in the turmoil, when there was nothing but disturbance and confusion, no favors could be obtained.

By Easter Sunday 1945 the Russians had begun shelling the suburbs of Vienna. Meanwhile, our family was still in the Collegium Hungaricum. Although Dohnányi continued to work diligently on his Symphony, he now seemed somewhat uneasy. He was most disturbed by the fact that I was in despair and quite hysterical. In the terrified confusion that had seized Vienna, there seemed to be no chance of escape.

We were rescued by Rudolf Frankovzsky, a Hungarian Colonel stationed in Vienna. Although he had never met Dohnányi, Frankovzsky had heard much about him when Frankovzsky had been married to the greatest Wagnerian soprano in Budapest, Ella Némety. He acted quickly when he heard that Dohnányi had no means of escape, agreeing to drive us toward Linz, Austria, where he had been sent by military command. This journey took us through St. Pölten, which happened to be enduring its most violent bomb attack. Both of the cars Frankovzsky had brought for us had barely passed a railway station where a train filled with women and children was standing when a thunderous swarm of bombers approached. At the Colonel's order we jumped from the cars and lay face downwards in a meadow next to the road. Dohnányi leaned on his elbows and, lifting his head, quietly watched the dreadful spectacle as the bombs leveled the train as well as the whole station in a few short moments.

In a later altercation, German soldiers, who had lost all of their discipline during the confusion, blocked our way and demanded the Colonel's weapons. At an SS Camp at the river Ens, some soldiers even attempted to confiscate our cars. After a brief stay in a miserable camp where we had to lie on flea-infested sacks of straw with fifty other refugees, we reached our destination. With the kind assistance of a Hungarian Count, we settled in the Upper Austrian village of Neukirchen-am-Walde, some forty miles northwest from Linz. Sheltered and protected on the top of a small mountain and reachable only by a minor road of no strategic importance, this village was far from the raging horrors of war.

❧

Dohnányi was instantly enchanted by Neukirchen-am-Walde and its tiny, neat, and colorful peasant houses, which were decorated with images

of the Holy Virgin. These houses bordered an unpaved, grass-covered street, where poultry and goats peacefully grazed under a bright blue sky. Dohnányi gazed at the bright, colorful flowers in the wide meadows, which were surrounded by the green woods after which the village had been named. "How lovely!" he murmured. "It's not as powerfully magnificent as the mountains of the Tyrol, but it does have charm and sweetness. This green around us is not only pleasing to the eyes; it soothes one's spirit." It was nice after those bitter experiences of war to breathe this fresh, clear air.

Unfortunately, we had no food; the official coupons we had received from the German government would not have satisfied even our little spitz. Dohnányi did not have any money; he had brought very little from Hungary and had no chance to earn more. In our search for food, the Maestro and I would walk to the peasant homes. Dohnányi would stand in front of the gates of the houses while I tried to persuade the natives to barter food for a dress or other pieces of clothing, since money had no value for them. In most cases, the peasants roughly and unkindly refused to exchange anything. In some cases they would eagerly argue that what they had to offer had a higher price. Because we had no other options, we were forced to surrender the few precious belongings that we had carefully safeguarded throughout our flight.

The peasants had hardly suffered anything from the horrors of war. They had not been bombed and had in fact grown fat and wealthy. Although they were required to deliver a certain amount of their products to the government, they had kept enough to live well. They would even sell excess merchandise on the black market to those who were stricken by disasters and starvation. Most of them were Catholic and prayed devoutly in their church, but their religious devotion did not seem to mitigate their insatiable greed. Despite this, Dohnányi was never offended by the selfishness. "Even though they might have been spared from bombs," he said, "they've also lost their sons and husbands, just as we did in Hungary. How can we expect a family who suffered such a loss to sympathize with the grief of others? Remember that everyone considers his or her own loss the greatest. Besides, there are many other refugees here, Hungarians as well as Germans, who surely pester them daily for food. It is no wonder that they have lost their patience."

It was just as difficult to find a place to live in the village. Neukirchen was already overcrowded with refugees. Dohnányi was lucky; a rather wealthy peasant, who was a clerk in the police office, offered him a clean and decent room on the second floor of his house. While the rest of our family was jammed into a windowless storage room formerly used by servants, Dohnányi's room had two windows and was light and airy. It was furnished with an old brown wooden bed, a big table with four chairs,

in which a fat hog had been installed in the bridal party, dressed in the solemn garb of a bride and covered with a veil.

As Dohnányi became more familiar with the natives, he grew to like them. He had many unforgettable experiences, including a visit from a young peasant named Ervin Polz, who repaired electric appliances in the village. Ervin came to ask Dohnányi to write down for him the tune of a song that he and his fiancée liked very much.

"What is the tune?" Dohnányi inquired. "Sing it to me."

"I have forgotten the melody, sir. But you're such a great man, you will surely know what it was like."

Dohnányi was amused. "Tell me the words of the song."

Ervin recited the poem, which had been composed by some friend of his in Neukirchen. Of course, Dohnányi had never heard it before. He told Ervin that since he could not remember the tune, there was no way to help him.

Ervin, however, desperately insisted. "You're such a fine musician, sir," he pleaded. "You can surely write down the song just as it was. We'll give you many eggs . . . even a whole ham!"

Dohnányi laughed with merriment. "Even if you offered me a whole hog, I couldn't do it," he said.

> Your case is very similar to the case of a man who once came to a painter and asked him to paint the portrait of his late father. The painter asked for a photo of the deceased, but the man did not possess one. He had nothing that could have shown what the father looked like. Nevertheless, he insisted that the picture be made. "I will describe him to you," he said, and began to tell the painter what sort of eyes, mouth, and nose his father had. The painter, since he was offered a big fee, completed the portrait. When the man came to see it, he called out in astonishment, "Ah, Father, how you've changed!" This would be the case with your song. I had better not try to do what the painter did.

When the war ended, the Americans were only a few miles from Neukirchen. The priest hung white flags from the tower of the church to show that no resistance would be made. All of the inhabitants decorated their windows with white cloths or paper. One afternoon, when the Maestro and I were walking on the slope of the hill, we noticed a dust cloud on the highway. Shining vehicles were rapidly approaching, and one could soon recognize American tanks, trucks, and jeeps climbing the hill to the village.

Everybody gathered to watch the vehicles of the victorious American Army thunder by on their way toward Linz. A few American soldiers stopped to disarm the Austrian policemen and arrest the members of the

Hungarian military, who temporarily became prisoners of war. A small crowd of villagers, including Dohnányi, stood and watched quietly. It was only now that everyone realized that the war was at an end and that it had been lost. Nobody felt hatred or hostility; everyone was relieved. When one of the American soldiers threw a handful of chocolate bars into a group of staring children, their gloomy faces brightened into smiles. Women began to wave their handkerchiefs at the Occupation Army. They did not stay, which was unfortunate because Neukirchen, disarmed and helpless without telephones or telegraphs, desperately needed their protection.

Neukirchen belonged to the Grieskirchen District and had to obey the orders of the American Military Government in the town of Grieskirchen. Large buses came to the village to pick up everybody who had been a member of the Nazi Party. Mothers were dragged away from their children, and fathers were torn from their families. Most of them had joined the Party just so that they would be allowed to keep their jobs. Many of those carried away were innocent and had been denounced only by some vicious and vengeful neighbor. Not even a good word from the priest could save these people. The authorities stated that those who were accused would be taken to a camp where they were to stay, whether guilty or innocent, until a trial took place. Only then would they have a chance to clear themselves. This trial was actually not held until twelve months later, when several victims were finally released.

Dohnányi had little time to think about political matters; he was concerned with his own fate. Numerous posters appeared upon the walls of the Mayor's office and other buildings, explaining the regulations of the new American Military Government. Most orders were for the Austrian natives, but there was a long list that bore the title "Regulations for D.P.'s: Displaced Persons." It took the other refugees and us a few minutes to grasp that these ominous regulations referred to us. The regulations made a great distinction between the D.P.'s from countries that fought on Germany's side and those who had been allied with the Western Powers during the war. The latter received separate rations, were helped by the Military Government, and had the support of the United Nations Relief Administration and other privileges. We, on the other hand, as Hungarians, never received the slightest aid throughout our stay of three long years in Austria.

As former "enemies," we were forbidden to leave. If we wanted to travel farther than nine kilometers, we needed a permit from the Military Government. This, however, was unobtainable because Grieskirchen lay more than twenty-five kilometers away. We were also not entitled to clothing coupons. Furthermore, we were granted only the same meager amount of food rations that we had received in the past, which had barely saved us from starvation. We were not allowed to earn money through any kind of work or to occupy any official position in Austria. The worst blow of all was the news that we had no right to stay in Austria and would be shipped back to Hungary at the first opportunity.[3]

At first, everybody smiled at these orders. They were so unfavorable and cruel that they were almost ridiculous. An Austrian newspaper even published a caricature picturing the Holy Virgin and Joseph with the baby Jesus, fleeing on a donkey, as the "First D.P.'s in the History of the World." Later, when we began to grasp the consequences of these regulations, we became uneasy and desperate. Deportations began, and the D.P.'s whose names were on the Mayor's list were mercilessly arrested and shipped home with no more than a rucksack of their belongings. Many of those who had deserted the Hungarian Army and did not wish to be delivered into the hands of the new Hungarian government committed suicide with their families. Dohnányi also became worried about his future. We were constantly alert for what would happen next and hardly dared to close our eyes at night.

One Sunday morning, two American officers were passing through Neukirchen in a jeep. When they stopped in front of the church to pray, they heard the music and were astonished. Being great music lovers, they wondered how a village like Neukirchen was able to produce such an artistically trained choir. After the Mass they learned from the priest that Ernst von Dohnányi was living in Neukirchen and leading the choir.

A few days later a jeep stopped in front of the house where Dohnányi was living and two American soldiers came to see him. They were the organizers of musical performances for the Army in Linz and asked Dohnányi if he would play gratis for the American soldiers and conduct the Philharmonic Broadcasting Orchestra, which was better known as the Bruckner Orchestra. Dohnányi gladly agreed to do so, and a concert was fixed for 6 July 1945. "But I have not had a piano and haven't played for months," Dohnányi said. The soldiers replied that this could be easily remedied. To Dohnányi's great surprise, a huge American truck arrived with a grand piano a few days later. It was carried up through the narrow, winding stairway and placed in his room under the direction of American soldiers. Dohnányi was deeply moved. He warmly thanked the soldiers and began a conversation with them.

One of the soldiers asked, "Do you know, sir, a chap named Bach?"

"You mean Johann Sebastian Bach?" Dohnányi asked.

"Yes, yes. Have you met him?"

3. These laws had come about on the urging of the Austrians, who were starving and wanted to deport the Hungarian refugees. They had obviously forgotten that in 1944 Hitler's government had brought an enormous quantity of ships and wagons loaded with food and clothing from Hungary that would have sufficed for ten times more refugees.

"Unfortunately I have not, since he died two hundred years ago."

"He did? What a pity," the soldier said with sincere regret. "He made such beautiful music!"

This little episode remained in Dohnányi's memory for long. He did not laugh at it; he was moved that a soldier, who was probably a simple laborer in private life, cared so much for Bach's music that he was interested in the composer as a person.

❧

Two days before the concert, a jeep came to pick up Dohnányi and take him to Linz, where he had a room in a hotel that was reserved for the American Army. Dohnányi was treated as a guest of honor in every way. General Reinhardt, the Governor of Upper Austria, gave a reception to introduce Dohnányi to the Staff Officers. On this occasion Dohnányi met several sympathetic people, including Captain John Kirn, who was the General's Aide-de-camp. Kirn was deeply impressed by this musical, cultured, and intelligent man. A friendship started between them that would deepen with every meeting.

The Bruckner Orchestra, which Dohnányi was to conduct, was an excellent orchestra. It had been assembled during the Nazi regime from the finest musicians in Germany. Hitler himself had considered it his own Orchestra and had offered it as a gift to the city of Linz. He had also given the musicians the privilege of exemption from the Draft. When Linz fell, the Conductor, who was a member of the Nazi Party, fled. It now became Dohnányi's task to rehearse the Orchestra. The program was Franz Schubert's *Unfinished* Symphony, Beethoven's *Emperor* Concerto, which was to be played and conducted by Dohnányi at the same time, and three movements of his own *Ruralia Hungarica*. The performance took place in the Linz Landestheater (Provincial Theater). No civilians were allowed to enter; only the Army. I was very proud to have the privilege of witnessing this great event as the only woman in a box otherwise filled with officers. The theater was jammed, and everybody seemed to be excited. This was the first classical concert in Linz since the end of the war.

An American soldier introduced Dohnányi with a few appreciative words. He pointed out that although Dohnányi was Hungarian and formerly an enemy, he was a great artist and it was a privilege to have him here. He asked the audience to show their sympathy and affectionately receive this great man who had undergone so many hardships and had lost practically everything in the war. The curtains parted, and Dohnányi was received with such a torrent of applause that it seemed it would never stop. It was touching to see the warm enthusiasm that these rough soldiers showed for a great artist.

The performance was very successful. The *Unfinished* was heart-gripping, and the Beethoven was magnificent and powerful. Everybody admired Dohnányi's artistic skill, conducting and playing at the same time. When the *Ruralia Hungarica* followed, the soldiers were thrilled, even though it contained pure Hungarian music and could have been considered music of an enemy. They broke out into an ovation. They had been warned before the concert not to whistle, because in Europe this had a meaning other than an expression of delight. They instead enthusiastically shouted European words, such as "Wunderbar!" and "Bravo!" The last movement of the *Ruralia Hungarica* had to be repeated as an encore. Dohnányi himself thoroughly enjoyed this performance. He had been deprived of the stage, which for him had a magic appeal, for many months. Besides, it was a delight to conduct this splendidly skilled orchestra.

After the concert, Dohnányi returned to Neukirchen. Since the success had been so great, he was asked to give other performances. The next one was on 20 July, when he performed Weber's *Oberon* Overture, Brahms's Symphony No. 1, and three selections from his pantomime *Der Schleier der Pierrette*. In addition to giving Dohnányi artistic pleasure, these concerts established a close contact between him and the American Occupation Army.

❀

Austria had been divided into four zones: American, English, French, and Russian. Each had its own regulations, and the borders of each zone were guarded by Customs Officers and authorities who strictly scrutinized every stamp and document needed by those who wanted to enter. We relied entirely on the aid of the American officers who visited Dohnányi frequently in Neukirchen. They would ask him to play something or would bring him little gifts that were trivial to them but meant a great deal to us.

Dohnányi also turned to General Reinhardt and his administration on behalf of others who asked him for help. People, mostly Hungarian refugees, quickly discovered that Dohnányi's influence with the American Army had enabled him to secure certain favors. It was only natural that in their tragic situation they would constantly pester him with the most complicated predicaments, and Dohnányi was always ready to help. Although his situation was very delicate and he was often warned by his American friends to remember that what they had done for him could not be done for others, he obstinately continued to support his compatriots. Most cases dealt with the violent deportations of Hungarians, who were deprived of all their belongings and shipped back, stuffed into wagons like cattle. Dohnányi advised the American Colonel who was in charge of the Displaced Persons in this area to put these matters into the hands of a Hungarian Colonel stationed near Neukirchen. The Hungarian Colonel could solve the problems to the advantage of these unfortunate people. After long discussions, the American Colonel convinced the Committee of the Military Government to officially entrust the deportation cases to the Hungarian Colonel. From then on, the refugees were able to carry home their belongings, which, although not numerous, were still precious to them.

In July 1945 Dohnányi heard that the Festspielhaus (Festival Play House) in Salzburg, having heard of his concerts in Linz but not knowing his whereabouts, was inquiring about him on the radio. They wanted to ask him to open the Festspiele (Festival) the coming August by conducting the first concert. Since railway transportation was still almost impossible, American officers took Dohnányi to Salzburg by jeep. Matters were quickly settled there, and a contract was signed for the opening concert as well as for other performances during the Festspiele, including a piano recital.

❧

The next concert for the Army soldiers in Linz took place on 3 August. This time the Maestro and I got rooms in a hotel where civilians employed by the American Army were allowed to stay. On the afternoon before the performance, Dohnányi was taking a nap when there was a knock at the door. A soldier handed me a letter that he said was extremely important. When Dohnányi read this letter, his face grew pale and his forehead twisted into a deep frown. The fateful message, written by the President of the Festspiele Committee in Salzburg, informed Dohnányi that they had to cancel his appearance at the Festspiele because of allegations that he was a war criminal.[4] One must consider the highly charged atmosphere of those days to understand what this meant. At that time, a single accusation, the slightest hint of slander, or just gossip could destroy the reputation of a most outstanding person. People were condemned without being interrogated. There was little possibility in that turmoil and chaos for any trial or procedure through which one could officially clear oneself from slanderous accusations.

Dohnányi's Hungarian friend Rudolf Frankovszky had been able to stay in Austria and had become Dohnányi's secretary. Frankovszky, who had been helping Dohnányi in his official affairs, now persuaded him to rush to the Military Government and prevent this slander from spreading. Dohnányi hurried to see Lieutenant Colonel Robertson, who was at the

---

4. This letter, written 1 August 1945, can be found in Appendix A.

Headquarters of the 65th Infantry Division, to explain what had happened. The Lieutenant Colonel indignantly said that before he had engaged Dohnányi for the concerts, the Americans had thoroughly investigated his political background. "If he was fit to play for our Army, he must surely be fit to play for Austrian civilians!" he retorted. Major John V. Hinkel, a musical and highly intelligent officer whom Dohnányi had always regarded as a wonderful man and friend, put all his energy into the effort to find out what was behind this accusation. Other officers also gathered around Dohnányi to discuss the matter. Some suspected that the accusations had come from a Hungarian organization recently set up in Salzburg. Although this committee had been established in connection with the Red Cross, its true intentions were trafficking in the black market and plotting against compatriot refugees in order to destroy them.

Dohnányi now recalled that friends had warned him that people who had become influential in Hungarian musical circles were spreading evil reports about him in order to prevent his return. They believed that his matchless authority in music would work against their own professional interests. What hurt Dohnányi most was that among these names was a man whom he had liberated from a concentration camp. Because Dohnányi had always wanted to keep his generous actions secret, that man probably never found out that he could have attributed his very life to Dohnányi, whom he now wickedly attacked with his false and dishonest accusations.

Dohnányi was eager to rush to Salzburg and confront the Music Officer who was his accuser. But there were still concerts in Linz and St. Florian to attend to, in addition to a benefit concert in the castle of the Jeszenszkys on the Attersee. The trip to Salzburg would have to wait for three more days. "Maybe things could be arranged here in Linz, without your going to Salzburg," Major Hinkel suggested. "I will phone the Music Officer in Salzburg, a man named Pasetti, and ask him to come here." Dohnányi felt deeply grateful to the Major, for it would have been so much more reassuring to face this meeting in Linz, in the presence of his friends.

Meanwhile, the Orchestra concert in Linz took place. It included Strauss's *Don Juan* and Beethoven's Fifth Symphony. As soon as Dohnányi mounted the stage, he seemed to forget all about this threatening affair and appeared completely at ease. After the concert, the Maestro and I were invited to a party at the home of a lovely young Austrian lady who was engaged to Captain Kirn. The guests were mostly Austrian ladies and American officers. Dohnányi took this opportunity to relate the whole affair to Captain Kirn, whose sympathy and understanding were a great relief.

The next day, 4 August, the concert in St. Florian took place in the convent where Anton Bruckner had once lived. This magnificent convent housed an ornately decorated church, the halls of which were lined with relics and paintings. This church also contained Bruckner's famous organ. The entire convent had the wonderful atmosphere of a period rich in art, music, culture, and great emotions. Before the performance, the Orchestra, the Maestro, and I dined in an intimate little restaurant as guests of a generous music lover, George Orberg, who was a member of the American Army. Mr. Orberg introduced himself after dinner, and he and Dohnányi had a pleasant conversation. Even though Mr. Orberg returned to the United States in a few weeks, he constantly wrote us letters and would send us packages of food whenever we were in need.

The concert was a solemn occasion. The program was the same as the night before in Linz, but different because Dohnányi never performed anything twice in the same way. Although during the performance he was again carried away by the music, it could not clear away the clouds that depressed him. This time, the members of the Orchestra shared his depression. The Bruckner Orchestra, consisting mostly of German musicians, had to be disbanded. Its players, many of whom were now married to Austrian women and had homes in Austria, were to be shipped back to Germany to face misery and starvation. The Austrians did not want to harbor Germans any longer. Although the Americans wanted to intercede on behalf of the Orchestra, whose performances they greatly enjoyed, they had to avoid interfering with Austrian civilian affairs. The musicians of the Bruckner Orchestra knew that this performance was their swan song. In spite of this, or perhaps because of it, they played so beautifully that my heart warmed up and sunshine seemed to illuminate the darkness within me.

The next morning, Dohnányi returned to Lieutenant Colonel Robertson's office in the hope that a meeting had been arranged in Linz with Mr. Pasetti. Major Hinkel informed Dohnányi that Pasetti was too busy at the moment to come to Linz, but would discuss matters with him in Salzburg. Because Dohnányi had a recital at Schloss (Castle) Kammer on the Attersee the next day, he decided to go to Salzburg on the following day. Lieutenant Colonel Robertson wrote a letter of support that Dohnányi was to convey to the American Music Officer in Salzburg.[5]

❧

Armed with the precious letter, Dohnányi felt confident when he set out for Salzburg with Mr. Frankovszky and me on the morning of 9 August 1945. Although Mr. Pasetti was an American Army Officer, he

5. This letter, written 6 August 1945, can be found in Appendix A.

trapped again. Because of constant bombing, trains were so scarce that one had to secure permission for rail travel weeks in advance. In addition, another permit was needed to enter the city to which one proposed to move. Even if Dohnányi had a specific destination in mind, the cities were already overcrowded with refugees and were giving no entrance permits. Of course, before the panic struck, it would have been easy for Dohnányi to acquire such documents. Now, in the turmoil, when there was nothing but disturbance and confusion, no favors could be obtained.

By Easter Sunday 1945 the Russians had begun shelling the suburbs of Vienna. Meanwhile, our family was still in the Collegium Hungaricum. Although Dohnányi continued to work diligently on his Symphony, he now seemed somewhat uneasy. He was most disturbed by the fact that I was in despair and quite hysterical. In the terrified confusion that had seized Vienna, there seemed to be no chance of escape.

We were rescued by Rudolf Frankovzsky, a Hungarian Colonel stationed in Vienna. Although he had never met Dohnányi, Frankovzsky had heard much about him when Frankovzsky had been married to the greatest Wagnerian soprano in Budapest, Ella Némety. He acted quickly when he heard that Dohnányi had no means of escape, agreeing to drive us toward Linz, Austria, where he had been sent by military command. This journey took us through St. Pölten, which happened to be enduring its most violent bomb attack. Both of the cars Frankovzsky had brought for us had barely passed a railway station where a train filled with women and children was standing when a thunderous swarm of bombers approached. At the Colonel's order we jumped from the cars and lay face downwards in a meadow next to the road. Dohnányi leaned on his elbows and, lifting his head, quietly watched the dreadful spectacle as the bombs leveled the train as well as the whole station in a few short moments.

In a later altercation, German soldiers, who had lost all of their discipline during the confusion, blocked our way and demanded the Colonel's weapons. At an SS Camp at the river Ens, some soldiers even attempted to confiscate our cars. After a brief stay in a miserable camp where we had to lie on flea-infested sacks of straw with fifty other refugees, we reached our destination. With the kind assistance of a Hungarian Count, we settled in the Upper Austrian village of Neukirchen-am-Walde, some forty miles northwest from Linz. Sheltered and protected on the top of a small mountain and reachable only by a minor road of no strategic importance, this village was far from the raging horrors of war.

❧

Dohnányi was instantly enchanted by Neukirchen-am-Walde and its tiny, neat, and colorful peasant houses, which were decorated with images

On Christmas Eve, Dohnányi sat at an empty table on which a small boxwood bush stood. Our chambermaid Bözsi, who hated the Germans, had stolen the bush from in front of the statue of Mozart in the square below. She had torn it from the ground with the excuse that Hitler had stolen enough from Hungary to give her the right to deprive him of this bit of property. We decorated this pitiful imitation of a Christmas tree with a few candles, which were very scarce in German-occupied territories, and a paper chain that the children had made. Dohnányi tried to force upon himself and us a Christmas mood by singing the Hungarian Christmas song "Mennyből az angyal." There was, however, no joy in our hearts, only dark and bitter despair.

As if all of these hardships were not enough, Julius suddenly became sick with the measles and a high fever. When we heard the call of the cuckoo, which the Viennese used as a radio warning of an approaching bomb attack, the Maestro and I carried Julius down into the coal cellar instead of the bomb shelter. Although it was evident that Julius had picked up this contagious disease in the bomb shelter, we refused to violate the strict regulation requiring those who suffered with infectious diseases to be quarantined. This included measles, which had become an epidemic.

Julius miraculously recovered, but in turn Helen and I caught the disease. Dohnányi decided that when a bomb attack came, we would stay upstairs in our room on the third floor. A four-hour stay in the coal cellar would have certainly killed us. Dohnányi stayed with us and our little dog, which kept moving around us excitedly, whining and wincing as though he knew what was happening. This raid, which took place on the anniversary of the Anschluss, was one of the worst bomb attacks on Vienna. Numerous private houses and public buildings were struck, including the Opera House, the Burgtheater, and even a wing of the Collegium. It was dreadful to hear the roaring engines of the attacking planes and the deafening explosions, followed by the clattering of windowpanes shooting out from their frames and shattering on the pavement below. Dohnányi sat calmly and a slight, ironical smile played over his face. The little dog howled with horror. I am ashamed to admit that I lost consciousness.

As Easter approached, the Russians began their assault on Vienna. We had known for weeks that they were approaching, but I was ill and Dohnányi had been occupied with his Symphony. There had been little time to consider our personal safety. Now that danger was imminent, Vienna was seized by the same panic that had struck Budapest. Everyone who had the means fled in terror toward the West, but our family was of the Holy Virgin. These houses bordered an unpaved, grass-covered street, where poultry and goats peacefully grazed under a bright blue sky. Dohnányi gazed at the bright, colorful flowers in the wide meadows, which were surrounded by the green woods after which the village had been named. "How lovely!" he murmured. "It's not as powerfully magnificent as the mountains of the Tyrol, but it does have charm and sweetness. This green around us is not only pleasing to the eyes; it soothes one's spirit." It was nice after those bitter experiences of war to breathe this fresh, clear air.

Unfortunately, we had no food; the official coupons we had received from the German government would not have satisfied even our little spitz. Dohnányi did not have any money; he had brought very little from Hungary and had no chance to earn more. In our search for food, the Maestro and I would walk to the peasant homes. Dohnányi would stand in front of the gates of the houses while I tried to persuade the natives to barter food for a dress or other pieces of clothing, since money had no value for them. In most cases, the peasants roughly and unkindly refused to exchange anything. In some cases they would eagerly argue that what they had to offer had a higher price. Because we had no other options, we were forced to surrender the few precious belongings that we had carefully safeguarded throughout our flight.

The peasants had hardly suffered anything from the horrors of war. They had not been bombed and had in fact grown fat and wealthy. Although they were required to deliver a certain amount of their products to the government, they had kept enough to live well. They would even sell excess merchandise on the black market to those who were stricken by disasters and starvation. Most of them were Catholic and prayed devoutly in their church, but their religious devotion did not seem to mitigate their insatiable greed. Despite this, Dohnányi was never offended by their selfishness. "Even though they might have been spared from bombs," he said, "they've also lost their sons and husbands, just as we did in Hungary. How can we expect a family who suffered such a loss to sympathize with the grief of others? Remember that everyone considers his or her own loss the greatest. Besides, there are many other refugees here, Hungarians as well as Germans, who surely pester them daily for food. It is no wonder that they have lost their patience."

It was just as difficult to find a place to live in the village. Neukirchen was already overcrowded with refugees. Dohnányi was lucky; a rather wealthy peasant, who was a clerk in the police office, offered him a clean and decent room on the second floor of his house. While the rest of our family was jammed into a windowless storage room formerly used by servants, Dohnányi's room had two windows and was light and airy. It was furnished with an old brown wooden bed, a big table with four chairs, a washstand, and a chest of drawers. This suite, which seemed almost luxurious to us, was completed by a worn rug and a tiny stove, which proved to be most useful on cold days. He shared the room with Julius, who slept on a straw pallet covered with a carpet. In the afternoons, those who dropped in to see Dohnányi would use Julius's bed as a couch. In the mornings, the makeshift couch was occupied by a cat, which most obstinately insisted on being, at least for a few hours, the third roommate.

Dohnányi's most frequent visitor was the priest of the village. He was kind-hearted, amusing, and had a sense of humor. Each time he visited, he brought a bag containing butter, eggs, or even a bottle of wine. The priest had long and intimate chats with Dohnányi and was delighted that Dohnányi could speak the Austrian dialect like a native.[2] On one occasion, the priest complained that the organist of the church had been wounded in the war and there was no one to play the organ.

"Would you like me to play the organ for you?" Dohnányi asked.

The priest's eyes flared up with joy, but then he sighed. "You are a great musician who used to receive fortunes for your performances. How could we pay you such a fee, in a village where only peasants live?"

Dohnányi assured him with a smile that he would not accept payment for a service to God. It was agreed that he would play on Sundays and on other solemn occasions without any remuneration. This duty became a pleasure to him. He organized a choir of Hungarian refugee officers, their wives, and local singers, who were amazingly skilled in music. It seems that the village had once had a musical schoolteacher. Dohnányi rehearsed them, and on Sundays and other festivals Neukirchen enjoyed beautiful Masses. Dohnányi became a popular and respected figure in the village. People never passed him without greeting him humbly. When they spoke of him, they would always say with deep reverence, "Der Herr Graf" (the Sir Count). They were told in vain that Dohnányi was not a Count, but they would just smile and continue believing that such a great man must be a Count.

The hostile attitude of the peasants changed, and they became willing to exchange food with our family. They would even go so far as give Dohnányi gifts of chicken, butter, milk, and fruit, without expecting anything in return. This made our lives easier, almost pleasant, because poverty was rapidly becoming a bitter problem in Austria. Even though black-market transactions were severely punished, people had to make them to survive. Black marketers maneuvered in the most curious ways to avoid being caught. Once the police discovered a suspicious wedding procession

2. Because Dohnányi had been brought up speaking Hungarian and German, he considered either to be his native tongue.

in which a fat hog had been installed in the bridal party, dressed in the solemn garb of a bride and covered with a veil.

As Dohnányi became more familiar with the natives, he grew to like them. He had many unforgettable experiences, including a visit from a young peasant named Ervin Polz, who repaired electric appliances in the village. Ervin came to ask Dohnányi to write down for him the tune of a song that he and his fiancée liked very much.

"What is the tune?" Dohnányi inquired. "Sing it to me."

"I have forgotten the melody, sir. But you're such a great man, you will surely know what it was like."

Dohnányi was amused. "Tell me the words of the song."

Ervin recited the poem, which had been composed by some friend of his in Neukirchen. Of course, Dohnányi had never heard it before. He told Ervin that since he could not remember the tune, there was no way to help him.

Ervin, however, desperately insisted. "You're such a fine musician, sir," he pleaded. "You can surely write down the song just as it was. We'll give you many eggs . . . even a whole ham!"

Dohnányi laughed with merriment. "Even if you offered me a whole hog, I couldn't do it," he said.

> Your case is very similar to the case of a man who once came to a painter and asked him to paint the portrait of his late father. The painter asked for a photo of the deceased, but the man did not possess one. He had nothing that could have shown what the father looked like. Nevertheless, he insisted that the picture be made. "I will describe him to you," he said, and began to tell the painter what sort of eyes, mouth, and nose his father had. The painter, since he was offered a big fee, completed the portrait. When the man came to see it, he called out in astonishment, "Ah, Father, how you've changed!" This would be the case with your song. I had better not try to do what the painter did.

When the war ended, the Americans were only a few miles from Neukirchen. The priest hung white flags from the tower of the church to show that no resistance would be made. All of the inhabitants decorated their windows with white cloths or paper. One afternoon, when the Maestro and I were walking on the slope of the hill, we noticed a dust cloud on the highway. Shining vehicles were rapidly approaching, and one could soon recognize American tanks, trucks, and jeeps climbing the hill to the village.

Everybody gathered to watch the vehicles of the victorious American Army thunder by on their way toward Linz. A few American soldiers stopped to disarm the Austrian policemen and arrest the members of the

Hungarian military, who temporarily became prisoners of war. A small crowd of villagers, including Dohnányi, stood and watched quietly. It was only now that everyone realized that the war was at an end and that it had been lost. Nobody felt hatred or hostility; everyone was relieved. When one of the American soldiers threw a handful of chocolate bars into a group of staring children, their gloomy faces brightened into smiles. Women began to wave their handkerchiefs at the Occupation Army. They did not stay, which was unfortunate because Neukirchen, disarmed and helpless without telephones or telegraphs, desperately needed their protection.

Neukirchen belonged to the Grieskirchen District and had to obey the orders of the American Military Government in the town of Grieskirchen. Large buses came to the village to pick up everybody who had been a member of the Nazi Party. Mothers were dragged away from their children, and fathers were torn from their families. Most of them had joined the Party just so that they would be allowed to keep their jobs. Many of those carried away were innocent and had been denounced only by some vicious and vengeful neighbor. Not even a good word from the priest could save these people. The authorities stated that those who were accused would be taken to a camp where they were to stay, whether guilty or innocent, until a trial took place. Only then would they have a chance to clear themselves. This trial was actually not held until twelve months later, when several victims were finally released.

Dohnányi had little time to think about political matters; he was concerned with his own fate. Numerous posters appeared upon the walls of the Mayor's office and other buildings, explaining the regulations of the new American Military Government. Most orders were for the Austrian natives, but there was a long list that bore the title "Regulations for D.P.'s: Displaced Persons." It took the other refugees and us a few minutes to grasp that these ominous regulations referred to us. The regulations made a great distinction between the D.P.'s from countries that fought on Germany's side and those who had been allied with the Western Powers during the war. The latter received separate rations, were helped by the Military Government, and had the support of the United Nations Relief Administration and other privileges. We, on the other hand, as Hungarians, never received the slightest aid throughout our stay of three long years in Austria.

As former "enemies," we were forbidden to leave. If we wanted to travel farther than nine kilometers, we needed a permit from the Military Government. This, however, was unobtainable because Grieskirchen lay more than twenty-five kilometers away. We were also not entitled to clothing coupons. Furthermore, we were granted only the same meager amount of food rations that we had received in the past, which had barely saved us from starvation. We were not allowed to earn money through any kind of work or to occupy any official position in Austria. The worst blow of all was the news that we had no right to stay in Austria and would be shipped back to Hungary at the first opportunity.[3]

At first, everybody smiled at these orders. They were so unfavorable and cruel that they were almost ridiculous. An Austrian newspaper even published a caricature picturing the Holy Virgin and Joseph with the baby Jesus, fleeing on a donkey, as the "First D.P.'s in the History of the World." Later, when we began to grasp the consequences of these regulations, we became uneasy and desperate. Deportations began, and the D.P.'s whose names were on the Mayor's list were mercilessly arrested and shipped home with no more than a rucksack of their belongings. Many of those who had deserted the Hungarian Army and did not wish to be delivered into the hands of the new Hungarian government committed suicide with their families. Dohnányi also became worried about his future. We were constantly alert for what would happen next and hardly dared to close our eyes at night.

One Sunday morning, two American officers were passing through Neukirchen in a jeep. When they stopped in front of the church to pray, they heard the music and were astonished. Being great music lovers, they wondered how a village like Neukirchen was able to produce such an artistically trained choir. After the Mass they learned from the priest that Ernst von Dohnányi was living in Neukirchen and leading the choir.

A few days later a jeep stopped in front of the house where Dohnányi was living and two American soldiers came to see him. They were the organizers of musical performances for the Army in Linz and asked Dohnányi if he would play gratis for the American soldiers and conduct the Philharmonic Broadcasting Orchestra, which was better known as the Bruckner Orchestra. Dohnányi gladly agreed to do so, and a concert was fixed for 6 July 1945. "But I have not had a piano and haven't played for months," Dohnányi said. The soldiers replied that this could be easily remedied. To Dohnányi's great surprise, a huge American truck arrived with a grand piano a few days later. It was carried up through the narrow, winding stairway and placed in his room under the direction of American soldiers. Dohnányi was deeply moved. He warmly thanked the soldiers and began a conversation with them.

One of the soldiers asked, "Do you know, sir, a chap named Bach?"

"You mean Johann Sebastian Bach?" Dohnányi asked.

"Yes, yes. Have you met him?"

---

3. These laws had come about on the urging of the Austrians, who were starving and wanted to deport the Hungarian refugees. They had obviously forgotten that in 1944 Hitler's government had brought an enormous quantity of ships and wagons loaded with food and clothing from Hungary that would have sufficed for ten times more refugees.

"Unfortunately I have not, since he died two hundred years ago."

"He did? What a pity," the soldier said with sincere regret. "He made such beautiful music!"

This little episode remained in Dohnányi's memory for long. He did not laugh at it; he was moved that a soldier, who was probably a simple laborer in private life, cared so much for Bach's music that he was interested in the composer as a person.

❧

Two days before the concert, a jeep came to pick up Dohnányi and take him to Linz, where he had a room in a hotel that was reserved for the American Army. Dohnányi was treated as a guest of honor in every way. General Reinhardt, the Governor of Upper Austria, gave a reception to introduce Dohnányi to the Staff Officers. On this occasion Dohnányi met several sympathetic people, including Captain John Kirn, who was the General's Aide-de-camp. Kirn was deeply impressed by this musical, cultured, and intelligent man. A friendship started between them that would deepen with every meeting.

The Bruckner Orchestra, which Dohnányi was to conduct, was an excellent orchestra. It had been assembled during the Nazi regime from the finest musicians in Germany. Hitler himself had considered it his own Orchestra and had offered it as a gift to the city of Linz. He had also given the musicians the privilege of exemption from the Draft. When Linz fell, the Conductor, who was a member of the Nazi Party, fled. It now became Dohnányi's task to rehearse the Orchestra. The program was Franz Schubert's *Unfinished* Symphony, Beethoven's *Emperor* Concerto, which was to be played and conducted by Dohnányi at the same time, and three movements of his own *Ruralia Hungarica*. The performance took place in the Linz Landestheater (Provincial Theater). No civilians were allowed to enter; only the Army. I was very proud to have the privilege of witnessing this great event as the only woman in a box otherwise filled with officers. The theater was jammed, and everybody seemed to be excited. This was the first classical concert in Linz since the end of the war.

An American soldier introduced Dohnányi with a few appreciative words. He pointed out that although Dohnányi was Hungarian and formerly an enemy, he was a great artist and it was a privilege to have him here. He asked the audience to show their sympathy and affectionately receive this great man who had undergone so many hardships and had lost practically everything in the war. The curtains parted, and Dohnányi was received with such a torrent of applause that it seemed it would never stop. It was touching to see the warm enthusiasm that these rough soldiers showed for a great artist.

The performance was very successful. The *Unfinished* was heart-gripping, and the Beethoven was magnificent and powerful. Everybody admired Dohnányi's artistic skill, conducting and playing at the same time. When the *Ruralia Hungarica* followed, the soldiers were thrilled, even though it contained pure Hungarian music and could have been considered music of an enemy. They broke out into an ovation. They had been warned before the concert not to whistle, because in Europe this had a meaning other than an expression of delight. They instead enthusiastically shouted European words, such as "Wunderbar!" and "Bravo!" The last movement of the *Ruralia Hungarica* had to be repeated as an encore. Dohnányi himself thoroughly enjoyed this performance. He had been deprived of the stage, which for him had a magic appeal, for many months. Besides, it was a delight to conduct this splendidly skilled orchestra.

After the concert, Dohnányi returned to Neukirchen. Since the success had been so great, he was asked to give other performances. The next one was on 20 July, when he performed Weber's *Oberon* Overture, Brahms's Symphony No. 1, and three selections from his pantomime *Der Schleier der Pierrette*. In addition to giving Dohnányi artistic pleasure, these concerts established a close contact between him and the American Occupation Army.

❧

Austria had been divided into four zones: American, English, French, and Russian. Each had its own regulations, and the borders of each zone were guarded by Customs Officers and authorities who strictly scrutinized every stamp and document needed by those who wanted to enter. We relied entirely on the aid of the American officers who visited Dohnányi frequently in Neukirchen. They would ask him to play something or would bring him little gifts that were trivial to them but meant a great deal to us.

Dohnányi also turned to General Reinhardt and his administration on behalf of others who asked him for help. People, mostly Hungarian refugees, quickly discovered that Dohnányi's influence with the American Army had enabled him to secure certain favors. It was only natural that in their tragic situation they would constantly pester him with the most complicated predicaments, and Dohnányi was always ready to help. Although his situation was very delicate and he was often warned by his American friends to remember that what they had done for him could not be done for others, he obstinately continued to support his compatriots. Most cases dealt with the violent deportations of Hungarians, who were deprived of all their belongings and shipped back, stuffed into wagons like cattle. Dohnányi advised the American Colonel who was in charge of the Displaced Persons in this area to put these matters into the hands of a Hungarian Colonel stationed near Neukirchen. The Hungarian Colonel could solve the problems to the advantage of these unfortunate people. After long discussions, the American Colonel convinced the Committee of the Military Government to officially entrust the deportation cases to the Hungarian Colonel. From then on, the refugees were able to carry home their belongings, which, although not numerous, were still precious to them.

In July 1945 Dohnányi heard that the Festspielhaus (Festival Play House) in Salzburg, having heard of his concerts in Linz but not knowing his whereabouts, was inquiring about him on the radio. They wanted to ask him to open the Festspiele (Festival) the coming August by conducting the first concert. Since railway transportation was still almost impossible, American officers took Dohnányi to Salzburg by jeep. Matters were quickly settled there, and a contract was signed for the opening concert as well as for other performances during the Festspiele, including a piano recital.

❧

The next concert for the Army soldiers in Linz took place on 3 August. This time the Maestro and I got rooms in a hotel where civilians employed by the American Army were allowed to stay. On the afternoon before the performance, Dohnányi was taking a nap when there was a knock at the door. A soldier handed me a letter that he said was extremely important. When Dohnányi read this letter, his face grew pale and his forehead twisted into a deep frown. The fateful message, written by the President of the Festspiele Committee in Salzburg, informed Dohnányi that they had to cancel his appearance at the Festspiele because of allegations that he was a war criminal.[4] One must consider the highly charged atmosphere of those days to understand what this meant. At that time, a single accusation, the slightest hint of slander, or just gossip could destroy the reputation of a most outstanding person. People were condemned without being interrogated. There was little possibility in that turmoil and chaos for any trial or procedure through which one could officially clear oneself from slanderous accusations.

Dohnányi's Hungarian friend Rudolf Frankovszky had been able to stay in Austria and had become Dohnányi's secretary. Frankovszky, who had been helping Dohnányi in his official affairs, now persuaded him to rush to the Military Government and prevent this slander from spreading. Dohnányi hurried to see Lieutenant Colonel Robertson, who was at the

---

4. This letter, written 1 August 1945, can be found in Appendix A.

was Tyrolean by birth and had been an American citizen for only a short time. Such was his power, however, that without his approval no musical event could take place and no musician could appear publicly in the whole American Zone.

On our way to Salzburg, we had to pass the notorious Glasenbach Camp. Here, surrounded by a double electric-wire fence, the Austrians who had been charged with political crimes vegetated in small wooden barracks, whether they were members of the Nazi Party or merely accused of being so. This gloomy place did not differ much from a German concentration camp. Because all of the Austrians who had played a part in the former regime were now incarcerated in such camps, the country was deprived of men whose abilities would have been indispensable in the work of recovery. While in Germany it was mainly the lower-class element who had joined Hitler's Party, in Austria prominent people did so knowing that their country was unable to exist and support itself without them. As a result, famous writers, actors, professors, and doctors, including the only brain surgeon, were now imprisoned. One American soldier appropriately remarked, "There are four types of Austrians: children, who pester us for chocolate; women, who give themselves away for a pair of stockings; men, who denounce each other; and an intelligentsia that sits under arrest in Glasenbach."

Meanwhile, Austria was governed by people whose only qualifications seemed to be that they had been punished by the former regime. In many cases, the former prisoners were not even asked for what crime they had been detained in those notorious concentration camps. There were several instances in which district leaders obtained their positions only because they had been arrested by the Nazis. It was later discovered, however, that many of them had been punished for smuggling opium or other contraband. One mayor became a hero after being delivered from a Nazi jail, where he had been imprisoned for black-marketing. One woman who enjoyed a privileged status under the new regime had actually been imprisoned by the old for murdering her own newborn baby.

The sight of that ill-fated camp made our hearts heavy as we arrived at Salzburg. Mr. Frankovszky drove us directly to the Mozarteum, where we were informed that the Music Officer was out of town for the day. Dohnányi explained to the Secretary that he had come to clear a most ominous accusation and it was imperative that he talk to Mr. Pasetti as soon as possible. She promised to phone Pasetti and ask him to receive Dohnányi the next morning. When Mr. Frankovszky returned an hour later, she confirmed that Pasetti would be in his office the next day to see Dohnányi. In addition to being disappointed by this delay, Dohnányi was hungry and tired. Unfortunately, almost every hotel that had not been bombed was overcrowded or had been requisitioned by the Occupation Army. We went to the Military Government, where a Colonel gave Dohnányi a certificate that entitled him and those in his company to be given beds in the Hotel Golden Löwe.

In the evening, the Maestro and I sat in the hotel's restaurant. We were served cabbage that had been prepared without shortening, a slice of stale bread, and a cup of coffee without sugar or milk. He was mechanically sipping the colorless liquid when Mr. Frankovszky appeared. Mr. Frankovszky's face was so pale that it was immediately clear that something dreadful had happened. "The radio has just announced," Frankovszky said in a shaking voice, "that Dohnányi's performance for the Festspiele is canceled because he was found to be a war criminal." Dohnányi listened with a frown. My heart stopped beating. It was obvious that Mr. Pasetti was responsible for this radio announcement, even though he had promised to give Dohnányi an opportunity to clear himself on the next day. For some unknown reason, Pasetti had disregarded the scheduled meeting and given this utterly false information to the radio station. Involuntarily, I remembered Glasenbach, the fatal camp with those pitiful figures crouching among the barracks, half-naked, with expressions of utter despair. Being D.P.'s, we could also be delivered into the hands of Dohnányi's accusers in Russian-occupied Hungary, where the wicked slander had originated.

Dohnányi continued to sip his coffee. Although he was very pale, he still kept his self-control. "I will fight them," he said. "You know I like to fight. The greater the injustice, the more I shall defend myself against it." In spite of everything that was happening, he still remained an optimist, believing that he would be given the opportunity to fight. He seemed to be absolutely unaware of the danger that was threatening him. He became upset only when he saw me burst into tears.

❧

The next morning, in the office of the Mozarteum, Dohnányi finally stood face to face with Mr. Pasetti. Pasetti spoke in English, but with a heavy Austrian accent. He seemed to be relieved when Dohnányi began to speak in German. After he read the letter from Lieutenant Colonel Robertson that Dohnányi had thrust under his nose, a cynical smile widened on Pasetti's lips. Briefly and somewhat ironically, he declared that this letter did not concern him at all, because he was not interested in whether Dohnányi did or did not play for the military forces in Linz. He was only interested in the welfare of the Austrian civilians, and he would not allow Dohnányi to perform for them. "I am building up a new Austria," he declaimed. "And I am building it up from musicians who are politically reliable and of a pure reputation; not like you, Professor, with your highly unsatisfactory political background."

"But what am I accused of?" Dohnányi demanded harshly, his blue eyes blazing. As he stood there, defiantly, it seemed as though he was the one who was interrogating Mr. Pasetti.

Under this firm and determined attitude, the Music Officer lost some of his self-assurance. He began to stammer. "There is a whole pile of accusations against you," he said evasively, carefully lowering his gaze.

"I want to know them," Dohnányi stormed.

"That is out of the question. I could not talk about them to you or to any of your friends," was the careful and confused answer. One could easily see that Mr. Pasetti was eager to end this most embarrassing conversation.

"I want to hear at least one of these accusations!" Dohnányi insisted, each of his words cutting with acid coldness. In spite of all of Dohnányi's protests, not one of the accusations was revealed. "If you try to blame me because I fled Hungary and Soviet control," Dohnányi declared indignantly, "then I must say there is nothing in my past I would regret or want to undo. In fact, if it were to happen all over again, I would act just as I acted before."

"We are allied with the Russians!" Mr. Pasetti shouted, having finally recovered his voice. "Those who are against them, we consider enemies. I could arrest you right now for this remark and attitude."

Still, he did not do so. Perhaps this was because, in spite of all his power, he was fully aware that he lacked evidence against Dohnányi; or maybe he only wished to threaten his victim. Regardless, there was nothing more for us to do or say. Realizing this, I tried to approach Mr. Pasetti myself to explain matters, but Dohnányi grasped my arm and dragged me away. "Come," he said almost roughly. "There is no reason for us to stay here. We are only wasting our time." Never in his life did he show as much contempt for anyone as he did now, looking at Mr. Pasetti. In spite of all his power, Pasetti suddenly seemed to shrink, almost shrivel, under the weight of Dohnányi's gaze. Then Dohnányi turned on his heels and left the dreadful office.

🌹

When we returned to Neukirchen, Dohnányi still seemed unaware of the full extent of the disaster. Fräulein Hermine and the children received us with the news that the whole village was in turmoil over the announcement that had been made on the radio. The Hungarians, including those for whom Dohnányi had done favors, had gathered in the square. They triumphantly discussed the possibility that Dohnányi, having turned out to be a war criminal, would be dropped from American favor and perhaps even shipped back to Hungary for a trial. It did not seem to matter to them that this accusation was obviously a lie. In their bitter jealousy and envy, they were rejoicing to see that Dohnányi had lost the protection and comfort that had been granted to him through his friendship with the Americans. Even the Mayor of the village smacked his lips over this sensational news. His reasons for rejoicing over our misfortune, however, were more practical. If we were removed from Neukirchen, our rooms would become vacant and could be rented on the black market for a much higher price.

When I complained to Dohnányi about how ungratefully and distastefully our compatriots were behaving, he replied with a lenient smile, "You seem to forget one fact: usually those who are bound to be grateful feel somehow humiliated by this gratitude. It is no wonder that they now feel almost triumphant to get rid of it. As to the danger we are in, since we cannot help it, we should not get upset by it. We should instead think of how we can get out of this mess. We must fight. I have never been afraid of a challenge; nor am I now."

Mr. Frankovszky suggested that we return to our American friends in Linz. They were, after all, very familiar with our case and would surely be able to help us. Their aid, however, would help only temporarily and locally. It was likely that every radio in the world had already broadcast the news that Dohnányi was a war criminal; this could not be undone. As it turned out, one of the first radios to announce this abominable news was the BBC, whose Hungarian Department seemed eager to publicize this disaster. We drove to Linz to see Captain John Kirn, who told us that although the Military Government had no power to enable Dohnányi to concertize, it certainly would do all it could to restore his reputation at least in the American Zone. An article was published in the military paper, clearing Dohnányi. The next day, Captain Kirn himself came with a friend to Neukirchen to show us the article, which explained that the rumor that Dohnányi was a war criminal was a mistake and that there was nothing in his political background for which he should be blamed.

When the jeep of the General's Aide-de-camp stopped before Dohnányi's home and the two high-ranking officers climbed out, the inhabitants of the village stared at them with gaping mouths. The news spread like wildfire that the radio announcement was a mistake and that Dohnányi had been falsely accused. Those who had been the loudest in condemning him a few hours earlier were now saying what nonsense the accusation had been. They declared indignantly that to accuse such a famous artist with political slanders was not only a blunder but also a crime. Who else was the loser, if he was banished from the stage, but the audience itself?

The next day, Dohnányi hardly had a minute to himself. All of Neukirchen streamed to his room to express congratulations over the solution of the disgraceful affair. Even the Mayor appeared with a bottle of sour wine to assure Dohnányi of his unwavering loyalty. Dohnányi only smiled. He was not upset by their offenses, nor did he rejoice over his triumph; he accepted it with perfect indifference. He was already preoccupied with a new composition, which was inspired by the beauties of the mountain village of Neukirchen.

🌹

For the next two weeks, we waited for more news. Although Dohnányi had been cleared by the Military Authorities in Linz, this was only a local action. By Mr. Pasetti's decree, Dohnányi was forbidden to make any public appearances, even at charity concerts. Although Captain Kirn tried to persuade Pasetti to remove this unjust order, he did not even succeed in discovering the secret behind the pile of accusations. It was not even possible for us to leave Austria and move into another country further west. The broadcast had spread the incriminating news all over the world.

The situation became even more threatening after the Soviet-controlled Hungarian Government began to demand the return of all Hungarian refugees. In most cases, their claims were fulfilled. Masses of refugees, criminals and innocents alike, were handed over to the Hungarian authorities and were in most cases executed. Some friends in Hungary sent Dohnányi a newspaper article with the heading "Dohnányi in Jail in Linz." The clipping told how Dohnányi had escaped Hungary, carrying with him a whole wagon full of valuables. The article also claimed that Dohnányi had stopped at a border town to hand over masses of sick Jewish musicians from a local hospital to the Gestapo. "Now he is in jail at last in Linz," the abominable article proclaimed, "to meditate over his evil deeds."

Such news, although absolutely false, nevertheless made us uneasy and unhappy. Even though Dohnányi was safe for the moment, his powerful American protectors could help only temporarily; officers were frequently transferred. Most of Dohnányi's friends, including General Reinhardt, had already left. This created positions for newcomers who were sometimes unable to understand the situation. Fortunately Captain Kirn was among those who remained. All of our hopes were based on him.

There was also another difficulty that weighed heavily on us: Dohnányi had not earned any money since he left Hungary. I gave English and piano lessons, but these earnings barely covered the expense of renting our rooms. Much of my time was taken up by working as an interpreter for the Hungarian Colonel who was the Commander of the Hungarian internment camp near Neukirchen. I also interpreted for the American Commanders who used to have their offices in the village. Although I could not expect remuneration for these services, I did receive food and other privileges. Helen worked as servant for the peasant woman in whose house we lived, while Julius walked miles daily to exchange our remaining bits of clothing for food.

In October, Dohnányi began to realize that we would have to spend the winter at Neukirchen. He had heard much about the biting cold that froze one's breath in the mountains. Because there was not one single log to warm the two rooms, we had every reason to be nervous about the future.

One afternoon, a luxurious car stopped before Dohnányi's house. The peasants recognized with a shudder that this had once been Hitler's car. An American Captain got out and hurried upstairs to see Dohnányi. It was Edward Kilenyi, Jr., a pupil of Dohnányi's who had been more like a member of Dohnányi's family during his stay in Budapest. Kilenyi was now stationed in Munich as Music Officer there. Although as a Music Officer in Germany he had no power in Austria, he had rushed to Neukirchen when he heard the rumor that Dohnányi was accused of being a war criminal. In spite of his best intentions, all Kilenyi could do was to spend an afternoon with Dohnányi in warm intimacy. During this time, there was very little talk. Dohnányi played his newest compositions for him, and Kilenyi was delighted to see that, in spite of all the troubles, his teacher was still in marvelous form.

After his meeting with Dohnányi, Kilenyi initiated seemingly endless arguments with Mr. Pasetti in Salzburg. Kilenyi explained matters to Pasetti, stating and restating the proofs based on his own experiences with Dohnányi. Kilenyi insisted that whatever the accusations were, they were wrong. All his efforts were in vain, and Pasetti eventually issued a decree stating that he would never be able to endorse Dohnányi's rehabilitation.[6] Kilenyi also tried to pave the way for Dohnányi to get either to Switzerland or Denmark. Unfortunately, the calumny had already reached both countries, and it was impossible to get an invitation to go there.

Dohnányi bore all these annoyances with his usual calmness. Although the political accusations irritated him and he felt an unprecedented contempt toward Mr. Pasetti, he still maintained his self-control. Nevertheless, he was no longer optimistic on the subject or on the political situation. As an admirer of the German philosopher Oswald Spengler, Dohnányi foresaw the decay of Western culture and was certain that sooner or later Europe would be lost. "When culture, civilization, and general welfare reach their peak," he would say, "they have to give way to a new culture and a new civilization." It was strange that he so calmly accepted this death sentence of Europe, a continent to which he clung with such passionate affection. "I am confirming facts that cannot be helped," he explained. "Conditions are so grave and everything is so mixed up politically that even the most experienced diplomat could hardly solve it in our favor. But in-

6. This decree, dated 21 February 1946, can be found in Appendix A.

stead, the West is committing one failure after another, as though they were blind and deaf at the same time."

In Neukirchen he completed his Symphony in E Major, which had been composed at various times and in various places. He had begun to work on it in Gödöllő and had finished it in Vienna. Now he made revisions on it in the Upper Austrian mountains. When he played movements of it, we were all deeply moved. "It seems like a good work," he agreed. "For I like it even after all these months. This is the way in which one has to judge a composition—after a lapse of time." Dohnányi also produced five piano pieces, which he entitled "Impromptu," Scherzino," Canzonetta," "Cascade," and "Ländler." Each one contained something that reflects the beauty of the mountain village's view. The "Cascade" imitates the splash of a waterfall in the mountains, and the "Ländler" is a melodious, charming country dance. The "Scherzino" and the "Cascade" would become Dohnányi's favorite encore pieces. While in Neukirchen, Dohnányi also made piano reductions of *Cantus vitae* and the *Suite en valse*.

Although the Americans had stopped the forcible repatriation of the refugees and extradited only those who were charged with political crimes, suddenly most of the Hungarians decided to return home. They felt that after living a Displaced Person's life in Austria, nothing worse could happen to them in Hungary. The military camp at which I had served as an interpreter was closed. As a farewell gift in return for the numerous services that Dohnányi had done for them, the returning refugees left him their remaining supply of food. This generous action eliminated our worries about the coming winter. Our chambermaid Bözsi was one of those who decided to return to Hungary. Weeks earlier, she had married a Hungarian soldier. At her wedding Dohnányi had played the Hungarian National Hymn on the church organ. This had brought tears to the eyes of the listeners. Rudolf Frankovszky departed with the other Hungarians. When he left, Dohnányi asked him to find out what slander had been invented against him in Hungary to transform him into a war criminal and cause all this misery.

When winter came and thick snow covered the streets, the first letters came from Hungary. Although censored to omit any hints of politics, they gave information about the deaths of many relatives and friends. Most painful of all was the news that Dohnányi's beloved son Matthew, a Captain in the Hungarian Army, had been taken prisoner by the Russians. He had been sent to a prison camp in Székesfehérvár, where he had died of typhus or, as it was suggested, starvation. The news wounded Dohnányi to the depths of his heart. Not wishing to burden others with his grief, he withdrew into solitude, withdrawing, perhaps for the last time, into his memories of the past. This blow did more than wound him; it made him bitter and resentful of his motherland. His son had not committed any political crime, but had served his country as a loyal and brave soldier. Dohnányi was outraged that Matthew had been abandoned by his own country.

In his solitude, Dohnányi erected an everlasting monument to the memory of his son: he dedicated the last of his *Six Pieces* for piano, op. 41, entitled "Cloches" (Bells), to Matthew. This magnificent chiming of bells is a somber piece, very different from the five lighthearted compositions that precede it.

On the morning of 20 December good news finally reached Dohnányi. It was a telegram from John Kirn and his fiancée Martha and ran thus: "Professor Dohnányi is cleared. Congratulations from the bottom of our hearts. Frankovszky is on his way with the documents. Martha and John."

Frankovszky had actually returned. His trip had not been easy, but he had defied all of the dangers and difficulties to bring the good news to Dohnányi. On this Christmas Eve, which was not much richer in material objects than the previous one, Dohnányi stood with us in front of a little tree that Julius had brought from the forest. Frankovszky placed a document on the table with tears of emotion.[7] The letter from the Hungarian Minister of Justice stated that Dohnányi was not considered to be a war criminal and was not listed as one on any official lists. The document proved that Mr. Pasetti's piles of accusations were nothing but absurd lies and wicked inventions that the Soviet-controlled Hungarian government itself rejected.

All of Austria welcomed Dohnányi's re-entrance into public life. His first recital was to be in Linz, and a charity concert was to follow in Grieskirchen. An interview was fixed for 15 January, on a broadcast from Linz, to give Dohnányi a chance to clear himself publicly. To Dohnányi's great annoyance, when he arrived at the radio building, he was informed that the interview could not take place. A representative of Mr. Pasetti in Linz had forbidden it. "It's not that Mr. Pasetti wants to forbid you to play at all," the man said in great confusion. "It's just that he doesn't want you to appear before the public . . . for a few more months."

"How so!" Dohnányi broke out indignantly. "Does Mr. Pasetti not know that I am in possession of a document from the Hungarian Government that declares that I am not and never was a war criminal?"

---

7. Frankovszky brought four official translations of this document that he was cautious enough to have made in Budapest. The notarized English translation of the Hungarian original, dated 14 December 1945, can be found in Appendix A.

"This may be so," the man stammered. "You might not be a war criminal, not even a Nazi, but you might be, let us say, an anti-Semite, and as such, might not be allowed to appear in public performances."

Dohnányi was dumbfounded at this accusation. Of course, it was impossible for him to disprove this lie on the spur of the moment. Furthermore, Mr. Pasetti was in charge; there was nothing more to say to this man. Dohnányi left the office with dismay and contempt. Outside in the corridor, one of the clerks who had been present at the discussion called Dohnányi aside. "Why the hell didn't you tell him that you did not drive all those Jewish musicians to the concentration camp, as Mr. Pasetti is accusing?" he advised. This had been one of the secret accusations that they had never dared to acknowledge. First Dohnányi's enemies had tried to make a war criminal out of him. When this attempt failed, they decided to destroy him with this baseless rumor, fully aware of the fact that even if it had been absolutely false, many Jews, in their bitter resentment against the Nazis, would accept the slanderous accusation as a fact.

The recitals that had already been booked had to be canceled, and once more the wretched debates started between Dohnányi's friends and Mr. Pasetti. This time, Captain Kirn was able to make some headway. He went to Vienna to a higher American Military Forum and explained the whole affair to them. Within a few days, Dohnányi received a certificate by which all four Occupation Powers in Austria gave him permission to appear on the stage.

It was on 31 May 1946 in Innsbruck that Dohnányi performed again. This recital had actually been booked before the document releasing him from those persecutions had arrived from Vienna. The French Zone had invited him to play regardless of what Mr. Pasetti or anybody else had dictated. When Dohnányi appeared that evening, his audience seemed to realize how deep his emotions were. The overcrowded hall listened to his interpretation almost breathlessly, overwhelmed with sympathy and enthusiasm. "To think that such an artist was kept from the stage for months!" the members of the audience whispered. "Just because of slanderous accusations!" The French Staff Officers who were helping to organize the concerts gave a reception in the Hotel Golf, in the picturesque outskirts of Innsbruck. It was in this hotel that Dohnányi, Julius, the driver, and I stayed. Dohnányi was delighted; he had not slept in such a luxurious room since leaving Hungary. When he noticed the bathroom with warm water, he felt as though he was no wretched D.P., but instead the celebrity he had once been.

Unfortunately, Dohnányi could not stay long. He had to hurry back to Linz to the wedding of Captain Kirn and Martha, who had both been so loyal to him. Dohnányi was now her witness. The wedding was a magnificent event and was attended by many high-ranking American officers, including the new Upper Austrian Governor, Colonel Lloyd M. Hanna, who later became Dohnányi's good friend. Eminent Austrian citizens and their families also attended.

Dohnányi, however, was not able to enjoy this wonderful festival without another painful shock. For months, he had been trying to locate his other son, Hans, through the American authorities. After Dohnányi lost track of him, Hans had been taken prisoner by the Nazis. On the morning of the wedding, Dohnányi was informed that his son was dead. He had been executed before the Americans had entered Germany.

After the wedding the young couple left for a long trip, and Dohnányi temporarily lost his defender. After his name had been cleared, concert invitations had begun to pour in from all parts of the country. Travel was still difficult, however; the trains were unheated, had no lights, and their windows had no panes. They were so crowded that people were unable to edge their way to the doors and often had to exit through the windows. Journeys took several hours longer than usual because of the interrogations the authorities made at the borders of the different Occupation Zones. Fortunately Dohnányi still had the use of a car. Since gasoline was hard to come by, he had to borrow some from his American friends before each trip. Although they were also suffering from the shortage, they shared their gasoline. It is no wonder that his only desire was to leave Austria as soon as possible and settle somewhere further to the west, where he could live in peace and safety.

In the meantime, Dohnányi performed in several concerts. There were four orchestral concerts in Innsbruck on 15, 16, 18, and 20 September 1946 that were especially significant to him. The highlight of each evening was a Brahms Piano Concerto. On the first two evenings, Dohnányi was the soloist, playing the B-flat Major Concerto, conducted by Fritz Weidlich, who was the Music Director of Innsbruck. On the second two evenings Dohnányi conducted, while Weidlich played the D Minor Concerto. Mr. Weidlich had a somewhat hard touch, but he was an excellent pianist and a fine conductor. All four performances were great successes. Another important performance was Dohnányi's first postwar recital in Vienna, which took place on 13 October 1946. "It is with the sadness of a farewell that we listen to the playing of the silver-haired Hungarian master; farewell to the piano's irrevocable past world of splendor, of men like Liszt, Rubinstein, and Sauer," the *Weltpresse* wrote on 14 October 1946. "Dohnányi is one of the last, if not *the* last, representative of it."

Several months earlier Dohnányi had received an invitation to play in England from his old agency Ibbs and Tillett. Although he had approached the civil authorities, he was still without the papers required for this trip. I made a trip to Vienna and tried to persuade the Hungarian Consulate to give Dohnányi a passport. After a delay of hours, the Consul's Secretary declared that if Dohnányi came home immediately and undertook a concert tour in Russia, he would be furnished with all of the necessary documents. If he did not agree to this proposal, they would have nothing to do with him and he would become an outcast in the eyes of the Hungarian Government.

Dohnányi became desperate and frustrated. The first concert date proposed by Ibbs and Tillett had already passed. He sent me to the British Consul, who persuaded the Austrian authorities to give Dohnányi and his Secretary—he could not have convinced them to allow a "niece" to accompany him—two sheets of paper that served as passports. Leaving the children in the care of Fräulein Hermine, the Maestro and I hurriedly left Vienna in an English military plane.

It was night when the plane crossed the Channel. Dohnányi showed me the green lights below that marked the banks of the Thames. The plane was above London! Only then did it become clear that this was no dream. Dohnányi watched the view below with deep emotion and immense relief. He was surprised when he turned to me and saw tears streaming down my face. It was hard to explain to him that these were tears of joy and gratitude. This was the beginning of a new life.

SEVEN

1946–1948

At the London airport, the official of the Home Office examined Dohnányi's disorganized papers and looked up at him with interest. "Are you the famous musician?" he asked.

Dohnányi nodded.

"You are welcome in England, sir," the official said with a benevolent smile.

These words warmed my heart. I was even more touched by Mr. and Mrs. Tillett, who met us at Victoria Station and then treated us to a delicious supper. Dohnányi talked calmly and composedly with them, while watching me as I expressed my obvious delight upon being served a cake covered with real chocolate. Although second helpings in restaurants were prohibited in England, the waiter brought us another plateful, which he said was by request of the other diners. Later that night, the Maestro and I continued our journey to Edinburgh. At the station, cocoa was served with real milk, and without coupons. England seemed like Paradise.

The concert in Edinburgh took place on 25 October 1946. The hall was packed, but this was not the audience of ladies wearing deep-cut evening dresses and gentlemen in immaculate tuxedoes that Dohnányi had seen on his earlier visits to Britain. The people now wore simple, everyday clothing. Some women even had shopping bags at their feet. I realized that in spite of the luxurious meals served at restaurants, conditions were still difficult here. When the conductor, Walter Susskind, appeared on the stage, everyone stood for "God Save the King." It was wonderful to be in a country where they had such a strong national feeling, where an anthem was respected, and where some things were still considered sacred. When Dohnányi appeared on the stage, the crowd received him with warm enthusiasm. Although many of them had heard that he had been labeled a war criminal, this did not seem to affect their respect or appreciation when they listened to the *Variationen über ein Kinderlied*. On the next day, Dohnányi went to Glasgow, where he played the *Variationen* in St. Andrew's Hall with Susskind conducting. On 27 October, Dohnányi played Mozart's

Coronation Concerto, K. 537, in Green's Playhouse. With all these performances, life was slipping past like a dream. This was a refreshing change from the constant procrastination and stagnation of Austria.

In London, Dohnányi and his friends worked hard to arrange for my children and Fräulein Hermine to come to England. Although this proved to be practically impossible, we hoped that after we returned to Austria we would be allowed to bring them with us and settle in England when we returned for the next season. One day, Dohnányi took me to pay a visit to his old friend Caroline Geisler-Schubert. Since the death of Mrs. Oliverson, "Lintschi" had lived alone with her loyal elderly housekeeper. Although she was almost ninety, Lintschi's eyes brightened up radiantly when she welcomed Dohnányi. They chatted about their old friends, most of whom had passed away. Dohnányi also met Bernard de Nevers, who was the head of the publishing firm of Alfred Lengnick and Company, which represented Dohnányi's German publisher, Simrock. Lengnick was interested in Dohnányi's new works, and de Nevers made a contract with Dohnányi to publish his Sextet, op. 37, the *Suite en valse,* op. 39, which Dohnányi had arranged for two pianos (op. 39a), his Second Symphony, op. 40, and the *Six Pieces,* op. 41, which Dohnányi had performed on a BBC program.

I would have liked to have extended our stay in this marvelous country, but Dohnányi was booked for concerts in Vienna and had to return. "There can be nothing more important than my concert obligations," he responded to my constant pleadings and arguments to stay longer. "Once an artist has accepted an engagement, he has to stick to it and cannot give it up even for a more favorable offer. It has very often happened that after I undertook to play somewhere, I got much more attractive offers. I always refused them, for I consider it to be a matter of honor to carry out my obligations."

On our way back to Austria, the Maestro and I spent two days in Switzerland meeting friends. There were many wonderful shops filled with all kinds of alluring merchandise, but we had no money to purchase anything. Dohnányi was still wearing the old, worn suit and mended shirts that we had saved from Hungary. The expensive trip to England had been funded by only two concerts, and the children and Fräulein Hermine in Austria were badly in need of money. Dohnányi still wanted to settle in Switzerland, but this was quite impossible after the evil radio propaganda of the previous year.

Dohnányi began to consider settling in Australia. He had experienced enough of the miseries of Europe and wanted to live in a free country. Dohnányi had already discussed this with the Tilletts, who had given him the name of a man who was connected with the radio and other musical organizations in Australia. When I argued that it was too far away, Dohnányi only smiled. "From where?" he asked. "If we settle there, it will be our home and will not be far away."

❧

In November 1946 Vienna was still devastated by the war. We came upon the ruins of bombed buildings everywhere. Political captives, mostly former high-ranking German officers, worked to clear away the debris under the harsh commands of their guards. Even more pitiful than the city's outward appearance were its living conditions. The city lacked all supplies that are crucial for survival, and the signs of extreme poverty could be seen everywhere. People strolled about, shivering in their shabby, worn clothing, because no new garments were available. To make matters worse, fuel was not available to battle the bitterly cold autumn weather. It was difficult to cook even a small meal, because gas and electricity were obtainable only at certain hours, which were announced on the radio.

The Konzerthaus Gesellschaft (Concert House Society) had furnished us with two rooms in a private home in the English Zone. Although a dozen English officers lived above our rooms, our hostess complained that a few weeks earlier two strangers had broken into her apartment, pointed their guns at her, and forced her into her own kitchen, where she was locked up while they helped themselves to all of her valuables. The Gesellschaft had also given us fuel for heating, but we had no food because our coupons from the American Zone were not valid. We had no choice but to buy food on the black market, where prices were outrageous. On the recommendation of friends, we once visited a restaurant where we were admitted to a secret basement room. There mediocre food was served at an exorbitant cost.

On 27 November 1946 Dohnányi performed Schumann's Piano Concerto in the Grosser Konzerthaussaal with Felix Prohaska conducting the Vienna Philharmonic. The hall was again packed, with the first rows occupied by representatives of the four Occupation Armies. After the performance, we spent the evening with the Manager of the Konzerthaus and Mrs. Heller, the widow of Hugo Heller. Dohnányi had told me much about Mr. Heller, who had arranged several concerts for him. Heller had often acted somewhat rashly out of anger. Eventually his wife, a lady of calm temperament, had advised him to write the words: "Auch dieses geht vorüber" (This too shall pass) on a piece of paper. He fastened it above his writing desk to force himself to always keep it in mind. Mrs. Heller praised Dohnányi's playing with deep emotion. She said had not heard anything like it for many years. "Nowadays," she said, "people in Vienna seem to have no money for concerts or any other entertainment. Every cent has to be spent on the black market for food and fuel. Yet tonight, the concert hall was so packed with people that not one more person could have been tucked into it. They knew why they had come, and they were not disappointed. It had been a long time since I had heard such enthusiastic applause!"

Dohnányi's lips drew into a melancholy smile. "The Viennese came," he said wistfully, "because they wanted to hear me once more. I am the last of those to whom they have so passionately clung. I am the last link to the School of Liszt."

"You are right," Mrs. Heller agreed. "Our young artists may be brilliant in their technique, but, as I heard this evening from several of my friends, our generation doesn't know how to play. I am not sure if this is due to a lack of feeling or if are they just incapable of expressing it. Regardless, they simply lack something that would speak to the heart."

On 30 November Dohnányi performed the first concert in a series of recitals of Beethoven sonatas in Vienna. The harsh, cold wintertime had begun, and the hall was unheated. Every member of the audience was shivering, and their teeth chattered from the cold. Dohnányi wore a sweater under his light evening suit, and his only source of warmth was a tiny electric heater that had been placed near his feet by some merciful soul, probably Mrs. Heller. Dohnányi frequently rubbed his hands together. He later said that he had felt as though all the blood had run out from his fingers. The performance, however, was one of the loveliest he had ever given, and people said that they had never heard Beethoven played so beautifully. For the following recitals of Beethoven sonatas, which took place on 3, 8, 11, 14, 15, and 17 December, the hall was equally cold but only half filled with sneezing, shivering people. The empty seats bitterly reflected Vienna's poverty. Those who were present were most enthusiastic, as though they wanted to compensate Dohnányi for the absentees.

Because I had fallen gravely sick with the flu and Dohnányi did not want to go to any more mysterious restaurants, he tried to prepare our meals himself with a few potatoes and some coffee that we still possessed from Neukirchen. It was a joyous surprise when one afternoon Martha Kirn's parents, who lived in Vienna, arrived with a wonderful *Kuglopf,* which they had made with flour that the Kirns had sent from their new home in Lancaster, Ohio. Martha's mother also brought a can of American marmalade and American butter. Another relief came when Frankovszky arrived one morning from Neukirchen with a rucksack filled with bread, butter, eggs, and milk packed by Fräulein Hermine.

We were greatly relieved when the last of the Beethoven evenings had taken place. That night, however, our hardships in Vienna increased. The electricity in our district did not function at all, and we had to dress in darkness, enjoying occasional flickers of light from a little candle that we blew out again and again, sparing it because it was the only one we had.

The trip back to Neukirchen was yet another problem. There had been no improvements in the condition of the trains; they were still crowded, windowless, and unlit. Mr. Frankovszky brought us a certificate in which the Commander of the French Supreme Headquarters granted us a compartment in the car of the Occupation Armies. Before we left Vienna on 17 December, we were politely ushered by French Officers into an empty cabin. This comfortable place did not remain ours for long, however; an hour into the journey, we were thrown out of it by some drunken French soldiers who were not interested in Dohnányi's certificate. The trip then turned into a nightmare. The passengers were jammed so tight that one could hardly breathe, and the icy wind streamed in through the paneless window.

Because we could only travel as far as Linz by train, we had arranged for a car to come from Neukirchen to pick us up. When we arrived in Linz, however, the snow was piled up in drifts almost six feet deep around the city, and the car could not come. We stood there, in the middle of the night in an unheated railway station, without anywhere to go. No hotel rooms were available in the overcrowded city. Dohnányi looked at me as though asking me what we should do, so I suggested that we telephone Governor Hanna.

"How could we wake him at midnight?" Dohnányi protested.

"I am sure he will not mind. Nor will his wife; she has is always been sweet and affectionate," I insisted.

I called and asked the Governor's help. Within minutes, a jeep came to pick us up and take us to their home, where we were welcomed as though we were members of their family. It was warm and cozy in the Hannas' living room. There was a table covered with delicious sandwiches, warm coffee, and whisky, which Mrs. Hanna had hastily prepared. We stayed with them for two lovely days. All that the Governor asked in return for this generous hospitality was that Dohnányi play him his favorite composition: Beethoven's *Appassionata* Sonata.

In Neukirchen the year 1947 began with an incredible amount of snow. Dohnányi, of course, was delighted by it whenever he peered through his window or walked with me down the road that had been cleared by the townspeople. We usually walked behind our little dog Csöppi, who, being light as a feather, almost flew over the heaps of glittering snow. The cold winter would have been much less enjoyable had we not been furnished with fuel, compliments of Governor Hanna. We were also able to obtain butter and other important food supplies through constant bargaining with the townspeople.

Dohnányi wrote letters to various countries, including Denmark, England, Canada, and the United States, asking for permission to start a new life there. Even Australia turned down his request. Dohnányi was unofficially informed that the man who was supposed have arranged an invitation for a position there had dropped the matter because he had been influenced by the slanderous radio proclamation of a year before. Arrangements to settle in the United States could have been made only if some important and influential musician had labored diligently on Dohnányi's behalf. As the Director of the Bank of Lancaster, Ohio, John offered an affidavit for Dohnányi. Dohnányi could have immigrated there if he had consented to go alone, but he would not leave Europe without us, because he now considered us to be his family. Since many of Dohnányi's former friends in the United States had either died or otherwise lost contact, John tried to contact famous musicians, including an elderly Austrian-born pianist. "Why on earth would you wish to bring Dohnányi here?" the musician said indignantly. "He's far too old to come to this country!" This man was actually only a few years younger and in fact died soon afterwards of old age. Although the Maestro and I would have been welcomed in England, it seemed impossible to also bring our family. A labor permit would have been available for Fräulein Hermine, but she would have been separated from us and would have had to serve a Scottish family for many years. Furthermore, there was absolutely no chance of bringing the two children.

Dohnányi did not seem discouraged by these obstacles. "If these countries don't accept us," he would say with a shrug, "there are still many others. There is for instance, South America." He remembered that a former Secretary of his, Árpád Bubik, was now a concert agent in Argentina. Promptly, which was very unusual for him, Dohnányi wrote to Bubik. The response included a contract with an offer for several concerts and the assurance that he would be able to settle there with his entire family. The fact that none of us knew Spanish did not worry Dohnányi because he expressed himself in music. He had already made up his mind to move to Argentina.

Meanwhile, Dohnányi had started his Second Piano Concerto, op. 42. The piano part is extremely difficult and requires a tremendous technical ability. Although the music rewards the pianist's effort through its brilliant effect, I could not help but wonder who would be able to play it. "I will play it myself," Dohnányi said simply. "I have written the concerto for myself. And, upon my soul, it doesn't tire *me*."

✿

Dohnányi was informed that an article had appeared in a Hungarian paper reporting that he was remaining in touch with Hungarian emigrants in the United States whom this article described as "reactionaries." According to the article, Dohnányi was to be given American citizenship as a reward for his treacherous activities against Russian-dominated Hungary. Although this article, like others of its kind, told the most abominable lies, Dohnányi wished with all his heart that he were to be given an American citizenship. The author of the article expressed his indignation that the Hungarian Minister of Foreign Affairs had not declared Dohnányi a war criminal. Soon afterwards, a communist obtained the position of Minister of the Interior and promptly declared Dohnányi a war criminal, putting him on a blacklist with thirty other victims. The new Interior Minister continued to pester the American authorities in Linz to hand him over.

Because the situation was growing increasingly dangerous, Dohnányi decided to move to Kitzbühel, Austria, which was in the French Zone. The French did not consider Hungarian refugees to be enemies and refused to deliver up anyone who sought refuge with them. It also seemed likely that Dohnányi, who had received the distinction of *Legion d'honneur Officier* from France in 1936, would easily obtain a *laissez-passer* from the French Authorities. The only disadvantage to the French Zone was its shortage of food. It was decided that Fräulein Hermine would stay in Neukirchen and send us parcels of food to augment our tiny rations. We also had no money, because at my request Dohnányi had not given any more concerts in Austria. I was trying to spare him from the horrible ordeal of traveling, which would have worn him out or made him sick. The trip was finally funded with the royalties I received when a publisher in Linz accepted one of my novels.

Although it was April, our trip to Kitzbühel was bitterly cold in the same windowless, unlit train. Dohnányi was in possession of a certificate from the American Government and Austrian Medical Authorities and had a seat in a compartment reserved for military invalids, who were sitting almost on top of each other. My daughter Helen and I had to stand in the pitch-dark corridor, where we were jostled and crushed by the impatient crowd throughout the eight-hour journey. Meanwhile, my son Julius balanced himself on the open steps of the coach, clinging desperately to the baggage that contained our food and our most precious belongings. One could not even turn to a conductor for help. A few days earlier, infuriated passengers had thrown a conductor out the window, and the conductors now did not dare to appear when the crowds of passengers were so agitated. It was a miracle that we got through the trip without any trouble, because I collapsed with a painful sciatic nerve. This kept me in bed for several weeks, just when my full energy was sorely needed.

Dohnányi either went alone or was accompanied by my daughter to those few concerts that he had accepted in spite of my protests. He gave recitals on 20 May in Innsbruck, which was in the French Zone; on 26 and

27 May in Kitzbühel with Wilhelm Werth; on 6 and 7 June in Linz in the Kulturamt der Landeshauptstadt (Cultural Office of the Provincial Capital); and on 14 June in Bregenz. On 5 July he contributed to a concert given for the benefit of International Displaced Persons in Innsbruck.

In the French Zone, Dohnányi made friends who stood loyally and helpfully by his side. These included Major Crussard of the French Military Government, who was a passionate cellist, and Crussard's wife, who was a fine violinist and pianist. Whenever Dohnányi had business in Innsbruck, which was two hours away from Kitzbühel by train, Major Crussard would help us and Mrs. Crussard would invite us into their home for dinner.

Among those who tried to lessen Dohnányi's hardships was Margarethe Frank. She had once been a concert pianist, and her husband had been an Austrian ambassador in Germany before the Hitler regime. Now they lived in comfortable retirement in their beautiful villa in Kitzbühel. They invited Dohnányi, who still had no piano, to use their Bechstein whenever he liked. Dohnányi took advantage of this opportunity to play parts of his Second Piano Concerto while he worked on the manuscript. Mrs. Frank, hiding in her kitchen, listened with excitement to the rapidly developing creation. She knew every melody of it, and every bar was imprinted into her memory. When the work was published years later, Dohnányi sent the first copy to her with a warm inscription. On his walk to the Frank house, Dohnányi would repeatedly stop to enjoy the surrounding mountains, which were now clothed in bright green with some patches of white on their peaks. He viewed the Ehrenbach-Höhe, the peak where he had spent his sixtieth birthday. How distant were those beautiful times now! "Can't you see the beauty of these mountains?" he asked me. "The magnificent beauty of nature?"

When Dohnányi admired something, he could concentrate entirely on the subject, forgetting its annoying context. The same was the case with his own faults. Whenever I blamed myself for something I had done wrong, he consoled me, "Do not regret anything you've done wrong in the past. No one has ever been without faults or errors; we are all human beings. I, too, have made mistakes and often could have done better. But I learned from it never to commit such a fault again. I have never lost time by bitter and torturing repentance, but I have taken good care not to repeat the error in future." It was also not his habit to blame others for causing him trouble if they had done so accidentally. "When, as a young conductor," he would say, "I noticed that someone in the orchestra playing badly, instead of blaming him I began to search for the fault in myself. If you must blame someone, blame yourself rather than others." Dohnányi's calmness and optimism helped to keep up the spirits of the family as we all worked diligently. Julius was now studying for his final Gymnasium graduation examination, while Helen was in charge of the cooking. This was perhaps the hardest job; at dawn she would join a line of people to buy bread and would sometimes come back weeping because, by the time her turn came, the bread had all been sold.

On 26 July 1947, the day preceding Dohnányi's seventieth birthday, the Hungarian colony in Innsbruck, which consisted only of poor D.P.'s, invited us to a surprise banquet in his honor. This banquet took place in a restaurant where the tables had been elegantly set with china and silver for thirty-four people. Delicious food was served: roast beef with potatoes, vegetables, a huge birthday cake, and bottles of French wine. This precious dinner had been prepared by the thirty members of the Hungarian colony, who had obtained eggs and butter from nearby villages, meat from Innsbruck, and wine from the French Army. They had purchased each item at high prices on the black market or traded their most valuable belongings, while continuing to work to feed themselves. This meal was a moving tribute to an artist and was a recompense for the stonehearted negligence that Dohnányi had suffered from his motherland.

A Hungarian lady greeted Dohnányi with a bouquet of roses that had been tied with a ribbon of the national colors of red, white, and green. With touching words she explained how they, the Hungarian colony of Kitzbühel, were trying to express all the best wishes of those Hungarians who now had to remain silent at home. Long speeches hailing Dohnányi followed. This time, they seemed neither boring nor tiring to him. Dohnányi was deeply moved and listened to every word. Later, when the wine made tongues looser, humor and merriment found their way into the banquet. Someone, not quite without irony, remarked that this was the first occasion when all members of the Hungarian colony were united. The whole evening culminated in cheerfulness when a young composer rose and, raising a paper napkin with an air of mock severity, announced that he had just received a telegram from the Hungarian communist leader Mátyás Rákóczi, who sent the following message: "Ernst! Come home! We would gladly detain you for seventy more years!" Everybody burst out in laughter, forgetting his or her troubles for an evening. Years later, Dohnányi would refer to this birthday as one of the most touching ones he ever had.

The celebration continued into the next day. Dohnányi was showered with gifts from friends, and even the hostess in the hotel surprised him with a birthday cake. In the afternoon, he went to Innsbruck to play his *Passacaglia* for a radio program that had been arranged to celebrate his birthday. Radio Salzburg, together with Radios Linz, Vienna, and Graz, dedicated a simultaneous hour to Dohnányi's birthday. After some warmly appreciative words describing his past life and compositions, they broadcast the *Variationen über ein Kinderlied*.

✿

In September Dohnányi frequently visited the home of German pianist Wilhelm Werth in nearby St. Johann, in the Tyrol. Dohnányi and Werth gave concerts of music for two pianos on 26 September in Kitzbühel and on 7 and 13 October in Innsbruck. On both occasions, they performed Dohnányi's two-piano arrangement of the *Suite en valse.*

Dohnányi was booked for a large number of concerts and recitals in England in the following autumn and winter. It was especially urgent for him to undertake this trip because the Hungarian Government was continually pestering the French Government in Innsbruck to deliver Dohnányi into their hands. Although they received a flat refusal each time, we did not feel safe. To make matters worse, Dohnányi received a telegram from a Hungarian friend who warned him to leave Austria as soon as possible because his life was in danger. Unfortunately, there was still no way for the children to come with us to England. Mrs. Frank finally suggested, "Why not get them a *laissez-passer* from the French Government?" she suggested. "They would be able to get into France, where they would be safe, and they would no longer be exposed to all kinds of danger as Displaced Persons. You could join them at the end of your English tour." Mrs. Frank even had a friend who lived in Beaulieux-sur-Mer, on the French Riviera, arrange for a hotel called the Pension Londres to look after Fräulein Hermine and the children on credit until we could pay their expenses.

These difficulties wore out even Dohnányi's strong nerves, and he was bedridden for days. He was feeling no pain, just weariness. The doctor said that the nervousness that he had carefully hidden within himself had affected his heart. His health was rapidly restored with some shots and pills, and he was once more ready to fight the obstacles that stood in our way.

On 2 October the Innsbruck Radio celebrated its twentieth anniversary. Its director, Mr. Schuschnigg, whose brother was the former Chancellor of Austria, asked Dohnányi to participate. This was a solemn event to which a hundred guests were invited, including several outstanding Austrians and members of the French Government. Speeches were given by the French Staff Officers and the leading members of the Radio. A chamber music performance followed, and then Dohnányi played Beethoven's *Pathétique* Sonata. The audience responded with stormy applause. At the end of the program, the assistant of the French Commander congratulated Dohnányi and in his enthusiasm asked what he could do to help him. "You could grant a *laissez-passer* to my children," I suggested boldly. Dohnányi explained our efforts to get the children to France.

"Granted," the Colonel nodded with a smile. "Come to my office tomorrow and everything will be arranged."

Just when Dohnányi was about to leave the hall, a man suddenly blocked his way. "I'm afraid, Maestro, that you will not recognize me in this civilian clothing," the man stammered in embarrassment, lowering his gaze. "You'll probably have disagreeable memories concerning me, for I have . . . hmm . . . somewhat annoyed you in the past. I'm Otto Pasetti, former Music Officer of Salzburg."

Dohnányi grew stiff. His blue eyes blazed with acid resentment and contempt. He ignored the hand that Pasetti had held out to him. "So it is you," he murmured. It was probably the first time in his life that he refused to shake hands with someone.

"I know you hold a grudge against me," Pasetti muttered in a broken voice, withdrawing his hand. "But you certainly don't realize that I could have acted even worse. Remember, at that time the Americans were allied with the Russians. I had the power to arrest you and hand you over to the Hungarian Government, had I chosen to."

"Rather, if you had *dared* to," Dohnányi corrected him with disdain. Then, bringing the unpleasant conversation to an end, he turned his back on Pasetti's apologies and, beckoning me, rushed from the hall.

❦

To make money for our trip to England we had to sell much of the silver that I had brought from my home, which we had safeguarded throughout our flight. Fräulein Hermine came to stay in Kitzbühel with the children, having left Csöppi, the little spitz, behind in Neukirchen. It hurt us to have to part with the dog forever, especially because he had gone blind in one eye and clung to us faithfully. There was, however, no possibility of taking him with us. Unfortunately, he had to be deserted at a time when he needed our help the most. A few days before our departure we discovered that the French Government in Innsbruck would not be able to give Fräulein Hermine a *laissez-passer* because she had once been a Sudeten-German, even though she was currently without a citizenship. The children would have stay with her in Kitzbühel until we found a way to get her a visa. Without the children, she could never hope to leave Austria. Although Mrs. Frank promised that she and her friends would watch over them, it was still hard to leave Fräulein Hermine and the children in such an uncertain situation. Naturally, it was a sad occasion when the Maestro and I said farewell at the station as we awaited the Arlberg Express. It was painful for me to part with my children and our friends, who had brought more flowers, cakes, and sweets than we were able to carry with us.

Even in those moments, Dohnányi was sensitive to the beauties of nature. He rested his gaze upon the mountains, which, with the approaching winter, were already covered with snow. "I feel almost sorry to leave these lovely mountains," he said with a sigh.

A Countess who was also a Hungarian refugee rebuked Dohnányi reproachfully, "Forget about those cursed mountains! Didn't you suffer enough, encircled by them as though you were in a concentration camp? Be happy that you can finally get away from this ill-fated place that is like a jail to us D.P.'s."

Then the Count informed us that he was soon leaving for Venezuela. "Not there!" I exclaimed in horror. "I have heard that Europeans cannot stand the climate of that country longer than for five years."

"Then it's just the right place for me," the Count remarked bitterly. "Five more years of this wretched life is more than enough."

The Count died of cancer exactly five years later in Caracas. He never returned to Austria, even though he had wanted to so badly that his friends in Kitzbühel sent him a boat ticket.

❧

Our stay in England was far from being as pleasant as our stay one year earlier had been. Food was scarce and clothing coupons were unavailable. Even more disturbing was the shortage of fuel. Heat was forbidden in hotels before Christmas time, and I had contracted influenza. Worst of all was our constant worrying about the children in Austria, who wrote increasingly desperate letters. In spite of the energetic help of Mrs. Frank and other friends, it was still impossible for Fräulein Hermine to obtain a *laissez-passer.* They also had no heat, and Kitzbühel was freezing. Furthermore, we began to hear rumors that, according to certain peace agreements, all refugees in Austria would be handed over to the Russians.

Dohnányi had numerous performances in the United Kingdom, to which the audiences responded just as enthusiastically as they had the previous year. He started with recitals in Dublin, Ireland, in the afternoon and evening of 3 November 1947. Then he played in Sheffield on 6 November, where he had such a success that the City Council asked Sir Thomas Beecham, who had agreed to conduct the premiere of Dohnányi's Second Piano Concerto, to premiere the Concerto with the Royal Philharmonic Orchestra in their city a month later. On 9 November Dohnányi played his *Variationen über ein Kinderlied* in the Cambridge Theater with Alec Sherman conducting the New London Orchestra. Dohnányi gave a recital on 11 November in the Southwest Essex Music Club for an audience of workingmen. He was deeply touched to see how the craftsmen had gathered after their hard, physical work to enjoy serious music.

Dohnányi's recital on 13 November at the Royal Academy of Music in London was a moving event. In spite of the hard conditions, the audience wore formal evening dress and received Dohnányi with spontaneous affection. After the last number the President of the Academy reminded the audience that Dohnányi was an "honorary member" of the Academy and had played there twenty years earlier on the same piano. The piano, he said, surely remembered that occasion, because pianos have souls, like human beings, and are tortured and tormented when played by someone without a sense of art. This evening, the piano had surely rejoiced, for someone had played it who knew his art well.

On 16 November, Dohnányi again performed his *Variationen* with the New London Orchestra. On 21 November he gave a recital in Bradford, and on the twenty-fifth he played for the Brentwood Musical Society. In Brighton, on 29 November, he performed Mozart's D Minor Concerto, K. 466, with the Southern Philharmonic Orchestra, conducted by Herbert Menges. Dohnányi also recorded his *Six Pieces,* op. 41, which he had composed in Neukirchen, for His Master's Voice in London.

Dohnányi's time in England was also consumed with business activities, including the attempts, aided by Mrs. Tillett, to claim the royalties that had been held by the Custodian Office of Enemy Property since the start of World War II. Since peace had been made with Hungary, as a Hungarian he should have had the right to his money. Unfortunately, he was a member of the Austrian firm A.K.M. (Gesellschaft der Autoren, Komponisten und Musikverläger—Society of Authors, Composers, and Music Publishers), which had merged with the German royalty organization GEMA under Hitler. Although it had since become Austrian again, there was no hope of getting even a cent of this money until peace was established with Austria and Germany. Dohnányi's royalties would continue to be frozen in the Custodian Office of Enemy Property because he could not join a royalty company in England or America.

Rehearsals continued with Beecham and the Royal Philharmonic Orchestra for the premiere of Dohnányi's Second Piano Concerto. This is a difficult work, not only for the soloist, but also for the orchestra. Beecham, with his customary humor, said that he would consider the performance in Sheffield to be a rehearsal, Birmingham to be the dress rehearsal, and only the performance in London to be the true premiere. The Sheffield performance of the Second Piano Concerto took place on 3 December 1947 in a new hall of which the city was very proud. The performance was more effective than one could have ever expected. A lady next to me had tears in her eyes. "I don't know why I should weep," she said, "I don't feel sad at all. This music has actually cheered me and stirred my emotions. Yet, my tears flow." The audience did not seem to want to stop applauding.

Then Beecham spoke to the audience, as he often did. At the previous night's rehearsal, Beecham had expressed disappointment with the new hall, which he said was so vast that he could not communicate with the Orchestra. He had cupped his hands over his eyes, saying that he needed a telescope to see his musicians and a telephone to communicate with them. Now he reproached the Mayor and his city for the tasteless hall and the stone lions that were placed just in front of him and at each side of the entrance to the artist's room. The Mayor and his friends were baffled and deeply hurt, for they were intensely proud of their new hall. The Mayor promptly left, and there was no reception that evening. The Maestro and I instead dined with Beecham's assistant conductor Norman Del Mar, who inquired about Dohnányi's compositions. The result of this conversation was that the next year, on 23 November 1948, Del Mar premiered Dohnányi's Second Symphony with his Chelsea Symphony Orchestra. Dohnányi did not hear this performance, the reviews of which, although favorable, were not exactly enthusiastic.

For the Birmingham performance of Dohnányi's Second Piano Concerto, which took place on 5 December, Beecham was suffering from lumbago and kept the audience waiting. Dohnányi was photographed in the artist's room as he involuntarily drew out his watch. The next day, the photo appeared in a paper with the caption: "Dohnányi, consulting his watch at Birmingham Town Hall last night, while waiting for Sir Thomas Beecham, the conductor." The Piano Concerto was performed the next day in London in the Drury Lane Theater.

Back in London, there was no letter from Austria waiting in the hotel. What had happened to the children? Were they able, after all, to obtain the much desired visa for Fräulein Hermine? Had they already gone to France? Even if they had managed to leave Austria, there was another threat; a railway strike had halted travel in France. Without trains or vehicles and with disorder and riots everywhere, anything could have happened to them. Sensing our nervousness, Mrs. Tillett advised Dohnányi to phone the Pension Londres in Beaulieux-sur-Mer to find out whether they had some news. He did so, and to his great surprise and relief Fräulein Hermine herself answered the phone and informed him that they had arrived there few days earlier, in spite of numerous hardships. Full of excitement, Dohnányi went out shopping with me. The only Christmas gifts that he could get, however, were very inexpensive because there were very few things that could be obtained in England without coupons. Dohnányi had wanted to buy a Christmas tree, but could find only a toy one no more than three inches high.

While in London, Dohnányi was reunited with his old friend Ludwig Lebell. Lebell gave him a gift that was one of the most precious he could have given: some clothing coupons that Lebell surely needed for himself. At first, Dohnányi refused to accept such a present, but after his friend insisted, he bought himself tuxedo shirts.

We left England on 17 December, traveling through Paris and arriving in Beaulieux-sur-Mer at noon the next day. After the damp, cold, foggy English winter, it was wonderful to feel the mild sunshine and refreshing breeze. It was an even greater joy to see the children waiting at the railway station.

❧

Beaulieux-sur-Mer, a little town on the French Riviera with the Maritime Alps to the north and the sea to the south, is a most picturesque, enchanting place. According to legend, the town was named when Napoleon came to conquer these regions and, admiring the scenery, murmured with wonder, "Quels beaux lieux!" (What beautiful parts!). In happier days, it had resounded with the laughter of the many foreigners who visited the French Riviera. Now the luxurious hotels were almost all closed, and the streets were empty and quiet.

The Pension de Londres was a two-story house with comfortable, tastefully furnished rooms. Dohnányi spent most of his time in his room or in the room that Helen and Fräulein Hermine shared, because theirs was the largest. Their room also had a balcony opening into a garden filled with orange and palm trees. Dohnányi sat here in the evenings and played a card game called tarok. This was the only card game he played, because it required no "racking the brains," like bridge. Although it was leisurely, it had enough challenge to not become boring. Dohnányi did not play chess because his father had once warned him against it. "Chess," Frederick von Dohnányi had said, "is too much of a game to be a science, and too much a science to be considered a game."

In the mornings, the Maestro and I would take walks to the beach, which was only a few blocks away. We would sit on a bench in the sunshine, listening to the splashing of the waves as they broke against the shore. It was a wonderful sound, and a great peace came upon our restless spirits. It was also good to feel that we were no longer Displaced Persons; we were free. The authorities on the French Riviera were surprisingly polite to foreigners because they were dependent upon money from tourists. Once Dohnányi phoned the Police to ask when he should come to register. They replied that it was not urgent at all and he could stay as long as he pleased.

It was hard to summon up the Christmas spirit on the evening of 24 December 1947. Outside, flowers were blooming and birds were singing. Nevertheless, Dohnányi placed the tiny Christmas tree he had brought from England on a table, arranged the modest gifts around it, and we sang Christmas songs. Everyone was merry, for a wonderful future had finally opened before us.

Dohnányi's contract for concerts in Buenos Aires was already signed and all he needed were the tickets to Argentina, but we could not relax from our worries. Although it was wonderful to live in Beaulieux-sur-Mer, it was also very expensive. Food in France was scarce and prices were enormous. We also needed clothes, since we had not been able to buy any in Austria. We had to make a trip to Paris for medical examinations and to obtain the various documents required for Argentinean visas. Dohnányi turned to his friend John Kirn in the United States and, using the anticipated revenue from his concerts in Buenos Aires as collateral, asked for a loan from Kirn's bank. Dohnányi's request was immediately granted. It would be hard to recount all the obstacles that hampered our departure at the last minute. The worst obstacle of all was the Italian Consulate, who until the last moment refused to grant a transit visa which we needed because our boat departed from Genoa. For a few days, they did not even recognize our Red Cross Passport. When we finally arrived in Genoa, we spent three days satisfying official formalities.

On the last night, Dohnányi sat at the table of his hotel room writing letters. It was unusual to see him occupied with this because he always detested corresponding and had become quite notorious for not answering letters. Dohnányi was conscious only of things that pleased him; he ignored everything else. People who admired him enough to make allowances for his weaknesses knew that he would not bother himself with inconveniences such as letter writing. His more candid critics objected to his way of looking at life without concern for things for which he felt no interest. When people wondered about his exceptional memory for music,[1] Dohnányi would say, "Some people have the ability to recollect poetry, books, or names. I happen to have a memory for music. Everything else just slips from my mind."

It was not laziness, however, that prevented Dohnányi from writing letters. He found it hard to express himself in words; his idiom was music. It was torture for Dohnányi to complete a letter, because he could not send it if he did not feel that it was perfect. Of course, it took him a great amount of time to complete such a precise work. When he did write, he took pains to do so precisely and in a concise style. "I hate receiving long letters," he would say. "Being a busy man, I usually skim the letter, trying to get to the point of what the writer has to say. It would be unfair for me to do to others what I don't wish for myself." He even tried to avoid telephone calls about important official matters because it was difficult for him to find the required expression rapidly.

---

1. In addition to having memorized all of Beethoven's piano sonatas, Dohnányi could perform by memory numerous pieces for solo piano as well as symphonies, operas, and chamber music on the piano.

As a result, his close friends did not expect him to answer their letters. Many years later, when Dohnányi made a telephone call to a Hungarian artist who had once been a pupil and friend of his, the former student did not recognize Dohnányi's voice until he introduced himself with the words, "It is he who has not answered your letters." The pupil then cried out in happy astonishment, "Ah, my dear Maestro! What a wonderful surprise!"

Dohnányi now took the time to write letters to his relatives, friends, and people from whom he had not heard for a long time but whom he now wished to bid farewell. Dohnányi knew that he was departing from Europe for not just a trip, but forever. He realized that any further visits or concert tours would be short. Although he was as calm and serene as always, it was breaking his heart to be parting from his "dear old Europe."

On 10 March 1948 at two o'clock, in sunny springlike weather, we waited at the port for the departure of the boat *Ravello*. It was a freighter carrying numerous passengers, mostly Italian immigrants who were leaving Europe, as we were, to settle in a strange, unknown land. Dohnányi sat with us in a little restaurant near the harbor for hours, because the ship was not scheduled to leave until late that evening. We were too tired to think and could not wait to board the boat, where we could lie down and rest. It was a magnificent sight to step out from the embarkation building and catch a glimpse of the huge, illuminated ship towering above us. When we went aboard, Dohnányi and the children became fascinated with the traffic on deck. They observed with delight the bustle taking place. These noisy preparations often covered up a loudspeaker that was blaring a gramophone recording of popular songs. It was just starting the song "Sorrento" when Dohnányi noticed that my eyes had filled with tears. "You seem tired," he said gently. He patted my face. "Better go to sleep in your cabin."

I quickly retired, grateful to be spared from the pain I would feel at the moment when the ship actually started toward the New World. Although I knew that this voyage could bring us wealth, fame, and comfort, I feared that we would instead remain unhappy aliens and wayfaring strangers forever.

EIGHT

1948–1949

We arrived in Buenos Aires on 4 April 1948. It was a perfect spring afternoon: the sun was shining and the plants were in full bloom. Dohnányi was welcomed by a solemn reception that included Árpád Bubik as well as several Argentinean journalists and musicians. Mr. Bubik smiled broadly when he told Dohnányi about the splendid house he had rented for us in Martinez, the elegant villa quarter of Buenos Aires. It had been difficult to find a house; lodgings were scarce because of the rent control enforced by the Government. As it was, we had to secretly pay a much higher rent then the regulations permitted. During the journey to our new home, Mr. Bubik told us about the cultural environment of Buenos Aires.

"Are the people here musical?" I asked.

Mr. Bubik shrugged his shoulders. "Who can tell? It seems like they are not very interested in music, but they do like piano playing. With good publicity a concert can be turned into a fashionable social event, and they will stream to it. It's good that you are a pianist, Maestro, because, as I told you, the people here prefer the piano to all other music instruments."

We were nevertheless concerned, because Dohnányi had never appeared in Argentina, and his records were not even for sale here. Other than the avid music lovers, the Argentineans knew little about Dohnányi. We also began to realize that Mr. Bubik could have done more to ensure the success of Dohnányi's recitals. For one thing, no season tickets had been sold for the six concerts. Although such subscriptions were customary in Argentina, the overly enthusiastic Mr. Bubik did not consider them necessary, and, having found difficulty in arranging them, had dropped the matter. "The hall will be sold out whether there are season tickets or not," he claimed.

In the meanwhile, we had no money. We had come to Argentina with first-class tickets because Mr. Bubik had told us that it was socially disastrous to be considered poor, especially if one was an artist. He had instructed Dohnányi to carefully avoid any sign that he was not financially well off. We had financed all our expenses with the loan from John Kirn and were now committed to paying a high rent for a luxurious house that we also had to furnish. "I could find a job," I volunteered. "I have learned to speak Spanish almost fluently. This would help."

"God forbid!" Mr. Bubik warned in horror. "What would people say if Dohnányi's niece had to work for a few wretched pesos? Class differences and conventions are more extreme here than in Europe. You may write books, if you would like, but there will be no need for money. It will stream to the Maestro."

Unfortunately, the first concert was not scheduled until the end of the month. After some discussion it was decided that Mr. Bubik would secretly take the jewelry I had safeguarded through all the disasters to a pawnbroker. Dohnányi insisted that his pearl tiepin and gold cufflinks should also be pawned, but we flatly refused. All of our bitterness vanished when we saw the elegant, richly decorated shops of Martinez. We all stopped in amazement to stare at a roast pork displayed in a store window, surrounded by all kinds of delicacies that made our mouths water. "Is all this for sale?" Dohnányi asked wonderingly.

"Naturally," Mr. Bubik said, laughing. "And without coupons. Let's buy some of it for your first supper in your new home!"

This new home was a splendid villa surrounded by a small but exquisite garden. With its balconies, huge rooms, and broad marble stairway, it looked like a luxurious home in a Hollywood movie. With Dohnányi leading we went from floor to floor and from room to room of our wonderful new home. We stopped for a moment on the spacious balcony adjoining his study and looked up at the stars. Dohnányi frowned. "I do not like these stars," he said. "They disturb me. I am too accustomed to the sky we had in Europe. I wonder if I shall ever be able to create under the strange constellations in this New World." Mr. Bubik had already furnished the dining room, of course on credit, and there were comfortable beds in each bedroom. While Fräulein Hermine warmed up the pork and whipped the cream in the marble kitchen, we discussed where to buy the rest of the furniture. The house had to be furnished quickly, because numerous important people belonging to the Press or music organizations wanted to visit Dohnányi in the following week.

Dohnányi's first recital in Argentina took place on 25 April 1948 in the superb Teatro Colón. Much depended on this performance, and Mr. Bubik was afraid that Dohnányi would lose his usual composure and become nervous. Nevertheless, Dohnányi seemed calm and confident when he appeared on the stage, and the crowd that filled the theater received him with courtesy. "They are a cold audience," I whispered to Mr. Bubik, who sat next to me in the box. "I'm afraid he'll be distressed by their indifference." Dohnányi, however, regarded their attitude as a challenge. For him this concert was a battle that had to be won.

The first number was Haydn's Variations in F Minor. It was played perfectly and received a polite, but cautious, applause. Beethoven's Sonata in C Minor, op. 111, was accepted with a little more appreciation. A Chopin Nocturne and Impromptu followed, and then came Liszt's *Legénde*, "St. François de Paule marchant sur les flots" (St. Francis of Paola Walks on the Waves). When this powerful piece resounded, the audience's attitude underwent a noticeable change. Their eyes lost their indifference and were filled with tension. There was such a silence that when Dohnányi came to the pause in the second part an audible sigh came from the audience. Then, after the gripping finish, they broke into a spontaneous roar of applause. From that point on the audience was fascinated. Dohnányi's own compositions, including the F-sharp Minor Rhapsody from *Vier Rhapsodien,* the delicate Scherzino from *Six Pieces* for piano, the Adagio ma non troppo movement from *Ruralia Hungarica,* and his arrangement of Schubert's *Valses nobles* won their hearts. When the recital ended, they streamed, just as an audience had long ago in Hungary, to the stage to request one encore after the other. The next day Mr. Bubik arrived triumphantly with a pile of newspapers. The leading paper, *La Prensa,* was most appreciative, and the others were all enthusiastic.[1] The whole family joyfully cried out, "What a triumph!"

Mr. Bubik smiled happily. "Yes, they are all excellent reviews," he agreed, but then he became more serious. "But there is an article in an obscure, third-class paper considered to be communist that makes the most outrageous attacks against the Maestro." He spread out on the table a rather small review that contained an insulting remark in each line. It declared Dohnányi to be hideous in appearance, disagreeable, and haughty. It criticized his ways and manners, attacked his compositions, spoke with ironical contempt of his age, and of course, did not fail to point to his allegedly incriminating political background.

"What harm could such a silly scribble do?" I asked indignantly. "Everyone knows that it's only meant to harm."

"It can do much harm," Mr. Bubik said with disappointment. "Maybe not here in Buenos Aires, but in other places where they've not heard the Maestro play." Months later, when Mr. Bubik went to Brazil to organize concerts for Dohnányi, the agency received him with boiling hatred, waving this article in his face. "Is it this criminal and anti-Semite you wish to force upon us?" they shouted with contempt. "We won't have anything to do with him, we assure you!" Poor Mr. Bubik had just as little chance of giving proofs and explanations as we had received in Austria.

---

1. The *La Prensa* review appeared on 26 April 1948; see Appendix C.

In spite of his great initial success in the Teatro Colón, luck seemed to be against Dohnányi in Argentina. At the next performance, on 6 May, the theater was only half-filled; the third, on 12 May, turned out to be a complete failure. Months later, after Dohnányi had become more acquainted with the Argentinean social attitude, he began to realize that this failure might have been because no season tickets had been sold. The concerts had subsequently lost their importance for those who would have attended them as social events. Those who would return only for the sake of good music were poor and could not afford to buy tickets for each of the six concerts. Furthermore, Dohnányi's publicity was not sufficient for a country where people knew little about him. Without the necessary funds, however, Mr. Bubik could do no more; he was only a refugee himself. Mr. Bubik also had to compete with the two powerful agencies that controlled all of the concert engagements in Argentina. He could have served Dohnányi better had he joined them in some way, or at least obtained their cooperation. Instead, his rivals made use of the hostile article, publicizing political accusations that made the Jews, who comprised the majority of the musical audience in the city, antagonistic toward Dohnányi.

Even the weather seemed to be against Dohnányi. On the days when the second and third concerts were given, rain streamed down without pause. In Buenos Aires, when there was a rain of this intensity, practically all traffic stopped, people were not expected to go to work, and schools were canceled. In addition, the humidity affected Dohnányi mentally and physically. Instead of his usual relaxed state when he played, he experienced considerable strain. This effort produced a soreness in his arm that swelled and bothered him for several days after his performances.

Dohnányi's arm was still swollen when he left for Montevideo for concerts that had been arranged for 4 and 11 June 1948. Mr. Bubik had finally acknowledged defeat and failure and had canceled the final three performances in Buenos Aires. Nobody could blame him; neither he nor Dohnányi could advance any more money for the expenses of further concerts in the Teatro Colón. Dohnányi's sore arm also forced him to cancel the first of two booked performances in Porto Alegre. He agreed to perform the second recital, on 26 June, only when Mr. Bubik urged him desperately to go. The tickets for this concert were sold out, and, after the first performance had been canceled, the prices of the seats had been almost doubled.

Before the 26 June 1948 recital, a reception took place in the castle of the Governor, whose wife occupied the balcony with her court during the concert. She was a music lover, as was her son, who told us that he had studied many of Dohnányi's compositions. The rest of the audience contained many appreciative listeners. Many Italians, Germans, and Hungarians had immigrated to Porto Alegre and had since enriched the cultural and artistic life of this fascinating city. Their applause must have compensated Dohnányi for the frigid reception in Buenos Aires. After the performance, a banquet was given in Dohnányi's honor in a luxurious restaurant.

Dohnányi also performed on 4 July in Montevideo, on 20 July in Rosario, and on 31 July in Córdoba. Unfortunately, Argentina was a country with few big cities where lucrative concerts could be given. Until Dohnányi's concert tour in the United States in November, which had only recently been arranged, we had no means of improving our financial situation. In the meantime, we had to maintain an appearance of wealth. We continued to attend parties and entertain those who came to see us, while wondering how we were going to pay for our plane tickets to the United States. "You must join Sadaic," Mr. Bubik advised. "This is the performing rights society that collects royalties here. Its members will be delighted if you leave the A.K.M., and I am sure they will give you a considerable sum as an advance against your future royalties and those still held by the Custodian Office of Enemy Property." Mr. Bubik tried to help us by hounding the Sadaic to get an advance, but they were so discouraging that Dohnányi withdrew his application.

❦

One morning in the middle of August two visitors arrived. One was George Serafini, a young Hungarian violinist who had once been a member of the Budapest Philharmonic and was now the concertmaster of a new orchestra in the North Argentinean town of Tucumán. The other visitor was Alex Conrad, who was the Director of a music school in Tucumán. "Tucumán?" Dohnányi listened in surprise. "I have heard of this place. Someone mentioned that concerts of a rather high level are given there."

"Tucumán is a place of high culture," Mr. Conrad affirmed, somewhat hurt by our ignorance concerning his city. "It also has a historical significance. It's probably the most important spot in our Republic, because it is where we declared our independence. Tucumán is also the home to a fine university with a powerful reputation. In particular, its faculty for architecture is world famous and acknowledged as the best in South America. We lack a music faculty, but now we are going to establish one. This is why we have to come to you, Maestro, because you are the man best able to help us."

"What is it that you want me to do?" Dohnányi asked. Although he was interested in the fact that a new music school, a new place for culture and art, would come into existence in some faraway North Argentinean city, he did not understand what this had to do with him.

"You may do whatever you would like to do," Director Conrad said, "that would be useful to our new institution."

Dohnányi still did not understand what they wanted of him, so Director Conrad explained that the Dean of Fine Arts, a man named Parpagnoli, who was also Director of the Institute of Superior Arts, wanted Dohnányi to become the General Director of the new Music School of the Universidad Nacional de Tucumán. "It will become the most prestigious music school in South America," Mr. Serafini affirmed.

When we had come to Argentina, Dohnányi had decided to give up teaching, which he found exhausting, to spend the rest of his life giving concerts and composing, because there was still much he intended to create. "I am sorry, but I cannot accept this offer," he said. "When I accept an obligation, I fulfill it to the best of my ability. But I am fully aware of how much administrative work a Director has to do, and no time would remain for my music. Besides, such work needs a younger man in possession of all his energies."

Director Conrad exchanged glances with Mr. Serafini. Then he quickly made a new proposal. "Because it's your name and personality that are so important to us," he explained, "we can arrange things in any manner you would prefer. You could have the title, distinction, and salary of a General Director, while someone, like me, would be Director under you, carrying out your ideas and plans. After you have organized our foundation, you can devote yourself to teaching only advanced pupils and have as much free time for your concert tours and compositions as you need."

Dohnányi was satisfied with this arrangement, and Director Conrad promised to send him a plane ticket for 4 September so that he could come to Tucumán to sign the contract and begin his work. Because I was going to accompany Dohnányi to Tucumán, we would have to pay the 500 pesos for my ticket. Unfortunately, we did not have the money or any means of getting it. We did not want to confide our distressing situation to our Argentinean friends, and our Hungarian friends, who would have understood our difficulties, were refugees themselves, struggling with their own difficulties. Finally, a Hungarian lady who was a friend of ours explained matters to the Reverend Luthor, a Hungarian priest who had once been the Ambassador to the Vatican. He immediately offered the money as a loan.

We counted the days until 4 September and were very disappointed when the day came and we had not heard from Tucumán. We knew that Argentineans, although they were nice and amiable, could be somewhat unreliable. This was caused by their code of etiquette; to say "no" in Argentina was considered impolite. One instead had to say *mañana* (tomorrow) or "Como no" (Why not) with an engaging smile, even if the request could not be granted. Although Argentineans knew each other and could judge whether a promise could be trusted or not, we ignorant foreigners could not. After 6 September came and went with no word from Tucumán, I gave up hope. Dohnányi, however, trusted Director Conrad's promise and felt that George Serafini would have found some means of informing us if the plans had fallen through. Dohnányi phoned Dean Parpagnoli and was told that the plane ticket had been mailed to the wrong address; it had been sent to Sanisidro instead of Martinez. They expressed their eagerness to see Dohnányi, and arrangements were made for us to leave the next day.

On 8 September 1948 the Maestro and I arrived in Tucumán.[2] We were welcomed by a committee of high-ranking officials, including Director Conrad and Dean Parpagnoli, who was a rather young, tall, dark-haired Italian with a beard. Dohnányi was introduced to the Conductor of the new Orchestra, which, although sponsored by the University, was a professional body consisting mostly of famous European artists who had sought refuge in Argentina. While Buenos Aires was an international city, Tucumán was a town that still preserved its ancient Indian traditions. As we rode in the Dean's car through the narrow cobblestone streets, we saw beautiful Spanish houses with spacious patios and trees covered with mauve blossoms that seemed like colorful clouds. At last we came to the University buildings, which were grouped close together because there was a shortage of space in the old town. Many of the libraries and other buildings were a distance away, among the houses.

In the evening we were invited to a cheerful party at the home of a Hungarian family that had been living in Tucumán for a year. Other Hungarians were present who had been there for more than twenty years, and we had an interesting time exchanging memories. Dohnányi observed wonderingly the appetites of the people around us who were devouring dish after dish. It was customary in Argentinean restaurants that one could eat as many dishes as one wished for the price of a single meal, and it seemed that people were able to eat through entire menus.

The next day, when Dohnányi signed his contract, he had the feeling that he was starting a very interesting period of his life. "Great things will happen here," he told me with a beaming face. "The Dean told me that the University intends to build a magnificent town a thousand feet up the slope of the mountain at the foot of which the city stands. An elevated railway is already being constructed. They intend this university town to be quite wonderful and unique."

"But when will this be accomplished?" I inquired.

"The Dean says very soon. The material has already been taken up to the site. The rest of the work will be easy. Only more money is needed, which the Government will surely grant."

---

2. The rest of our family would not move to Tucumán until 22 October.

Dohnányi worked with characteristic thoroughness on his plan for the new Music School. It improved the existing Argentinean educational system to accommodate an international music faculty. Letters poured in from musicians who were applying for positions in the new faculty, and Dohnányi carefully selected teachers who could ensure that the institution would be of the highest quality. He chose many great foreign musicians, including a Hungarian-born violinist who had once spoken out against him. It was due to this man's evil activities that a radio engagement sponsored by General Electric had been canceled. The violinist had said that twenty years earlier Dohnányi had been on a committee that had opposed his becoming a member of the Budapest Philharmonic because he was Jewish. Dohnányi was absolutely indifferent to one's religion, race, or nationality, so if he had spoken out against this man, it was only because the violinist had not been a good musician. "Don't you remember that this man ruined your chances of a lucrative engagement?" friends reminded Dohnányi.

"He was already among the candidates of the University," Dohnányi said coolly. "And I agree and have put him on my list. From the reports, I judge that he must now be a good musician, and our faculty needs such men. My personal feelings shouldn't influence me when I am working on plans for the general welfare. How can you expect me to be so narrow-minded?"

The violinist was accepted on the faculty of Tucumán. Two years later, when he became disgusted with the climate as well as the authorities of the University and left abruptly, the only person to whom he said farewell was Dohnányi. When they shook hands, he said simply, "Thank you, Maestro." These words may have been a vague apology for the injustice he had once ignorantly committed.

An all-Beethoven concert, the first performance of the new Orchestra, took place on 7 November, with Dohnányi as the soloist in Beethoven's Third Piano Concerto. The house was packed, and the concert was a striking success. Everyone in Tucumán was talking about the wonderful performance, which was also broadcast. Nevertheless, Dohnányi began to lose his enthusiasm for his new job. He realized that this atmosphere was far from the ones to which he had been accustomed in Berlin and Budapest. Dean Parpagnoli, who as Director del Instituto Superior de Arte (Director of the Superior Institute of Art) and Decano de la Facultad de Culturales y Artes (Dean of the Faculty of Culture and Art) had to approve all of Dohnányi's plans, did not appreciate the Dohnányi's directness, who, ignoring "mañana" and "como no," expressed his opinion openly and briskly. Relations became so strained between them that Dohnányi refused to have anything to do with the Orchestra and limited his activities to the affairs of the music faculty. Of course, it would have been easier and much more profitable if Dohnányi had simply appeased the Dean, but this would have been contrary to Dohnányi's principles. "Throughout my life I have always said what I thought and stuck to my principles," he said. "I am certainly not going to change at seventy-two."

We avoided further friction by leaving Tucumán on 9 November and returning to Buenos Aires, where we were to stay for four days before our departure to the United States. On the last day, Dohnányi collapsed with severe food poisoning, which he had contracted by eating some tainted meat at a party on the previous night. Two doctors kept vigil by his bed the whole afternoon and evening, treating his high fever with powerful drugs and injections. At night he felt better, but he was still so weak and ailing that our departure the next morning seemed out of the question. With the help of his devoted doctors and aided by a strong constitution and an even stronger will, however, he was able to make the journey.

❦

Andrew Schulhof and his wife Belle were waiting at the airport in New York. They took us to the Great Northern Hotel, where we discussed Dohnányi's U.S. tour. Mr. Schulhof had arranged numerous concerts, recitals, and master classes for Dohnányi.[3] "I am glad you have come at last," Mr. Schulhof said warmly. "Perhaps you remember that ten years ago in Budapest I tried to persuade you to take a most lucrative trip to this country and accept the conductorship of a most eminent orchestra here. You warded me off, saying that you were too tired to undertake the journey and the job."

"True," Dohnányi nodded. "I wanted to live a quiet life and intended to dedicate myself to my home and my compositions. But Fate has willed otherwise. As you see, I have lost all I once possessed. Although I hate to do so, I must now start working again to make money." He did not say this as a complaint, simply as a fact. He even accompanied his words with a smile.

Everything seemed wonderful in New York. Dohnányi liked the superb technical inventions such as elevators, cars, refrigerators, and tape recorders, and he especially appreciated the high standards of concerts and the enthusiasm of the audiences. "The United States has made tremendous progress in music since I was last here," he said with approval. In the United States, he felt nearer to his old life in Europe than he ever had in South America, partly because he could see the stars just as he had once seen them at home. He also enjoyed the cold winter, with its blanket of fine white

3. During the 1920s, Andrew Schulhof had arranged several concerts in Berlin for Dohnányi. In 1938, Dohnányi had helped Schulhof acquire the funds necessary to flee to the United States.

snow, even if it felt twice as biting as before because he was no longer accustomed to it.

We found out that even in the United States some sparks of the old accusations had spread from Austria. In March and April 1947, *The New York Times* had published four articles about Dohnányi. The first, written in a hostile tone, called him "an excellent pianist, but a mediocre composer and conductor" and accused him of using all his power in Hungary to prevent his "rivals," Bartók and Kodály, from succeeding. Egon Kenton, who had been the violist in the original Waldbauer String Quartet in Budapest, indignantly answered all these accusations, deflating and destroying them one by one with the simplest arguments. A week later Emil Havas called attention to an accusation in a Hungarian paper, *Az Ember,* which was published in America that called Dohnányi a war criminal. This was followed by a firm declaration by Edward Kilenyi, Jr., that Dohnányi had been completely cleared by the American Army.[4]

After Dohnányi read these articles, he asked Mr. Schulhof what kind of paper this *Az Ember* was that published such lies. Mr. Schulhof told us that it was a weekly Hungarian paper edited by a Hungarian-born Jew named Ferenc Göndör. We later found out from friends that Göndör, whose real name was Nathan Krauss, had founded the paper in Hungary under the communist regime of Béla Kun after World War I. When the Horthy Government had come into power, he had fled to the United States and obtained shelter. The Schulhofs informed us that he had attacked Dohnányi in his paper in such a vulgar and insulting manner that they did not even want to show Dohnányi these articles for fear they would excite or enrage him.

"We should sue this man!" Dohnányi broke out with indignation.

"It would take plenty of money," Mr. Schulhof explained, "which unfortunately you don't have at this moment. Besides, even if you were to win, and I don't doubt you would, you probably couldn't get a single dollar from this man. I'm sure he doesn't possess anything." Dohnányi decided to ignore the whole affair because he thought that very few people would read this paper. Besides, we were in a hurry to leave for Boston for a recital at Wellesley College.

❧

On 17 November 1948, the afternoon before the concert at Wellesley, the wife of David Barnett, who was the Concert Manager, wanted to see

---

4. The four articles in *The New York Times* had appeared on 9 March, 16 March, 23 March, and 20 April 1947; see Appendix C.

Dohnányi. Because he was resting in his hotel room with a bad headache, I went to meet her. "I have some bad news," she said uneasily. "It's very unpleasant indeed. Three days ago *The Boston Sunday Herald* published this attack on Dohnányi." She held out to me the paper. "Do you see this headline: 'Jewish Agencies Strongly Oppose Dohnanyi's Wellesley Concert'? The writer says that the Maestro was a . . . well . . . a war criminal."[5]

I gasped and then flew into a rage. Here it was again, this horrible persecuting accusation, which never stopped but grew new heads like the Hydra when the sword of truth cut the old ones off.

"I cannot understand," she complained, "why this article appeared only now, three days before the concert, although the date was announced more than two months ago and everybody knew about it!"

I knew why. Mr. Göndör's disgraceful articles had been sent to the Jewish Agency. The strange thing was that its members had credited the charges without personally looking into the matter. I read the article and was perplexed. What could I say about the absurd lies it contained? Not one of them was even near the truth. It seemed as though Dohnányi had been publicly ruined and nothing could be done to clear him. I had to struggle to keep my self-control.

"Surely this isn't true," the lady said, somewhat embarrassed. She could read from my expression of indignation that there must be some mistake.

"From the first to the last word, they are the most absurd lies," I said flatly. "Dohnányi never belonged to any party, whether it be Arrow Cross, or anything else. He had no connection whatever with Szálasi; he saw him only twice at public meetings where more then two hundred people were present, including those who are now musical leaders in Hungary. And the most reliable source they quote, *Az Ember,* is a paper of which I should not give my opinion."

"Can you prove that what they affirm here isn't true?" she asked, hopefully.

I thought for a moment and then remembered that Dohnányi had brought a statement that he had officially resigned as Director at the Budapest Academy in 1943 and the document written by the Hungarian Government stating that he was not on the official list of war criminals. "I can prove it," I said triumphantly, telling her about the documents. I quickly hurried back to the room and returned with it.

Before the concert, David Barnett read the documents to the audience. It is to the great credit of Americans that very few had returned their tickets after reading that incriminating article. Dohnányi was then received with

5. This article appeared on 14 November 1948; see Appendix C.

warm applause, and the performance was a complete success. After it was over, the audience streamed into the artist's room to congratulate him.[6]

The next day the New England Conservatory held a reception for Dohnányi in their Music Hall. The Director, Harrison Keller, who had studied violin in Berlin while Dohnányi was Professor there, led him onto the stage and introduced him with warm words. Dohnányi received a standing ovation and then sat in one of the four armchairs placed on the stage. The other chairs were occupied by the Director and two Professors, Miklós Schwalb and Boris Goldovsky, both former pupils of Dohnányi. The program was a touching event: Mr. Schwalb and Mr. Goldovsky played two of Dohnányi's *Vier Rhapsodien,* and Dohnányi himself played the other two. Although he still wore a suit he had brought from Hungary because he refused to buy anything new for himself while our funds were low, his appearance had such a dignity and distinction that everyone was impressed. Mr. Goldovsky confessed that he had never felt as nervous and embarrassed at a performance as he did when he played the Rhapsody in the presence of his former teacher.

Returning to New York, Dohnányi told Mr. Schulhof what had happened before the Wellesley concert. Mr. Schulhof was extremely upset and now, at last, showed Dohnányi the 15 March 1948 issue of *Az Ember* as well as a more recent issue attacking Dohnányi.[7] To avoid further trouble, Mr. Schulhof came with us to Detroit, where Dohnányi was scheduled to perform his Second Piano Concerto with the Detroit Symphony Orchestra conducted by Karl Krueger. In Detroit, however, not a word was mentioned about this ominous affair. The two performances, which took place on 25 and 26 November 1948, were unforgettable triumphs.[8] Dohnányi also had the pleasure of reuniting with General Reinhardt and John Kirn with his young wife Martha. On the following day Mr. Schulhof returned to New York while we drove with the Kirns to their home in Lancaster, Ohio, where we were to stay each weekend in December and during Christmas while Dohnányi led three weeks of master classes at Ohio University in Athens, Ohio.

❧

The Kirns told us that the President of Ohio University, Dr. John Calhoun Baker, had also received some warnings about Dohnányi. As soon as

---

6. Reviews of this concert were published in *The Boston Globe* and *The Boston Herald* on 18 November 1948 (see Appendix C for the latter review). This was followed the next day by a letter to the editor of *The Boston Herald* attacking Dohnányi (see Appendix C).

7. Two of the three vile articles that appeared in the 20 November 1948 *Az Ember* can be found in Appendix C. They were written in Hungarian, of course, but anyone trying to translate them would have difficulties; some of the words were so vulgar that I was unable to find them in a dictionary.

8. See Appendix C for a review that appeared in *The Detroit News* on 26 November 1948.

it was publicly announced that Dohnányi was booked to appear at the University, allegations of Dohnányi's political crimes had reached Dr. Baker. Naturally, the President had become rather concerned and, knowing that John Kirn was closely acquainted with Dohnányi, had turned to him for an explanation. John had all the necessary documents in his possession and was able to give the President a true picture of this ominous affair.

Dohnányi, Martha Kirn, and I were worried on the morning of 29 November when we entered the President's office. As soon as Dr. Baker welcomed us, however, our concern vanished. His tall figure, his composed attitude, and every word he spoke showed dignity, while his eyes expressed kindness. With a straightforward openness and witty remarks, he quickly dissolved the tense atmosphere. There was something so firm and trustworthy in Dr. Baker's character that one had the feeling of security in his company. He was the type who stood up without hesitation for those he cherished. What aroused Dohnányi's admiration and made him feel so close to him, however, was his sense of humor. Dr. Baker not only found a solution for almost every problem, but he also tried to ease one's mind with a good-natured remark that aroused merriment and laughter. Dohnányi began to feel a deep affection, as well as confidence and respect, for Dr. Baker. These feelings grew deeper when the President invited us to his home to introduce us to his wife.

Elizabeth Baker was in every way an exceptional woman. She was noble, gentle, highly musical, and intelligent—in every way worthy of her husband. She had been a music student in her youth and had spent much time in Europe to develop her voice. Now she became a true friend to us both, and their home, which was cheered by their three charming daughters, became a place to which Dohnányi would return every year as "permanent Guest Professor" at the University.

Dohnányi made several friends in Athens. We spent many pleasant hours discussing music with the Director of the Music School, Dr. Thomas Gorton, and his wife in their home. Dohnányi also enjoyed working with American youth, whom he found to be somewhat more familiar with their superiors than he was accustomed to, but still just as affectionate and loyal. The students displayed a passionate eagerness and listened to Dohnányi's playing with awe. Dohnányi always liked young people, and now, surrounded by them, he felt lighthearted once again.

Dohnányi's visits to Ohio University consisted of a one-hour Convocation recital, an evening recital, a lecture, and several master classes for Composition and Piano, to which the general public was also admitted. During the master classes, Dohnányi would sit on the stage with the pupil who was playing. After the performance, Dohnányi would critique it thoroughly. Sometimes Dohnányi would play the piece himself, or parts of it, so that everybody could judge the difference. Dohnányi was happy to be able to pass on his knowledge and experience to the young artists.

On one occasion Dohnányi gave a lecture on sight-reading. Although it took him several hours to prepare this lecture, he welcomed the opportunity to show young people the importance of sight-reading. He explained that sight-reading was not a special gift and could be acquired by anyone who had musical intelligence. On another occasion he lectured on Romanticism in Beethoven's piano sonatas.[9] Through these lectures Dohnányi discovered that he was able to speak fluently and with a sincerity and warmth that delighted his audience, who did not seem to mind his slips and grammatical errors. Sometimes his witty and humorous remarks made people burst out with laughter. Lecturing became easy for him, and in the future he undertook it willingly.

President John Baker was not a fanatical music lover, but he did appreciate good music. He loved Dohnányi's playing and even listened to him when he was practicing. His respect for the performer was so great that he would not tolerate the slightest noise or whispering at such times. Dr. Baker's favorite composition was the "Träumerei" (Reverie) from Schumann's *Kinderscenen* (Scenes from Childhood), op. 15, and Dohnányi often played him this piece in the evenings. Sometimes the President's party guests became absorbed in conversation and delayed their departure, even though their hosts were tired. Dr. Baker would remark in his direct, somewhat mocking tone, "Well, ladies and gentlemen, we had better ask Maestro Dohnányi to play us the 'Träumerei' so that we may sleep well." Dohnányi would smilingly sit down at the piano, and afterwards the guests would leave in response to the gentle hint.

Noticing the indefatigable energy with which his friend supervised even the smallest detail of his beloved University's activities, Dohnányi tried to persuade him to relax occasionally. "In Argentina people certainly don't rush in their work as you do," he remarked. Dohnányi himself preferred a slower pace of life.

"Good for them," Dr. Baker would answer, in his mocking way, with a shrug of his shoulders. "But unfortunately I cannot afford that way of living. Not unless I was granted a life of at least 150 years."

We spent the Christmas holidays in Lancaster, in the cozy home of the Kirns, which was furnished with Martha's antique Viennese furniture and decorated with artistic paintings, delicate china figures, and embroideries that gave Dohnányi the feeling, especially in the evenings when we talked about the past, that he was once more in his beloved Europe. On Christmas

---

9. These lectures can be found in Appendix B.

Eve we celebrated a European Christmas with the Kirns. On the following morning we went to the home of John's parents for an American Christmas celebration.

One musical activity followed another. On 29 December Dohnányi gave a recital in Columbus, Ohio. He performed again on 5 January 1949 in Austin, Texas, and 9 January in El Paso. On 10 January Dohnányi joined Frederic Balázs, who had once been a very talented student at the Budapest Academy, in giving a recital of violin sonatas in Wichita Falls, Texas. Dohnányi's recital and master class in Fort Worth, Texas, on 12 January were so successful that the Dean of Music at Texas Christian University invited him to come there as Professor and Composer-in-Residence. On 20 January Dohnányi performed at Marycrest College in Davenport, Iowa, and on 23 January he played the *Variationen über ein Kinderlied* with the Tri-City Symphony Orchestra in Davenport. On 24 January Dohnányi gave a recital in Iowa City. This was followed by a master class and two recitals in Kansas City from 30 January to 5 February. Each concert was reviewed with the highest praises.[10]

One of the most pleasant events during this tour was a four-day visit to the home of the Waldbauers in Iowa City. Imre Waldbauer was a fine Hungarian violinist who had once been the leader of the Waldbauer Quartet. He had left Hungary a few years after we had and was now Professor at the University of Iowa in Iowa City. Although he and Dohnányi talked about unforgettable times that were gone forever, they spoke smilingly, almost serenely, and never bitterly or resentfully. I admired Mrs. Waldbauer's sense of humor, courage, and perseverance in building a new life. Like us, the Waldbauers had lost everything. Although Mrs. Waldbauer was struggling hard to keep up their house, she could always see the humorous side of life. She was extremely amusing, and we had to laugh at her story of their misfortunes, even though it was tragic and we were near to tears with grief.

The U.S. tour was pleasant for Dohnányi. He enjoyed meeting people, teaching enthusiastic and talented youngsters, and giving concerts. Above all, however, he enjoyed the comfort, high standard, and security of the American way of life. If one had a job here, one could more or less rely upon it regardless of the political party that was in power. "America is a

10. Selected articles, taken from *The Columbus Citizen* (30 December 1948), the *Wichita Falls Record News* (11 January 1949), the *Fort Worth Star-Telegram* (13 January 1949), and *The Kansas City Star* (6 February 1949), can be found in Appendix C.

wonderful place," he used to say with deep appreciation. "I have known this country for fifty years. Its merits far outweigh its faults, and I must say that I am very fond of it and its people." As usual, Dohnányi made enemies as well as friends in the United States. He could not help it; it was in his nature to stir up people. Those who were in his company could not remain neutral or lukewarm. Either they admired his greatness, his frankness and outspokenness, and his realization of what his art and experience meant to humanity, or in their pettiness they became jealous and envious because they could not compete with him.

When the tour came to an end in the middle of February, we returned to New York to join the Schulhofs. Dohnányi was in high spirits, thrilled with memories of the delightful events we had experienced. The news Mr. Schulhof had for him was quite a shock: Mr. Göndör had continued his filthy intrigues and accusations. He had translated his abominable articles into English and turned them over to the American Veterans Committee. Mr. Schulhof had subsequently requested Leon Goldstein, in the name of this organization, to start an investigation. Mr. Schulhof was optimistic that it would be easy to prove that these slanders were all based upon lies. He was going to start by using the declaration Dohnányi had officially made during his stay in Detroit.[11]

While we were in New York City, Dohnányi and Kilenyi recorded the two-piano arrangement of *Suite en valse* for His Master's Voice. On 17 February 1949, the Maestro and I were married. Our friendship and love of so many years had convinced us both that we wanted to stay together for the rest of our lives. As soon as he had divorced his former wife, Dohnányi had made arrangements for us to get married. This had to happen in the United States because Argentina still had Catholic laws under which they would not grant divorces. Considering the disturbing situation caused by Mr. Göndör, it was only natural that Dohnányi wanted us to marry in the greatest secrecy. Therefore, except for the Schulhofs, not even his closest friends were informed. He only asked the Kirns to come because John Kirn was to be my witness. In Austria, Dohnányi had been Martha's witness at her wedding, and we knew they would be happy to return the favor. Mr. Schulhof was to be Dohnányi's witness. Kilenyi was the only invited guest to share our great moment, but even he was not told in advance what was to take place. He came to the registrar's office at Mr. Schulhof's request, but could not understand why Dohnányi happened to be there so early in the morning, why the Kirns had suddenly arrived from Ohio, and why we all seemed in such a ceremonial mood.

11. This declaration was signed on 26 November 1948; see Appendix A.

❧

On 24 February we flew from New York back to Buenos Aires. We had delayed our return for a few days because just after our wedding I had fallen sick with a grave attack of influenza. Even during our journey I was feverish and had a tormenting cough. A most touching reception was given to us at the airport by our close friend Emanuel Puente, who was a Radio Director and a music lover, his wife, and other friends, who told us that my historical novel *Tambien dios lo quiere* (God Wants It as Well) was to be published by the Circulo Literario in Buenos Aires.

At our hotel we read letters from Fräulein Hermine and the children, who wrote that they were practically penniless. After we had left Tucumán, the University had paid no salaries to any of its employees. It was not uncommon in South America for state offices to not pay salaries for several months and then pay their arrears in one sum. It was also disappointing to read that they were unable to find a larger apartment, which meant that in the oppressive heat we would be packed into three tiny, airless rooms. After the luxurious, comfortable hotels that the Maestro and I had enjoyed in the United States, this prospect was not alluring. Although we wanted to hurry to Tucumán, we were told that flight reservations had to be made four weeks in advance. With the help of influential friends, however, we were able to obtain tickets within a few days.

When we reached Tucumán on the evening of 4 March 1949, there was a crowd waiting at the airport to welcome Dohnányi. While we were receiving this cheering demonstration of appreciation, we were almost bowled over by the damp heat that enveloped us as we descended from the plane. When we got home, we found that the subtropical autumn, which we had never experienced before, had practically turned our tiny rooms into ovens. Furthermore, the political affairs had become so shaky that some of our acquaintances were asking Dohnányi to help them get jobs in the reliable security of the United States.

The next morning Dohnányi came home from his office depressed. The construction of the wonderful university town had not started yet, and the prospects of it ever starting had become almost hopeless. Although numerous students had enrolled in the Music School and were eager to start their studies, there was no building. Dean Parpagnoli had tried to reassure Dohnányi that the cornerstones had already been laid for the music building, but Dohnányi found not one pebble in the undisturbed meadow where cows were peacefully grazing.

In addition to the problem of the University still withholding salaries, we could not find another apartment. Although Dohnányi had purchased some land before his United States tour, he was not allowed to build a house. There were also no apartments available within the city, and residing outside it was impossible because one could not obtain a car and the buses were irregular and always overcrowded. We could not even obtain a telephone for our apartment, although Dohnányi held the prestigious position of the General Director of the Music School.

Dohnányi's annoyance was increased by the constant friction and conflicts with Dean Parpagnoli, who now seemed anxious to reverse all of Dohnányi's decisions. For example, the Dean had formerly agreed that the Orchestra's concerts should be free to the public. Later, as the expense of maintaining the Orchestra grew, he charged high prices for tickets and even made the students pay. Dohnányi protested that those who attended the Music School should at least be allowed free seats in the balcony. The Dean opposed this until two hours before the performance, at which time he conceded that students could be admitted to the balcony with no charge. It was too late, however, to inform anyone about this sudden decision, and the seats remained empty. The next day Dean Parpagnoli triumphantly told Dohnányi that it was useless to fight for the rights of students because they would not make use of such privileges anyway. There were many other clashes, especially over the selection of the faculty members for the Music School, and the relationship between the Dean and Dohnányi grew worse, almost hostile.

Eventually Dohnányi lost all his enthusiasm to create an outstanding music institution. Alex Conrad, who had come to Buenos Aires with George Serafini to offer the position to Dohnányi, had exactly the same opinion about matters. Although Conrad loyally sided with Dohnányi in every dispute, he had even less power. Dohnányi finally became tired of all these conflicts and began to yearn for the comfort and security of the United States. This longing was increased by the daily letters from Mr. Schulhof in New York, who kept assuring Dohnányi of the possibilities of settling there. Texas Christian University in Forth Worth still wanted Dohnányi to join their faculty as Pianist and Composer-in-Residence. Then one day Mr. Schulhof informed Dohnányi that Dr. Baker wanted him to come to Athens, Ohio, as a member of his music faculty. This possibility seemed so alluring that Dohnányi immediately dispatched a letter in which he accepted the position. He then started making arrangements for our departure to the United States. The Kirns excitedly rented a spacious, comfortable house for us.

Before matters were officially sealed, however, Mr. Schulhof forwarded Dohnányi an offer from Dr. Karl Kuersteiner, Dean of the School of Music at the Florida State University in Tallahassee, Florida. Dean Kuersteiner had known of Dohnányi when Kuersteiner was in Europe studying violin with Géza Kresz, who had once been a Professor at the Budapest Academy. Florida had always seemed like a dream to us; it was a land of beauty where azaleas and camellias bloom in winter and the air is perfumed with blossoms in summer. "I have had enough of cold winters," Dohnányi declared. "I don't want to freeze any longer. I want eternal spring." When people told Dohnányi that Florida could be intolerably hot, he remarked that it was hot in the summertime almost everywhere, and in Florida at the least winters would be enjoyable. Even if one had to suffer from the heat, at least there was compensation for it. Mr. Schulhof had assured Dohnányi that he would have to work less at the Florida State University and have an easy schedule, which was also very important. Dohnányi accepted the University's offer to become Professor of Piano and Composition starting in the fall of 1949.

Dohnányi's heart was heavy when he made his final decision to leave Argentina. This country had, after all, given refuge to him and to thousands of Hungarian refugees who were practically forgotten by the rest of the world. Argentina had opened its gates to many Hungarian aristocrats, scientists, artists, priests, and nuns who had fled from the Russian assault and could not enter the United States. Dohnányi had met many friends there whom he had known in Hungary. "In a way, Argentina has become a second Hungary to me," he said, with a sigh. "When I leave, I shall have the feeling that I have left Hungary forever." It was also painful for Dohnányi to leave the lot he had bought ten miles from Tucumán. "If I were young, I would like nothing more than to settle in this country, which has such a variety of beauties, and so many possibilities," Dohnányi said. "But I no longer have the strength and patience to be a pioneer."

The United States, in exchange, offered comfort and financial security. Mr. Schulhof wrote that in addition to the monthly salary from the University, he had already arranged concerts that would amount to twenty thousand dollars.

To actually get to Florida with our family and our new belongings, however, seemed almost impossible. The biggest problem was that the United States would not accept the Red Cross Passports that Fräulein Hermine and the children had obtained in Paris. It seemed to take us forever before the children received student visas and Fräulein Hermine obtained a temporary visitor's visa. It took a few more weeks to update the visitor's visas for Dohnányi and myself, which were still valid from the previous year. It was already October when we departed. Fräulein Hermine and Julius traveled by boat, carrying the belongings that we had decided to take with us, while Dohnányi chose to take a plane with Helen and me.

At Miami, unfortunately, we did not receive a hearty welcome. We learned that with a visitor's visa one was not allowed to earn money, and Dohnányi, who was unaware of this regulation, had displayed all his papers, including the document which showed that he was engaged for a yearly income by the Florida State University. We were driven to the office of the Immigration and Naturalization Services, where, after a long investigation, we were finally released with the warning to obtain permanent visas as soon as we could. We were told that to obtain permanent visas, we would have to travel to another country in order to be admitted to the United States again. This sounded absurd, and Dohnányi smiled at the warning. He was in high spirits, starting a new life in a country where he felt at home, and not even this annoying incident could discourage him. "This man is being silly," he said laughingly. "Surely the President of the University or a Senator can help us to obtain a permanent visa without having to wander out of the country just to re-enter again. What nonsense! After all, I have come here at the invitation of a University."

NINE

1949–1953

It was late in the evening when we arrived at the Tallahassee airport. Dean Kuersteiner was out of town, so we were greeted by his charming wife and Owen Sellers, the Dean's Assistant who would later become one of our closest friends. Mr. Sellers and Mrs. Kuersteiner drove us to a spacious wooden house with four big, furnished rooms and a porch, which Dohnányi decided would be his study. The large kitchen included a refrigerator, an electric stove, and numerous cooking utensils. There was also a telephone, and Mr. Sellers reminded us to call if we needed something. We hardly slept that night because we wanted to explore every corner of our new home. The house was surrounded by a garden fragrant with blooming flowers and was illuminated by stars. When Dohnányi recognized the same stars that he had known so well in Hungary, he gave a sigh of relief. Dohnányi heard the song of a bird; it was beautiful, resembling the voice of a nightingale. We learned later that it was the "Nightingale of the South," the mockingbird. There were red robins fluttering around in the moonlight, and a gray squirrel climbed up the screen of a window and stared at us with his wide, shiny little eyes.

"So we now have flowers, squirrels, and birds—many birds," Dohnányi said with a smile. "I am pleased; I have always loved birds. We must never have cats, because they could destroy our birds." A year later, however, we adopted a cat. Dohnányi had not changed his mind; in fact, he energetically opposed our keeping the cat. He only conceded when he learned that the poor animal was sick and homeless. It was against Dohnányi's principles to refuse asylum for destitute creatures, even if they happened to be cats.

The next day, when Dohnányi first visited the University, his enthusiasm increased. "We have a wonderful music building," he said. "Many tell me it's one of the finest in the United States. It's all air-conditioned, with a fine hall. I have a comfortable, spacious room, with two pianos. Also, my schedule is easy: just six hours weekly. I can teach without exhausting myself and relax as my doctor in New York advised." Dohnányi told us that his room was next to the room of Professor Franciszek Zachara, who was a Polish pianist and composer. He became Dohnányi's closest friend, and they met daily to share all their little joys and sorrows. Likewise, Mrs. Zachara became my best friend. They, and most of the faculty members at the Florida State University, welcomed Dohnányi warmly and did their best to make Tallahassee an enjoyable place for him.

Mrs. Schulhof in New York informed Dohnányi that Fräulein Hermine and Julius were being detained at Ellis Island by the Immigration Office, even though their papers were perfectly in order. It seemed that one of the Immigration officials was suspicious because they were traveling with twenty-one cases, and he had held them back for further investigation. Before the two could be released Dohnányi had to pay a guarantee of five hundred dollars for each of them. After some difficulty, Dohnányi managed to borrow the thousand dollars from the bank, further increasing his debt.

Dohnányi's relaxed schedule at the University allowed him to dedicate sufficient time to his new composition, his Second Violin Concerto, op. 42, which he dedicated to the talented young American violinist Frances Magnes. Dohnányi had started this work in Tucumán, where he had completed the first two movements, and was now completing the last one.

Although it was November, the days were still hot. The breezes at night, however, were cool and refreshing. After sunset the Maestro and I would take long walks on the streets, which were bordered by ancient oak trees with Spanish moss hanging from their huge branches. During the days, Dohnányi would happily walk along the paths of the University campus, enjoying the oak trees, the flourishing shrubs, the green palms, and the bright green lawn that was usually buzzing with young people. Dohnányi often spent his free time in the garden admiring the lawn and plants. "Tallahassee is a most picturesque town," he would say with an affectionate smile. "Although a capital, it's as silent and tranquil as a country town." Tallahassee, with over forty thousand inhabitants and a University of almost six thousand students, was a rapidly growing city that focused chiefly on the activities of the University. The city would be swarming with life on weekdays, but be almost empty and silent on holidays.

The tranquility we had found in Tallahassee lasted only a few weeks. When Dohnányi asked Mr. Schulhof about his future concerts, Mr. Schulhof told him that, except for a few concerts in Ohio that were to take place in February and March of the following year, there was not one single concert. All, without exception, had been canceled as result of the continuous attacks on Dohnányi's reputation that had been inspired by Göndör's slan-

ders.[1] These attacks had continued throughout the summer, but the Schulhofs, eager to have Dohnányi in the United States and believing that they
could ward off the blows themselves, had kept them secret from him. Mr.
Schulhof, however, had not realized that some stains on a reputation cannot be completely cleared in the public eye. Evil news spreads like wildfire,
and while everybody reads slanders, only very few read retractions. In our
case, there were still no retractions because Mr. Göndör was considered to
be a reliable source.[2]

Supporters began to write letters to defend Dohnányi, some even defying the dangers and difficulties of writing from behind the Iron Curtain.
Jenő Sugár openly declared from Budapest that Dohnányi had saved him
and his daughter from certain death in Nazi-controlled Hungary. Letters in
support of Dohnányi had also been written by Edward Kilenyi (8 February
1949), Tibor Serly (10 February 1949), Miklós Schwalb (12 February
1949), Imre Waldbauer (14 February 1949), and Leo Weiner (18 March
1949).[3] All the witnesses who tried to stand up for Dohnányi, however,
were dismissed as biased friends.

Meanwhile, the Maestro and I received a letter from the Immigration
and Naturalization Service declaring that we had to leave the United States
before 11 June 1950 or we would be deported for violating the country's
laws. We had dismissed the warning of the Immigration official in Miami
who had told us to obtain a permit at a U.S. Consulate outside the country.
Dr. Doak Campbell, who was the President of the Florida State University,
enlisted the aid of a senator and a congressman in Washington, D.C., as
well as a lawyer in Miami, but nothing could be done to help us.

On 1 June the Maestro and I decided to go to Cuba to obtain a Non-
Quota Visa with which we could return for a permanent stay. Because we
did not have a permit to stay in the United States, however, the Cuban Immigration Office refused to let us enter their country, as there was no guarantee that we would not become a burden on them. In three days, Mr.
Schulhof hastily arranged a recital in Havana, even though it was not the
concert season. The engagement allowed us to board the plane to Cuba.
When we entered the U.S. Consulate in Havana to apply for the Non-

1. On 5 February 1949, Göndör had written a letter to Tom C. Clark, Attorney General of the
United States, to which Clark responded on 8 February 1949; see Appendix A.
2. Eventually, Göndör lost interest in persecuting Dohnányi. He risked only one or two more articles, comparing Dohnányi to a flea that had managed to cling to the country. In 1951, however,
Göndör intended to appear at a party in honor of Dohnányi at the private home of friends in New
York, presumably to bring about some kind of reconciliation. Dohnányi found out in time and did not
attend the party.
3. These letters can be found in Appendix A, along with letters condemning Dohnányi that had
been written by John Katona, Legation of the Republic of Hungary (16 September 1949), and Leon
Goldstein (17 September 1949).

Quota Visa, we were received by a sympathetic gentleman extending his hand toward Dohnányi. "You are welcome, Dr. Dohnányi," the Consul said warmly. "I was delighted to hear that you were coming here and that I would have a chance to meet you. I can assure you that we shall do everything we can to enable you to return quickly to the United States."

The concert hall was crowded with an enthusiastic audience. It was a real pleasure for Dohnányi to play for them, and he was further rewarded with an honorarium that Mr. Schulhof in his haste had not even demanded. After the concert, we were invited to the houses of wealthy plantation families and enjoyed the splendor of their hospitality.

Although we returned as the proud possessors of permanent visas, our dealings with the Immigration and Naturalization authorities were not yet settled. We had to initiate the entire process again for the children. They, too, had to go to Cuba, one by one. Their difficulties with the Cuban Immigration Office were even greater because they were not able to perform. Fräulein Hermine obtained her permit only through a private bill generously presented and supported by a senator and a congressman.

Meanwhile, Mr. Schulhof was still unable to schedule performances for Dohnányi because of the accusations. Although this did not defeat Dohnányi, he began to resent those who had treated him unjustly. He was ready to face any number of attacks with his usual courage, but he was bitter that he could not raise his voice in self-defense against his anonymous accusers.

Nevertheless, Dohnányi had no reason to complain that he was not welcomed in the United States. Most of those who came in contact with him fell under the spell of his personality and enveloped him with affectionate admiration. Among these were several Jewish friends who tried with all their power to correct those who had been misinformed about Dohnányi. Even though all of the orchestras and musical organizations stayed aloof, the universities, one by one, welcomed him to their campus. The younger generation realized that they could profit from a man with his background, knowledge, and experience. Although they could not offer the payments that professional organizations would have given to artists of his renown, Dohnányi gladly accepted their invitations. The affection he had always felt for young people strengthened in his heart and gave him an aim, a purpose, to bestow upon them the gift he himself possessed.

❧

Except for his work at the University and a performance on 1 December 1950 of the *Variationen über ein Kinderlied* with the Charleston, South Carolina, Symphony Orchestra, the only activity Dohnányi was able to undertake in 1950 was an autumn visit to New York to make recordings for the Remington Gramophone Company. He welcomed this opportunity to be reunited with, after twenty years, his old friend, the famous violinist Albert Spalding, with whom he recorded sonatas. Dohnányi's life had changed dramatically since Spalding had visited his splendid home in Budapest. Even his family conditions had changed, and I was most embarrassed when I opened the door of our hotel room in New York to admit a gentleman who, holding his violin under his arm, introduced himself with the faintest trace of surprise as Albert Spalding. I had to explain that the Mrs. Dohnányi he had known had not grown a few years younger, but that I was actually a different person. He smiled and with the exquisite manners for which everyone called him a "real gentleman" put me completely at ease. When Dohnányi finally entered, the two friends embraced each other with affection.

When, at an interview, Spalding was asked how their friendship had survived those years of distance and world war, he answered, "In a friendship like ours time or distance cannot count." Their friendship was built upon mutual understanding, taste, and musical opinion. When they played together they did not have to rehearse because both had exactly the same ideas. Although Spalding had given up public concertizing and his only activity now was to teach at the New England Conservatory in Boston, he volunteered to come to Tallahassee and play with Dohnányi.

In the meantime, we received an eviction notice from our landlady on Christmas Eve 1950. She had an opportunity to rent our house for a higher price and wanted us to vacate it within four weeks. We were unable to find a furnished apartment that was large enough for us. Our friends assured us that renting a home, especially for such a high rent, was a waste of money when we could buy a house for a minimum down payment and afterwards pay off the balance at the same monthly cost as our current rent. This was a delightful idea, and nothing would have made us happier than to own a home. We found several houses and started to negotiate over their price, but, although they were simple and inexpensive, the down payment for them was far more than we could afford. We had almost given up hope when we were offered a beautiful old house for twice the price that we had anticipated, but with a low down payment that we would not have to pay immediately. Dohnányi was happy to have a home he liked, and he grew more and more fond of it every day.

Dohnányi's first guest in the new home was Albert Spalding. Spalding spent the winter on nearby Captiva Island, and so in January 1951 he came to the Florida State University to give classes and to play recitals with Dohnányi. Spalding would teach at the University during the day and spend the evenings with us, enjoying our Hungarian meals. Afterwards he and Dohnányi would play for their own entertainment, but were generous enough to allow me to invite some of our closest friends so that they, too, might enjoy the music. After each sonata they would smile at each other,

music agent Arthur Judson, but he was not successful in reinstating the concerts. John, who was ready to make every effort for a cause he believed just, felt very bitter. "I always thought of banking as a rather cut-throat business in which people treat each other relentlessly," he told Dohnányi, "but now I realize that it is nothing compared to the music business." Dohnányi regretfully stayed at home in Tallahassee and did not witness the Concerto's tremendous success. Mrs. Schulhof, who was present, wept with emotion throughout the performance. The newspapers acknowledged the success next day,[5] and it pleased Dohnányi that his work was so warmly received. It pleased him even more, however, that Frances Magnes, whose art and abilities he highly appreciated, had achieved such a success by performing it.

Dohnányi's friends never ceased working to end Dohnányi's blacklisting. One of these friends was Harriet Pickernell, a music lover and the manager of a summer orchestra in New York. Dohnányi had met Mrs. Pickernell on his tour in 1927 in the United States when she was the Secretary of Mr. Wagner, President of the Chickering Firm. Mrs. Pickernell arranged for Dohnányi to give a recital in Miami, Florida, on 19 February 1952, as a charity benefit for poor musicians. She believed that even his enemies would not have the indecency to protest against him when he was contributing to such a noble purpose, and those who would attend the concert would discover the magic spell of his music and spread the news of what they had experienced. When we arrived at Miami, Mrs. Pickernell personally greeted us at the airport with her friends. She led us to a stupendous reception given by Bertha Foster, who was the Director of the Musician's Club. Dr. Foster had invited more than two hundred people and had even arranged a musical program of Dohnányi's music performed by his former pupil, Joan Holley.

The next morning, Mrs. Pickernell informed us that information was being circulated declaring Dohnányi to be a violent pro-Nazi. Upon hearing this news people had stopped buying tickets and some had even returned tickets. There were a few people who declared with apologies that they would have gladly attended the concert but they were afraid of losing their jobs. Once more Dohnányi had to endure this hostility because no one admitted responsibility for it. Indeed, several people who undertook campaigns against him afterwards flatly denied it. A millionaire, in her passionate hatred and eagerness to harm, wanted to buy all the tickets to leave the hall entirely empty for the performance. We actually wished she had succeeded, because then at least the poor musicians for whom the concert was planned would have benefited. On the morning of the recital, how-

---

5. One review of the Second Violin Concerto appeared in *The New York Times* on 15 February 1952; see Appendix C.

ever, she apologized to Mrs. Pickernell, explaining that she realized she had been wrong to judge Dohnányi so harshly. She even attended the concert.

Naturally, there were many empty seats at this concert. Those who came, however, were enthusiastic and applauded heartily in support of Dohnányi. An article in the Miami paper the next day praised the performance with real enthusiasm.[6] Nevertheless the benefit concert was a failure, and what made this failure even more bitter was that there seemed to be no way to ever overcome the same obstacle. Our friends were all upset, and although Dohnányi remained imperturbable, it hurt him to be defeated without being able to fight back.

From that point on, however, it seemed as though the campaign against Dohnányi was beginning to weaken. This became more obvious to us when Van Lier Lanning, who had founded a new orchestra in Atlantic City, New Jersey, invited Dohnányi to play his Second Piano Concerto at their inaugural concert.

We arrived in Atlantic City four days before the concert. Despite torrential rain the Conductor was waiting for us at the airport with several important people. Somebody, on behalf of the Mayor, presented Dohnányi with a small jewelry box containing a gilded key that was a symbolical entrance key to the heart of the city. A Hungarian-born lady, Bertha de Hellebranth, gave Dohnányi a lovely bouquet of red tulips and feather grass decorated with a ribbon of the Hungarian colors of red, white, and green. She became such a close friend that we came to regard her as a member of our family. Ms. Hellebranth was not a musical scholar, but she was an enthusiastic listener and a sincere admirer of Dohnányi. She made it one of her duties to make us happy, and whenever Christmas, Easter, or a birthday took place in our family, she would send a gift that she had thoughtfully chosen with profound sentiments and resourcefulness. Once, she painted a portrait of Dohnányi by memory. All we could do in return was occasionally send her homemade records of Dohnányi's music; he had not recorded a professional one since the few completed in 1950 for Remington.

Dohnányi found Atlantic City to be an interesting, luxuriously fashionable town. The seemingly endless walk along the seashore, with the stupendous shops and the throngs of people, made a fascinating picture in the sunshine. The Maestro and I sat on a bench, holding hands, and in this whirl of people we had never felt so forlorn and lonesome in our lives. I do not know exactly how he felt, for he was silent, but for my part, the sight of all the wealth around us made me feel like a wayfaring stranger. I wondered if there would ever be a time when we, too, could undertake a trip just for

---

6. See Appendix C for the *Miami Herald* article that appeared on 20 February 1952.

rest or enjoyment, or even a summer vacation to escape the tormenting heat of Tallahassee, which, in spite of the air conditioning recently installed in our bedroom, was very unpleasant.

Thanks to a great effort made by people whom we had met only a few days before, not one comment was publicly made against Dohnányi, even though Atlantic City was fairly close to New York and its influence. The concert hall was almost overflowing for the 9 April 1953 performance. Although the concerto is a difficult work, especially for a new orchestra, the performance went well.[7] Much of the evening's success can be attributed to the President of the Orchestra, Dr. Victor Ruby, in whose house we were staying as guests, and by two very nice ladies, Sylvia and Stella Woolman, who gave a reception after the concert to honor Dohnányi. The big crowd at the reception made me feel that at last people had begun to realize the absurdity of the accusations.

We made a three-day visit to New York, and Dohnányi tried to make arrangements to join the American royalty company B.M.I. (Broadcast Music Incorporated). Unfortunately, the royalties that were due to Dohnányi from the wartime and even afterwards were still tied up by the Custodian of Enemy Property. The only solution to safeguard future income was to join an American organization for at least the royalties in America. It deeply grieved Dohnányi to cut connections, even if only partly, with the A.K.M., which had served him well for fifty years. Dohnányi was always loyal in business as well as artistic matters, especially to those who had worked with him for so long in the past and had become true friends.

From New York we flew to Athens, Ohio, for Dohnányi's fifth annual three-week residency. We now had so many good friends there that it was almost like a homecoming. People began to receive us happily, saying, "Spring is coming, and the Dohnányis fly north." Dr. Baker asked Dohnányi to write a composition for the University's student orchestra to perform in the following year for the 150th anniversary of Ohio University. Dohnányi and the Bakers decided that a work containing old American folk melodies would be best, and Dohnányi started to search for suitable songs. Unfortunately, all the songs he found had actually originated in some other country and had merely been brought to the United States. Dohnányi eventually managed to find several songs that had been sung in this country for many years and could justly be considered American folk songs.[8] Dohnányi dedicated his *American Rhapsody* for orchestra, op. 47, to Ohio University and Dr. Baker.

7. A review appeared in the *Atlantic City Press* on 10 April 1953; see Appendix C.
8. These folk songs include "On Top of Old Smoky," "I am a Poor, Wayfaring Stranger," "The Riddle," "Turkey in the Straw," "Sweet Betsy from Pike," two "country dances," and the Ohio University Alma Mater.

❦

Dohnányi's biggest triumph in fighting his opposition was a concert in New York that was arranged through the efforts of the loyal and affectionate Mrs. Pickernell. Dohnányi was to play his Second Piano Concerto on 9 November 1953, in Carnegie Hall, with the National Orchestral Association conducted by Leon Barzin. Mrs. Pickernell warned Mr. Barzin in time that New York was probably the very center of wicked accusations against Dohnányi, and that he, too, might be attacked on account of Dohnányi. Barzin shrugged his shoulders. "I will consider it a privilege," he said. Since the National Orchestra consisted of young musicians, most of which had only just graduated, it needed several rehearsals. Dohnányi, however, could not stay for such a long time in New York, because he had work to do in Tallahassee. Instead, he sent his former student, Joan Holley, who knew the concerto well, to play at those rehearsals. To reward her for her pains, she was also the soloist for the dress rehearsal, which was broadcast.

The concert was a great excitement, not only for me, but also for all those who were loyal friends of Dohnányi. It was touching to see how they poured into New York from various parts of the country to be present at this event. Mrs. Pickernell worked as hard as ever, planning a stupendous reception with Mrs. Barzin, in whose house the reception was to take piece.

On the day of the concert snow fell unceasingly. When we exited the taxi in front of Carnegie Hall, we could hardly see through the steadily falling curtain of snow. Nevertheless, the hall was full, and even in my anguish I noticed the tense atmosphere: almost everyone here knew that something unusual, something important was going to happen, and they were curious and uneasy. Joan Holley was pale with excitement, Ms. Hellebranth plucked nervously at her handkerchief, and Mrs. Schulhof pinched me every minute, whispering encouraging words although she herself was just as agitated. Mrs. Pickernell did not even appear among the audience; in her nervousness she preferred to remain backstage and cross her fingers in the hopes that everything would go as she had expected.

The concert surpassed every expectation. Dohnányi probably forgot all the tension and excitement when he sat at the keyboard and was quite unconscious of what was at stake. I had rarely heard him play with such vivacity, such energy, such passion, and such delicate finesse. He showed the audience what it had missed by having not heard him for all those years. The concerto went "like the wind," according to the *New York Herald Tribune,* and when the last chord was played, roaring applause stormed up, which was rare for the usually blasé New York audiences. People not only applauded, but were quite frantic and beside themselves with passionate ecstasy. Again and again they shouted "bravo," and Dohnányi repeatedly returned to the stage to thank them. When he turned to the orchestra and motioned for them to rise, Barzin gave them a wink to remain seated; the glory of the evening belonged to Dohnányi. This gesture aroused even more enthusiasm. Ms. Hellebranth wept with joy and suddenly she found herself in the arms of her neighbor, a complete stranger who was just as overcome as she was.

When I tried to edge my way through the crowd to the artist's room, I was blocked at every step. I overheard people's excited remarks. "To think that such an artist was kept from the stage for some idiotic political calumny!" shouted a man whom I knew to be Jewish, and I heard similar comments from others. I was blinded with tears and I could hardly see my way, but luckily I was carried along by the crowd into the artist's room, which was decorated with so many gifts from friends that it looked like a flower garden.

The success was immortalized by three articles in leading New York papers. A paragraph of the *New York Herald Tribune* was so touching and characteristic that it became widely quoted. Part of it ran: "How, at the age of seventy-six, Mr. Dohnányi is able to career so glibly about the keyboard is no question this writer can answer. But the fact remains that the composer darted to and fro as though he had just graduated cum laude from a conservatory and was prepared to tackle single-handedly the entire virtuoso repertoire. Hearing Mr. Dohnányi play made the youngsters on the scene feel ancient and worn."[9]

9. In addition to the *New York Herald Tribune*, reviews appeared in the *Brooklyn Eagle* and *The New York Times* on 10 November 1953; see Appendix C.

EPILOGUE

1954–1960

In 1954 Dohnányi received an honorary doctorate degree from Ohio University, and in 1955 we became citizens of the United States of America. Dohnányi's reemergence as an internationally acclaimed virtuoso pianist, which had begun in Carnegie Hall on 9 November 1953, was solidified by performances in the 1956 Edinburgh Festival. One year later, Dohnányi received another honorary doctorate from the Florida State University. Dohnányi's final compositions were an *Aria* and a *Passacaglia* for flute, op. 48, which he dedicated to Ellie Baker, daughter of Dr. and Mrs. Baker.[1]

Dohnányi taught at the Florida State University for eleven years. Although he had started with a six-hour weekly schedule, his workload later doubled when the Board of Control of the State of Florida reduced the funding for the Music School. In addition to Dohnányi's regular teaching schedule, there were seminars, rehearsals, and conducting on occasions when his pupils played with the Florida State University Symphony Orchestra. Dohnányi was past seventy when he came to the University, so he was not legally eligible for a pension. Because the University did not grant paid summer vacations, he also taught during the summer sessions.

The continuous strain took its toll on Dohnányi's heart. In spite of this, he continued to perform all over the United States, including performances in Toledo, Chicago, Cincinnati, Milwaukee, and Minneapolis. Dohnányi also continued to return to Ohio University every year. In October 1959 the eighty-two-year-old Dohnányi gave a concert in Atlanta after which he was hailed as a "Musical Whiz."[2] Dohnányi endeavored to maintain his strength and spirits because he was convinced that as long as he

---

1. Ellie Baker (1936–2001), who was later known as Eleanor Lawrence, went on to have an active career as a flutist and a conductor. She recorded both of the op. 48 pieces for Musical Heritage Society.
2. Dick Gray, "Ever-Young Octogenarian Dohnanyi at 82 a Musical Whiz," *The Atlanta Constitution* (23 October 1959).

kept up a semblance of youth he could continue living. Although he clung desperately to life, nature could not be cheated. The grueling work and the trauma of starting all over again so late in life undermined his strength.

We went to New York on 21 January 1960 in happiness and good health; a recent physical examination indicated that Dohnányi could live for many more years. During his recording sessions for two records by the Everest Company, however, everything seemed to conspire against him. In addition to being fatigued, Dohnányi was upset about the serious illness of his friend and agent Andrew Schulhof, who was unable to help us in the difficult and exacting work of preparing a record. The studio in which Dohnányi was recording was too cold, and he contracted influenza. On 5 February, despite his illness, he refused to go to the hospital and stubbornly insisted on finishing his last record.

The life of Ernst von Dohnányi, which was so triumphant in youth and so hard, painful, and humiliating in the twilight of his life, ended on 9 February 1960 at 10:40 P.M. in the Madison Avenue Hospital. Throughout his illness, Dohnányi had never complained. He had been as patient and serene as always. Even in his last sleep, a few hours before his death, a smile had wavered on his lips. He must have had a cheerful dream; perhaps God wanted to compensate Dohnányi in advance for taking him so abruptly from his beloved earth. Dohnányi's loyal friend and doctor, Elmer Wahl, who kept daily vigil at Dohnányi's bed, told the *New York Herald Tribune,* "The composer had been under 'great strain' at the recording session. Dr. Dohnányi was a perfectionist and made as many as nine recordings of each of the works. He wore himself out."[3]

Dohnányi's body returned to Tallahassee in a coffin, on the same plane on which he had planned to return with me to nurse his beloved camellias in his garden. He was buried on 13 February in Roselawn Cemetery. There he rests under the bright blue Florida sky he so ardently loved, shaded by dogwood trees and listening to the songs of his favorite birds, the mockingbirds. A lyre is engraved on his white marble tombstone under his name: "ERNST VON DOHNANYI / July 27, 1877–Feb. 9, 1960." On the back of the tombstone is his name as he was once called in Hungary, when his compatriots still admired, praised, and loved him: "DOHNANYI ERNÖ"

3. "Von Dohnanyi, Hungarian Pianist and Composer, Dies," *New York Herald Tribune* (11 February 1960).

Appendix A. Selected Correspondence

14 September 1894. Dohnányi, Budapest, to his parents, Pozsony.

On the ninth, I went to the Academy of Music (Pecskai was also there) and waited for the Director. After a little while, he arrived and entered his office, followed somewhat later by a professor. A few minutes afterwards I knocked at his door. The Director was involved in a most animated conversation with the professor, and he told me to wait. So I waited while they talked with each other in a low whisper, probably discussing secret matters. Suddenly, I heard the voice of the Director. Although I did not quite catch what he said, I guessed his words were meant for me: "It seems one can never have privacy. I want to be left alone, my dear boy. I have matters to discuss." I went out into the antechamber and waited.

When the other gentleman left, I returned and introduced myself. The Director asked if I was the son of the Professor in Pozsony. I nodded and handed him the letter. He began to scold me for not coming sooner, because the piano examination was on the tenth and the eleventh. I made the excuse that I had not known when the examination was to take place. "You say you did not know? Then why did you not inquire? Is it not you who wants to attend the Academy?" Then he asked whether I was already enrolled. I told him I was not. "Come at three in the afternoon, get enrolled by the secretary, pay five florint, and tomorrow at nine you may attend the examination for composition. Have you some special request?" I told him I would like to study with Professor Thomán. "Well," he said, "Professor Chován will also be present at the examination. Now, goodbye."

At three in the afternoon, I went to the secretary, who was a Hochschule teacher named Harrach. I introduced myself and told him that I wanted to be admitted for piano and composition. "You are already late for the piano test," he said, "but for composition the exam will be tomorrow. But, by the way, why do you choose two main subjects? You could study piano as a side subject."

"No, please, I want piano as my main study. I have already spoken about this to the Director."

"Are you the one from Pozsony? We have kept a place reserved for you. Go into the antechamber and complete two matriculation forms. Hurry up, for your exam should have begun at three."

I went out, completed the two pages, and was ready when the secretary came out. Then I entered the classroom. The Director told me that Professor Chován was conducting the examination. I quickly paid the enrollment fee and sat at the piano. Professor Chován took a seat next to me and began: "Play the E-flat Minor scale."

After I played the E-flat Minor scale and all kinds of dominant chords and told them what etudes I had studied, they judged my sense of pitch. Chován struck the E-flat Minor triad. I would have had to have a very poor sense of tonality not to recognize it so soon after having played the E-flat scale. Then he struck some other notes.

They require every student to name the remaining notes when a chord is named.

Chován exclaimed repeatedly, "He definitely is a talented boy!"

Director Michalovich nodded.

Then I played parts of Bach's "Chromatic F[antasia] and F[ugue]" and scales in thirds and sixths. With this, I did not succeed too well. I told them that I had not practiced this type of scale much. Then the Director inquired about my compositions, and at his request I played the "Romance." He was very touched and gave me a pat. He then had to go downstairs to attend a violin examination (that was the reason why my exam was so short). In the corridor, he told me what a talent I had, etc., etc. He went into the office and wrote a note: "You will be admitted into the III Class" (Junior year).

I was delighted and dashed down the stairs, jumping five at a time in my joy.

The following day (this morning) at nine, the entrance examination for composition took place. I was the first. I had to play some of my compositions, including half of the first part of my Sextet (the Largo part), the Scherzo from my String Quartet, and a song, "Das verlassene Mägdlein." Then Koessler (a rather young and handsome man) went to the blackboard and gave me the following test: chords that, after getting stuck once or twice, I finally resolved. Then I had to improvise variations on this theme on the piano. After I had played six or seven variations, Dr. Koessler made the following judgment: "You will be officially admitted into Class II, but if you seem to be advancing too quickly, I will release you from the II and III class in the same year." I was pleased. I could complete both subjects in two years.

The professors were not pleased to hear that I was also enrolled at the University. Michalovich was worried about my health and asked why Papa wanted me to attend the University of Philosophy. I told him that it was not Papa alone who wanted it, but also myself.

10 February 1895. Dohnányi, Budapest, to Frederick von Dohnányi, Pozsony.

I am in such a solemn mood that I am hardly able to collect my thoughts. Yesterday will always be a remarkable day in my life. I have obtained a triumph as never before. The concert had a wonderful success. Goldmark himself was present and was exceedingly pleased with the Quintet. He congratulated each of us, but especially me. He said: "Es war kein Schülerproduction, sondern eine, wie man sie von Künstlern erwartet" (This was no student production, but one such as is expected of artists). Michalovich and the professors were also touched, and I could hardly escape their praise. After the concert Goldmark repeated his appreciation and shook my hand three times. Koessler immediately mentioned my Quintet, and Goldmark told that he would very much like to hear it. This, of course, was impossible, since my Quintet is not finished yet. Finally he said, "I hope we shall often meet in life," and it seemed as though he may someday invite me to visit him.

1 August 1945. President of the Festspiele Committee, Salzburg, to Dohnányi, Linz.

According to a communication which I have just received from the I.S.B. of the Military Government in Salzburg, this office has to cancel your appearance at the Salzburg Festivals for political reasons.

Therefore, I regret to have to forgo your contribution to the Festival as conductor of the first orchestral concert and must consider all other engagements canceled.

6 August 1945. Lt. Col. James N. Robertson (Headquarters of the 65th Infantry Division), Linz, to Whom It May Concern.

1.) The undersigned is writing this letter for the express purpose of stating that the above-named Professor Donyani [*sic*] has been checked thoroughly by this Headquarters prior to the time that he has directed the Linz Symphony Orchestra and prior to the time that he has given piano recitals for the Enlisted Men and Officers in Linz, Austria, and [we] could discover nothing in his past history which would indicate that he was a security threat or in any way detrimental to the interests of the Soldiers of the U.S. Army and Allied Forces in Linz.

2.) Professor Donyani [*sic*] has done some excellent work for members of this command and is to be highly commended therefor [*sic*]—and as entertainment for soldiers and civilians, he is considered completely cleared by this Headquarters.

14 December 1945. Dr. Benkö (Hungarian Minister of Justice), Budapest, to Col. Rudolf Frankovszky, Budapest.

On your request I certify that the conference of the parties convened to this effect did not comprise Dr. Ernest Dohnányi in the draft list of war criminals, i.e., cancelled his name from the list which had been published previously without authority.

21 February 1946. Otto Passetti, Salzburg, to Edward Kilenyi.

This is to inform you that Ernst von Dohnanyi's rehabilitation could not be approved by this section, because of his anti-Russian tendency.

There is some possibility of reopening the case with the Austrian Governmental Commission in Vienna and the quadripartite commission as counterpart.

26 November 1948. Dohnányi, to whom it may concern:

I, Ernst von Dohnányi, herewith declare that

1.) I never was a member of any national socialist party. It is, therefore, not true that I was a member of the Arrow Cross "Nyilas" the Hungarian fascist party.

2.) It is not true that I was Szalasi's "musical aide," or "advisor." I had nothing to do with Szalasi or with his regime whatsoever. Szalasi came to power on October 15, 1944, and I left Budapest for good in November 1944.

3.) It is not true that I made the Hungarian Academy of Music "Judenrein" or "Aryanized."

4.) I resigned my position as Director of the Liszt Ferenc Academy of Music in 1941, and left finally in May 1943. My successor was Mr. Ede Zathureczky who has held, and is still holding, this position since then, and during all regimes (Szalasi's, etc.).

5.) I was honorary president of "Harmonia," a concert agency, which had as its aim the promotion of young talent. This organization was not influenced in any manner by racial prejudice. The founder and executive manager was Mr. Miklos Rékai who was [of] Jewish descent. (Mother is Jewish.)

5 February 1949. Ferenc Göndör (Editor and Publisher of *Az Ember*), to Tom C. Clark (Attorney General of the United States of America).

This country has applauded the action of the Immigration and Naturalization Service of your Department to make German pianist, Walter Gieseking, leave the United States as an undesirable alien, because of his war-time activities in Hitler's Germany.

Your attention should be called to another undesirable alien now in the United States, Ernest von Dohnanyi, Hungarian pianist and composer, who sided with the most vicious enemies of the United States and of humanity during World War II.

Those enemies were the Hungarian Arrow Cross war criminals, who declared war on the United States and wanted to wage it until they and their Allies, the Nazis, would reach—in their own words—the shores of the United States. Those Hungarian criminal leaders waged war on humanity by slaughtering hundreds of thousands of Hungarian Jews and those of their non-Jewish political opponents on whom they could lay their hands.

This newspaper has published the criminal record of Ernest von Dohnanyi in all its details.

Ernest von Dohnanyi was the musical "Fuehrer" of the Hungarian Nazis and served them as the director of the Hungarian radio and of the famous Academy of Music of Budapest. In those capacities he saw to it that no decent person should obtain a public hearing on the Radio or the platform.

His hatred of the Jews was so great that he forced them out of public view as musicians even when it was not absolutely necessary for him to do so. He followed the Nazi line in eliminating the music of the great Jewish composers of the past.

Ernest von Dohnanyi not only served Hungary's criminal wartime masters, but publicly demonstrated his solidarity and affection for them. Moving pictures have been made of his bowings and scrapings to the Arrow Cross leaders.

He left Hungary for fear of falling into Allied hands and hid himself in the West. The name of Ernest von Dohnanyi is on the list of the Hungarian war criminals. Many of his friends in Hungary's war governments were publicly tried and hanged.

He made his way to Argentina where he associated with known war criminals. He came to the United States under conditions which call for urgent investigation and action.

The presence in this country of a man like Dohnanyi is an insult to the memories of the young people who were called upon to lay down their lives in defense of the United States against the danger which was represented by Dohnanyi and his Fascist friends.

"Az Ember," a liberal Hungarian-language newspaper written in the spirit of America, backed by many of its readers, asks you to instruct your Immigration and Naturalization service to look into the past history of Ernest von Dohnanyi and the circumstances under which he reached the United States, with a view to instituting deportation proceedings against him.

8 February 1949. Tom C. Clark to Ferenc Göndör.

This will acknowledge your communication of February 3rd enclosing a copy of the February 5th issue of "Az Ember," calling attention to the marked portion, an open letter to me, commenting on the Walter Gieseking case and the presence in the United States of the Hungarian composer, Ernest von Dohnanyi.

I appreciate your interest in the situation described and shall be glad to look into the background circumstances and advise you further.

8 February 1949. Edward Kilenyi, New York, to whom it may concern.

In my capacity as Music Control Officer for Bavaria, a position which I held from June 1945 until April 1946, at which time I was a captain in the U.S. Army, I had occasion to investigate the case of ERNST VON DOHNANYI.

On the basis of cross examinations, reports of numerous witnesses, documents and letters, I recommended that Dohnanyi be cleared by the Military Government authorities. Having had considerable experience in the investigation of Nazi musicians, I came to the definite conclusion that Dohnanyi was not an intellectual supporter of Fascism, but held the views of a conservative, ruggedly individualistic, perhaps indiscreetly outspoken anti-Bolshevik. There is ample proof that he could not have been guilty of the actions attributed to him, as he was not in a position of authority (Director of the National Academy of Music, Head of the Budapest Radio) at the time they had taken place. In fact, he had resigned as Director of the Academy as early as 1941, three years before these events.

I have documentary evidence that: 1.) The only reason why the so-called Music Chamber (for the purpose of removing Jews from musical life) could not be established was that Dohnanyi sabotaged it. 2.) He was not on the war criminal list of the post-Nazi, pre-Communist Government (in power from November 1945 until February 1947), but only on that of the Communist-dominated government still in power.

He was forced to attend the first meeting of the Hungarian Nazi Cultural Council and photographed while shaking the hand of the Hungarian Arrow Cross leader Szalasi. This photograph was widely publicized at the time without Dohnanyi's approval. This is the one "crime" which is neither disproved nor denied. Mr. Zathureczky attended this meeting with Dohnanyi. That the attendance of this gathering is not considered a crime is proven by the fact that Mr. Zathureczky is still Head of the Academy of Music, as he was at that time.

Dohnanyi left Hungary one month later, having been such a violent anti-Communist that he was naturally on the Russian proscribed list.

10 February 1949. Tibor Serly, to whom it may concern.

It is a sad commentary that the aftermath of World War II has brought upon us (particularly here in America) the strange paradox of individuals and factional periodicals proclaiming to pass verdicts on the behavior of certain European artists of note. Were their allegations in all cases the truth and nothing but the truth, there would be no need of any open statement by private citizens such as the present letter. By all means let the war criminals be exposed! But not before all facts have bean proven and each point has been considered. Then, let judgment be passed by the proper authorities only. This is the core of our democratic system.

As a recent such instance, I have in mind attacks leveled upon the famous Hungarian pianist and composer, Ernest Dohnanyi. While I am not in a position to refute alleged war crimes attributed to him, not having been present at the time, I can however attest to his absolute moral and artistic integrity over a period of twenty-five years. This includes information gathered during a recent visit to Hungary.

As an American student at the Budapest Academy of Music in the early Twenties, I knew him as a kind, helpful and sympathetic guide and teacher. As I recall it at the time, his scholarship pupils of Jewish origin outnumbered the gentiles. In 1923 I brought him a young pianist, an American Jew, Eli Miller, whom he heard play and immediately recommended for a scholarship at the Royal Academy.

As a conductor and music director of the National Hungarian Radio, he not only performed the works of Jewish composers—to mention a few: P. Kadosa, Leo Weiner, G. Kosa, Geza Frid—but in addition, helped a number to secure positions in the Radio.

Although conservative in his musical tastes, he nevertheless performed and championed the then radically modern works of his colleagues Bela Bartok and Zoltan Kodaly. Bartok often expressed sentiments of gratitude toward him. As early as 1907 (by which time Dohnanyi was already famous in Europe), Bartok, then an unknown composer, hoping to find a publisher for some songs, wrote to his mother as follows: "I asked him (Dohnanyi) does he think it would be possible to find a publisher for this group of songs. He not only volunteered to use his influence, but in addition offered to include some new songs of his own if it were necessary as an inducement." (From the published letters of Bela Bartok.) To his last days Bartok spoke of Dohnanyi with fondness and respect.

While attending the Bela Bartok Memorial International Competition as the American representative member of the Board of Judges, September to November 1948, I made it a particular point to seek information regarding Ernest Dohnanyi's activities during the Nazi occupation from both Jewish and gentile musicians of prominence. Not one expressed any bitterness regarding his behavior during the Nazi occupation. His only crime, if such it could be called, was not exposing himself to open hostility which for one in his position would have meant death or concentration camp.

Finally, it is a curious coincidence that *not one Jewish musician of any reputation* living in Hungary lost his life or perished during the entire period of World War II.

12 February 1949. Miklós Schwalb, New York, to whom it may concern.

Reading a new attack against Mr. Dohnanyi, in which an irresponsible newspaper calls him a war criminal, I feel that I cannot let it pass again without answering it. For a long time I have felt the necessity of clearing up the situation about nazi collaborationists, who should not appear in this country—nor in any country—and, on the other hand, people who are being picked on by persons who hate them and by calling them names try to ruin them.

The latter is the case with Dohnanyi, who was my teacher for many years—during the most important years of my life—and whose influence on my career may have been greater than the influence of my own parents.

Without having been introduced by anyone, I went to Dohnanyi's home when I was eleven years old and asked him to let me play for him. He smiled and told me to do so. After listening to me, he took me as his pupil and I studied with him for four years. I don't think Dohnanyi ever asked me one question about religion, my financial status, or similar. He never asked one penny for his lessons. He had many students of whom 90% were Jewish. On Sundays we used to go to his house for tea. He was and is an artist of the greatest integrity and nothing could affect it. One of his pupils, Georg Farago, became a member of the Faculty of the Music Academy. In 1941 they discovered that Farago's father was Jewish and fired him. Dohnanyi resigned his directorship at once in protest. I was staff member of the Budapest Radio from 1934 to 1938. Dohnanyi was Musical Director.

I know that Dohnanyi was never influenced by religious hatred or political reasons. I was in Budapest this past summer and inquired about him. I did not hear one bad word about him—on the contrary, many good artists expressed their desire to have him back, and this included artists who had suffered in concentration and labor camps and had more reason to hate than people who sat back in the United States, comfortably in their easy chairs, thinking up new hate campaigns.

In any opinion there has to be an end to this and a line must be drawn. Artists who have been cleared by official authorities, should not be molested anymore—even criminals are sentenced only once and innocent people should not be punished for what they did not do. On the other hand, artists who were nazis should not be granted visas.

I would be ashamed all my life if against my belief and convictions I had let Dohnanyi down. If this letter serves to clear the situation up just one little bit, it would be a great relief to me, who has a great admiration for Dohnanyi's art, in which I am joined by many great artists who had more chance to form first-hand opinions of his activities, being on the spot, than people who sat next to the fireplace all the time.

14 February 1949. Imre Waldbauer, Iowa City, Iowa, to whom it may concern.

Erno von Dohnanyi has been a very close friend of mine for forty years. I have known him as a great musician, composer, wonderful teacher, and administrator. As a teacher of the Academy of Music of Budapest I was in close touch with him during the entire period while he was director (1919–1943) of the same Academy before he resigned the post because he disagreed with the anti-Semitic views of the Hungarian Government. He never played any part in Hungarian politics. He never was a Nazi; he was not anti-Semitic. On the contrary, he effectively sabotaged the acts of the semi-Nazi Hungarian Government before the Nazis came to power, by protecting all the good Jewish musicians like Annie Fischer, Heimlich, Weiner, Farago, Kosa, and many others.

As a prominent person in Hungarian music, he was compelled to attend the first meeting of the Hungarian Nazi Cultural Council. A moving picture taken at this time shows him shaking hands with the Hungarian Nazi leader Szalasi. This photograph has been used by his enemies to compromise him politically. However, Mr. Zathureczky, who was Director of the Hungarian Francis Liszt Music Academy at the time of the meeting and who is still Director of the same Institute, also attended the meeting, and with him many other cultural leaders of the country.

18 March 1949. Leo Weiner, Budapest, to Leon Goldstein (Chairman, Musicians Chapter, American Veterans Committee).

I am very glad to take the opportunity to inform you about the anti-Nazi activities of Erno Dohnanyi, whom I consider one of the greatest musicians of your day.

In his evidence may I quote the following:

1. Most of his pupils, to whom all he imparted the highest standards of artistic education, were Jews or of Jewish descent. Just to mention a few names; Anni Fischer, Andor Foldes, Lajos Heimlich, Gyorgy Ferenci, Endre Petri, Ivan Engel and Jeno Zeitinger.

2. When during the Nazi regime he could not manage to have Gyorgy Farago, his favorite pupil, of Jewish descent, appointed professor to the Academy of Music of which Dohnanyi was Director at the time, he had resigned.

3. It is the merit of Erno Dohnanyi that the "Chamber of Music" had not actually been created in the face of the repeated declarations of urgency. The task of this chamber would have been to deprive by exclusion the Jewish musicians of their livelihood.

4. My experience in person is this: Whenever, even at the time of actual persecution, I applied to Erno Dohnanyi for the execution of any of my compositions, he always accepted with complete readiness conducting same or performing it on the piano. It was he who had presented many of my compositions including my "Concertino" composed for the piano and my "2nd Sonata" for the violin and the piano, as well as many of my orchestral compositions. He always did this with the full devotion of the artist. Had his attitude been anti-Semitic, he could easily have declined to execute my compositions or at least would have performed them less often.

I should be extremely glad if by the present declaration I could contribute to do away with the unjust incriminations against as great an artist as Erno Dohnanyi.

16 September 1949. John Katona (Legation of the Republic of Hungary), to Leon Goldstein.

In reply to your letter of 12 September 1949 we wish to advise that we have received no further information from Budapest regarding Erno Dohnanyi. Although we do not know if he is on the War Criminal List we can verify the fact that he has been banished from the Liszt Academy of Music in Budapest. Also, we can further state that Dohnanyi is indisputably considered to be a Nazi collaborator by the Hungarian Republic. Proof of this may be found in the listing of his collaborationist activities brought forth in our letter of 5 July 1949.

17 September 1949. Leon Goldstein to Andrew Schulhof.

Your most recent letter, demanding that the Musicians Chapter of the American Veterans Committee "clear" Ernst von Dohnanyi by September 19, was as impertinent as it was late (in reply to ours of August 1).

Dohnanyi's case was weak enough for Mr. Meeder to remind you—as you have since discovered—that organizations other than AVC would be sure to protest any further United States appearances by Dohnanyi.

At the offices of the American Federation of Musicians, we agreed to help uncover the true facts in the case, no matter what side they favored, and to let the facts speak for themselves. In the event Dohnanyi was cleared, we were to withdraw our opposition—and in the event Dohnanyi was proved guilty of Nazi collaboration, you were to drop his management.

The facts have thus far shown Dohnanyi to be a confirmed Nazi collaborator. We are expecting further official word from Hungary and from the British authorities in Germany (see enclosure). Unlike yourself—and you have never offered us any of your evidence—we shall withhold nothing from you.

Despite the facts, and the agreement in Mr. Meeder's office, we note that Dohnanyi is still under your management.

In fairness to all parties, we are advising the organizations who requested of us the listing of musicians who were blacklisted by their European governments, that altho [*sic*] Ernst von Dohnanyi is still blacklisted by Hungary as a Nazi collaborator, there is doubt as to his status on the War Criminal list.

5 April 1951. Herbert Monte Levy (Staff Council of the American Civil Liberties Union), to Louis C. Pakiser, Jr. (Executive Director, American Veterans Committee).

Our Mr. Malin yesterday conferred with Mr. Schulhof who is Mr. Dohnanyi's manager . . . he did state that shortly after the original blacklist was issued, he conferred with Mr. Goldstein of the Musicians Chapter and presented him with the evidence about Mr. Dohnanyi. Since all the evidence he presented was favorable, and since the only unfavorable evidence that Mr. Goldstein had was a letter from the Consulate of Communist Hungary, Mr. Goldstein thereupon promised to retract the blacklisting. However, according to Mr. Schulhof, though this promise was allegedly made some time ago, it has never been carried out. I would greatly appreciate if you could investigate this matter for us. If you would prefer that we take up the matter directly with the Musicians Chapter, we would be glad to do so. However, since this might be considered to be "questionable behavior" by them, you might want to take direct action yourself.

Appendix B. Dohnányi's Lectures at Ohio University

SIGHT-READING

When I decided to talk to you about sight-reading, it was because in my broad experience, this branch of music education is not given the attention its importance requires. Surely there is no musician who would not admit that sight-reading is a useful thing and that a good sight-reader enjoys many advantages in the practice of his art, but there are very few who realize the *necessity* of it, otherwise there would not be so many poor sight-readers, even among the teachers.

Before I go in more detail into the subject I want to emphasize that sight-reading is not a special gift, it does not require special talent, it is a matter of mere practice and can be acquired by anyone who has musical sense. If this were not so, we would not find comparatively more good sight-readers among amateurs of the better class than among any other classes of musicians. These amateurs have no ambition to display their skill before others, but want to enjoy their more or less good playing themselves, do not spend time in endless practicing of one or two pieces, but, longing for variety, play all sorts of pieces which they can manage fairly well to their own satisfaction. In this way they learn—not to play well, but to play at first sight, and besides, if they love *serious* music, they learn to know a considerable part of the literature.

Here I am at the main point of my talk. The piano literature is so enormous, the standard works, which an average pianist who aspires to be called an "artist" *should* know, are so many, that it is *impossible* to get to know them without the knowledge of sight-reading. One might reply, that nowadays most of the standard works are recorded by first-rate artists, and one can learn to know them by listening to the gramophone. This is partly right. And the fact that the kind of amateurs I spoke about just now is vanishing is surely due to the invention and development of the gramophone. It is a great pity! Because it is *not* an equivalent. Apart from the fact that it gives more satisfaction to be active than passive, the listening to music on records is never so attentive as the playing of it; consequently you learn to know a piece better when you play it yourself. The records have besides the danger that—unless you have several and different records of the same piece—you get accustomed to the interpretation of *one* artist, who may be not always the best.

If it is important enough to get an idea of the whole literature, it is still more important the effect which this has on your playing, on your interpretation of masterworks. To play *one* Beethoven sonata *well* you have to be familiar with the style of Beethoven; this is impossible by knowing only that one sonata. This applies equally to other composers too. A great composer's style is something that can hardly be taught, because it is a matter of feeling, obtainable only by close knowledge of a great part of his works. This alone makes the necessity of sight-reading obvious, but there is another advantage which lies on the technical side. The sight-reader—while he is playing—especially, in "ensemble" with others—has no time to look for proper fingering in the passages and is obliged to take whatever fingering—sometimes just the most awkward one—that comes to his fingers. For instance, one learns to play the C-sharp Major scale with the fingering of C Major, which may be very useful. But here many of you, ladies and gentlemen, will reply that this might lead to a "sloppy" playing. Yes, it *might*. But it *need not*. Just as well as the occasional rhythmical unevennesses need not lead to sloppiness, the sometimes unavoidable "sloppiness" can be thoroughly balanced by the demand of absolute correctness in practicing and executing of the pieces which are the objects of our regular studies. And besides: if the practice of sight-reading is done *reasonably*, this danger is almost null.

You ask me now how this "reasonable" sight-reading should be done. To my mind the practice of sight-reading should begin almost with the first instructions in piano-playing, at a time when the pupil is not yet allowed to practice alone unaided. The simplest little pieces for four hands can be used, of which kind there exists a lot, the teacher playing "seconds" and thus controlling the pupil, chiefly paying attention to the rhythm. This four-hand playing should continue, even when the pupil can play easy pieces for two hands; the sight-reading of these should also be done under control of the teacher. If the pupil is fairly firm in his rhythmical feeling, he may do his sight-reading exercises alone without control. But care must be taken in the selection of the pieces. It is of great importance that these be in closest accordance with the technical skill of the pupil and by no means be more difficult than the material he is regularly studying. By observing these directions, "sloppy" playing is easily avoidable. The best school for sight-reading is the "ensemble," the playing with others, when you strictly have to observe the beat, otherwise the executants get in a mess of discords and have to stop. I cannot highly enough recommend playing chamber music sonatas with violin or violoncello, trios, quartets, etc. However, this is easier said than done.

Not everyone is in the fortunate situation of having friends who play the violin or violoncello well enough to be able to take part in an ensemble. But what is easy to accomplish is to play with another fellow pianist on about the same level of technical skill the works written for four hands on one piano, and when the players are more advanced, the works for two pianos. The literature for two pianos is not very big, but contains valuable works: the literature for four hands on one piano is enormous and contains works from the easiest caliber to the most difficult. It is a pity that four-hand playing on one piano went so much out of fashion—again a result of the diffusion of mechanical instruments. Playing four hands was in my youth so general in Europe that it was even used in courtship between couples, and—incredible nowadays—quite a number of marriages were contracted in consequence of such four-hand playing. But it had other advantages too. The miniature scores with which people nowadays go in orchestral concerts—just to show their music understanding—were at that time not yet invented, and it was quite usual for amateurs as well as professional people to play the symphonies at home in arrangements for four hands in order to be well prepared for their listening at the concert. This was very useful, certainly more than the miniature scores, which most of the people cannot read anyhow. Almost all orchestral music of value exists in arrangements for four hands. But not only arrangements, the number of *original* compositions for four hands is considerable, unfortunately now not very well known. Schubert, for instance, wrote volumes of beautiful and charming four-hand pieces.

All this is very well adopted for sight-reading. When I say "sight-reading," I do not mean a reading only once. The more valuable works should be played through more often, because a full knowledge of the literature can be obtained only by playing each work a number of times. Now I hear your objections: "How can we do all this? How can we find time to spare for sight-reading when we have to study and practice so much?" Ladies and gentlemen, the thing is not so bad as it looks at first sight. Of course, children who begin to learn piano should get lots of lessons, but they ought to get that anyhow, because it is important not to let beginners practice alone without control. But then you will find that the time devoted to reading is not wasted; the child who sight-reads will progress much quicker. So will the others. About a quarter of the time which is devoted to practice should be spent on sight-reading. The benefit will be seen later. A good thing would be when the music school would offer courses in sight-reading combined with chamber music lessons. If proficiency in this would also bring "credit" to the students, I am sure the number of good sight-readers would rapidly increase.

ROMANTICISM IN BEETHOVEN'S
PIANOFORTE SONATAS

Before I go into my subject, I have to explain what Romanticism means. The word comes from "romance," a poetical narration in verse, which began in the seventeenth century, after the epical chivalrous poetry had fallen in decadence. The word "Romantic" was then used at various times in various meanings: as individualism, as religious or national feeling, as sentimentality, as irrationalism, as idealism, as liberty in poetry and art, but generally as opposed to the word "Classic," which always meant the conserving spirit. Towards the end of the eighteenth century, in different European countries a Romantic school in literature developed. This school had its biggest development in Germany, where in the so-called "Sturm und Drang" period the writers almost celebrated excesses.

In music we understand by Romanticism a style in opposition to the Classical, by the Romantic period the school represented by Weber, Schumann, Chopin, and others, in one word the music of the nineteenth century, while that of the eighteenth we call the Classical. Perhaps it is superfluous if I point out that I don't use the word in the sense in which still many people use it, who think that classical music is the music they do not understand. By "Classical" we mean always the music of the eighteenth century. Their greatest representatives are Haydn and Mozart.

Classicism is law and order. Classical music is placed on formal elements, is of symmetrical proportions, is impersonal, objective. Romantic music is of loose-jointed structure, of strong personal feeling, impulsive, subjective. The greatest Classical composer is Mozart, the most significant Romantic is Schumann, and between these two poles stands Beethoven. In fact, Beethoven is both Classical and Romantic, so much so that in the time after him, when the dispute about Classicism and Romanticism arose, both parties claimed him as their own. He combined the expression of his subjective personal feeling with the objective architecture of the Classical forms in a perfect manner which cannot be surpassed, and perhaps this is why we admire him so much, why he is in the eyes of most of us "*The* greatest" composer; and this may have been the cause why he was so highly esteemed even during his lifetime. Because Beethoven did not belong to those geniuses who were misjudged. Though he was not understood, he was recognized.

I am, or rather was, in the possession of a first edition of Johann Nepomuk Hummel's Piano Method. Hummel was a great virtuoso, pupil of Mozart, and a contemporary of Beethoven.[1] In this book I found an

---

1. Dohnányi's sister Mitzi later took great efforts to smuggle the three large volumes of Hummel's *Ausführliche theoretisch-practische Anweisung zum Piano-forte-spiel* to Dohnányi.

advertisement of a subscription for a complete edition of the works of Beethoven, which began with the following words: "Beethoven! Sagt dieser Name nicht Alles? Sagt er nicht: Grösster Componist *aller* Zeiten?" (Beethoven! Does this name not say everything? Does it not say: greatest composer of *all* time?) Astonishing words if you imagine that this work of Hummel appeared in 1828, only one year after Beethoven's death.

But let us come to our subject. The Romantic elements in Beethoven's music are best shown in his pianoforte sonatas, where he could pour out his innermost soul easiest, while in his symphonies he naturally had to be more objective and general. We distinguish three periods in Beethoven's music: in the first we find Beethoven still much influenced by Haydn and Mozart, though he shows already his own personality. The striving to extend the scheme of the sonata form especially in the so-called development and the coda are quite Beethoven-like. But in the works of this period we scarcely find Romantic elements, they are Classical throughout. The second period is of more individual character, and shows already many specimens which could belong to the Romantic school. The third and last period—without abolishing the Classical forms—is music influenced throughout by personal feelings! Here Beethoven is entirely Romantic.

We do not want to occupy ourselves now with the first Classical period, though the Sonata, op. 13, the so-called *Pathetic,* which belongs to this group, has some Romantic features already. But we have to come to the Sonatas, op. 27, the E-flat Major, and the C-sharp Minor, the so-called *Moonlight,* to find Beethoven in the Romantic field. Beethoven must have felt himself that these sonatas have not much to do with the Classical ones, because he did not dare to give them purely the title "sonata," but he called them both: "Sonata quasi una fantasia." And especially the second, the *Moonlight,* drew the attention of the world. Not unjustly, because it is one of the finest works of Beethoven. Of course, it has nothing to do with moonlight, and the stories, which have grown up around it, are mere legends. Nevertheless the music itself is from the beginning of the twilight-like first movement till the end of the crashing finale full of passion, thoroughly Romantic.

The next conspicuous example of Romanticism is the first movement of the D Minor Sonata, op. 31, no. 2. The movement begins with two bars "largo," which sound like a question. The two bars are followed by a stormy passage and the conflict begins. The whole movement is dramatic, yet strictly in sonata form. When it comes to the recapitulation, a recitative is placed between the two largo bars and the stormy passage. What did Beethoven mean? One is inclined to put words under the notes of the recitative, but words can never explain music. Music is a language of ideas, which cannot be expressed by words. Schumann's F-sharp Minor Sonata contains also a recitative, which, however, can be explained much easier, as the Sonata is dedicated to Clara, and this recitative indicates most probably a dialogue between Robert and Clara.

The next sonata, which deserves the title "Romantic," is the F Minor, op. 57, the *Appassionata,* which is perhaps the most dramatic of Beethoven's works. Even the restless last movement with the minor ending is full of dramatic elements. It is remarkable that the preceding great Sonata, the *Waldstein,* op. 53, has scarcely any Romantic elements. This Sonata, like the C Major, op. 2, no. 3, has obviously pianistically virtuosic tendencies.

With the Sonata in F-sharp Major, op. 78, we come to Beethoven's last period. Here is everything personal, everything self-revelation. Here Beethoven is the poet: with the exception of the "Les adieux," the *Farewell* Sonata, which is program-music, the others all belong to the Romantic school, or better expressed: they laid the ground for it. Here is the trail which Schumann followed, only he was not capable enough to maintain the symmetrical architecture of the bigger forms, for which reason he preferred the smaller ones. Because Beethoven is even in his most Romantic movements Classical in form. There lies his greatness. Also remarkable is that with the intimate revelation in his music, he begins to use instead of the international Italian tempo indications German instructions, like Schumann. For instance, in the Sonata in E Minor, op. 90: "Mit Lebhaftkeit und durchaus mit Empfindung und Ausdruck" (With animation, and with feeling and expression throughout). Does this not sound Schumann-like? Could you imagine these words on a Classical composition?

And what shall I say of the last three sonatas? They are mere Romanticism, mere poetry. And there are no words to express what this reveals. Although Hans von Bülow, the celebrated Beethoven interpreter, characterizes the two movements of the Sonata, op. 111, with "Sansara and Nirvana" or "Auflehnung und Ergebung" (Revolt and resignation), what the Sonata tells us is still very far from that. Do compare the three movements of this Sonata with the three movements of a Classical one. Here the first movement like a free fantasy, there a conventional allegro; here a nervously agitated prestissimo as a second movement, there a calm andante; for the third here an *adagio* with variations, there a rondo. What a difference! And what a difference between the Beethoven of the first period and the Beethoven of the last!

Appendix C. Selected Articles

13 December 1889. "Quartett-Soireé Dohnányi-Ungarn," *Grenzbote* (Pozsony).

The public received the pieces, especially the Schumann Quintet, with the most hearty applause. Ernst von Dohnányi, a child of eleven [*sic*], surprised the audience with his precision, confidence, and power. The young man has evidently inherited the talent of his gifted father. If his physical development keeps up with his musical talent, for which God shall give him strength, and if he does not become one of the many young virtuosos who overestimate their own capacities, he will easily become a very famous musician.

29 December 1890. "Konzert des Singvereins." *Pressburger Zeitung* (Pozsony).

It was a thrill to witness the artistic triumph of the first public recital of fourteen-year-old [*sic*] Ernst, the son of the very talented Frederick von Dohnányi. With perfect poise and without stage fright or obtrusiveness, the young artist performed a Nocturne by Chopin, a Scherzo by Mendelssohn, and the Eighth Rhapsody of Liszt. He played with a powerful touch as well as with a clear understanding and feeling. But most applauded, and rightfully so, for the two compositions of his own: a little Fantasy in Schumann's spirit, and, played as a much deserved encore, a fiery, charming Scherzo.

17 June 1897. Title unknown, *Budapesti Hírlap* (Budapest).

Today's concert at the Royal Academy seemed like one long ovation for Ernst von Dohnányi, who performed Liszt's "Don Juan Fantasy." His performance surpassed every expectation. Very few pianists can play like this young man of such powerful talent can. He is one of the titans of modern virtuosity, who, as soon as he appears before the public, will be ranked with d'Albert and Sauer. We can compare the power and sincerity of his performance only to these two masters.

At the end of the Fantasy, something happened that is unheard-of in the history of examination concerts. The audience crowded around the stage, cheering and applauding, until Dohnányi returned to the piano to play encores. The professors watched this break from school discipline with astonishment.

This time, the school performance turned into a real concert, into an artistic achievement. A Hungarian boy started his triumphant career on the stage of this school, to which the echo of his fame will always reverberate.

25 October 1898. "Richter Concerts," *The Times* (London).

Even the most genial and encouraging hearers could hardly have been prepared for such a surprising display of the highest executive art as was made in Beethoven's lovely pianoforte concerto in G major by Herr Ernest de Dohnányi, a young Hungarian player, who immediately established himself in the good graces of all his hearers. Not only is his technique absolutely faultless, his tone exquisitely clear, his enunciation distinct, but he already possesses a most rare maturity of style, and in the manipulation of his phrases he yields to none but the very greatest artists. It is perhaps unsafe to assign to any executant a place among the greatest on the strength of any one performance, however successful, but it will surprise most of those who are best qualified to form an opinion if he does not rapidly attain the very highest position. He was completely in sympathy with the beautiful instrument he used, with the conductor, and with the audience, and the result was a musical treat of a very remarkable kind.

11 November 1898. "Herr von Dohnányi's Recital," *The Times* (London).

Seldom in the recent history of music has a success so immediate or an impression so profound been made by an unknown artist as has been made by the young Hungarian pianist who lately appeared at a Richter Concert. Though Herr Ernst von Dohnányi's first recital, given yesterday at St. James's-hall, drew an audience nearly as small as that which attended M. Paderewski's first recital, the enthusiasm his wonderful playing aroused can be compared with nothing in the experience of recent years. Wonderful is, indeed, the only epithet that can be applied to the young artist's performances, but the word is not meant to convey the idea of a technical dexterity to which everything else is sacrificed; technique there is, and of a superbly finished kind, but is entirely held in subjection to the higher things of interpretation. Those who heard him a fortnight ago, and these who were present yesterday, were not long in realizing that in the depth of poetic feeling, in the apparently infinite command of tone-gradation, and in the intellectual insight to the soul of music he plays no pianoforte-player now living can approach him. The union of these qualities suggests a comparison with Mme Schumann; but in Herr von Dohnányi, while there is the most beautiful tenderness of expression, there is also a virile power and a brilliancy of tone which that illustrious artist no longer possessed in her later years. A tone of greater volume or sonority has seldom been heard, and it need hardly be said that it is produced, even in the loudest passages, with no harshness and with little apparent effort.

22 October 1925. Olin Downes, "Music: Ernst von Dohnanyi Conducts," *The New York Times.*

Technically the performances were in every way superior to those of previous seasons. They were superior in point of intonation, attack, phrasing, tonal balances; musically they were energized by a conductor of unquestioned authority and communicative feeling. . . . It was clear last night that the State Symphony has secured, for a new beginning a man of an artistic stature equal to his reputation, and that the new conductor's heart was in his task.

28 July 1937. *Pesti Napló* (Budapest).

Dohnányi did not take his place on the throne of the d'Alberts or the Busonis. Instead, after his professorship in Berlin, at the outbreak of World War I he returned to his fatherland, where he displayed to us Hungarians, through the unforgettable performances of his piano and chamber music, the treasures of his poetical soul. We shall preserve these treasures at the bottom of our hearts, with unending gratitude, as the real treasures of our musical culture. Music-loving Hungarians, indebted for their noble musical education to Dohnányi's art, will preserve in their minds the results of his great accomplishments. I am not referring to the results Dohnányi has obtained on the official forums of our music life. The results of Dohnányi's art consist of secret, spiritual threads with which he has linked the Hungarian audience to the most intimate poetry of music. The intoxication of triumphant youth may have already left him; but here in Budapest we all know that he, who is living among us, is the greatest interpreter of the musical works of Beethoven, Schubert, and Schumann. And this is enough. No worldly success can surpass in importance the deep and profound gratitude of even one single listener. Therefore Ernst von Dohnányi cannot receive a more beautiful birthday gift than the true and deep understanding of his Hungarian concert audience that will accompany with unchanged devotion the great artist on his future ways.

Not long ago our Radio celebrated the first decade of its life, and we all joined in this celebration, we, who have started with it on this wondrous interesting road. Through the seven of these past ten years the name of Dohnányi has been completely linked with the Radio. He planned programs and opened up a new way. He acted as pianist, conductor and composer, but he was present, in the background, invisibly, at every event where the presence of a great artist was indispensable.

Only on this event, which was his birthday celebration, did he withdraw into the Austrian mountains. The announcement took place in three languages. It has probably crossed the whole world. It has penetrated the sanatorium on the huge mountains, knocked at windows in Rome, carried the news to London and Marseilles, mounted the rocks of Heligoland, etc. . . . "Please, listen to us," it said. "Radio Budapest is speaking, the blue Danube, the radiant Hungarian grain fields, the pale green forests, the Radio of ardent Hungarian hearts. Listen to us, for we are celebrating Ernst von Dohnányi, who is ours, and whom we have given to the world."

9 March 1947. "Hungarian Revival: Country's Music Struggles to Feet Despite Woes," *The New York Times.*

The success of Zoltán Kodály in America, plus the fact of Hungarian artists having won three first prizes abroad, has reawakened the interest of the Hungarian public in serious music from which it turned away for a time after the war.

Kodály and Bartók have become popular abroad, but at home they did not become popular—chiefly for political reasons. Both Kodály and Bartók were convinced democrats and refused to introduce politics into music. The music dictator of the last twenty years, Ernoe Dohnányi, director of the Academy of Music, looked upon their activity with suspicion.

Dohnányi, an excellent pianist, but a mediocre composer and conductor, did everything in his power to prevent his rivals from asserting themselves. Bartók's opera, "The Remarkable Mandarin," lay about for ten years in the Opera House without being produced.

"Does not lend itself for performance," was the official standpoint, because the libretto writer was a Jew.

16 March 1947. Egon F. Kenton, "Another Report from Hungary," *The New York Times.*

The curious unsigned article from Budapest about the revival of music in Hungary, which appeared on last Sunday's music page, is, on closer examination, a fabric of malicious insinuation and half-truths that cannot go unanswered.

For the sake of brevity this answer will confine itself to refuting the letter point by point.

1. The unqualified allegation that the Hungarian public "turned away for a time after the war" from serious music should be considered in the light of gutted concert halls, deported performers and the natural preoccupation of the listening public with the precarious business of staying alive.

2. The works of Bartók and Kodály, far from being neglected by the pre-war regime, were widely and continuously performed in Hungary from about 1910 on. The alleged "lack of popularity—chiefly for political reasons"—of Bartók and Kodály is simply not true. Their popularity is attested to by the fact that, with negligible exceptions, all their compositions were repeatedly performed in Hungary.

3. Dohnányi, far from "looking with suspicion upon the activities of Bartók and Kodály," conducted and played their works constantly. He has always been a champion of their music, and his "preventing" their self-assertion is a plain untruth.

4. Dohnányi was never a "music dictator," as alleged. As a matter of fact, his appointment to the post of director of the Academy or Music during the season of 1918–19 by Minister of Education Kunfy under the republican regime of Count Károlyi was followed by his removal in 1920 by the Horthy regime for purely political reasons. He was reinstated only in 1934, after the death of Hubay, who had replaced him.

5. The "mediocrity" of Dohnányi as a composer may be the personal opinion of the anonymous writer of the article—an opinion not shared by many performers, authoritative critics and listeners. His works are frequently heard on the radio and in concert halls all over the world.

6. Dohnányi's position as director of the Music Academy gave him no say whatever in the management of the opera. Both of Kodály's operas, "Háry János," and "The Spinning Room," were performed in the Budapest Opera House, as were Bartók's one-act opera "Bluebeard," and his pantomime "The Wooden Prince." Bartók's pantomime "The Wonderful Mandarin" was indeed not produced in Budapest, but because the libretto seemed risqué to the official in charge of the state-controlled opera, and not because, as the article declares, the librettist was a Jew. In fact, the librettist of both other Bartók works mentioned was also a Jew, Béla Balázs.

7. The charge that radio "gave few opportunities to Bartók and Kodály" is unfounded. Their works were played on the Hungarian radio, in proportion not less than that which an American station would devote to "serious" as opposed to light and popular music.

The only heartening fact to emerge from the article is that Kodály, as well as young students of the academy, are winning successes abroad. To this observer it would seem that the revival of music in Hungary could proceed faster and more easily without trumped-up imputations of rivalries—on alleged political, non-musical grounds—between Hungary's great contemporary musicians.

23 March 1947. Emil Havas, "Dohnanyi," *The New York Times.*

I dislike taking part in the discussions now going on about Ernest Dohnanyi, the famous Hungarian composer and conductor, but I would like to call your attention to this one fact.

Az Ember, weekly Hungarian democratic organ, published at 320 East Seventy-ninth Street, New York, recently (March 15, 1947) published a dispatch, dated Budapest, stating that the Hungarian Government had forwarded a note to the Allied Control Commission demanding the arrest of twenty-two Hungarian war criminals living outside of Hungary. The list begins with the name of Albrecht Hapsburg—who fled to the Argentine. The seventeenth name on this list is Ernest Dohnanyi, presently residing in Austria.

20 April 1947. Edward Kilenyi, "More on Dohnanyi,"
The New York Times.

Since there have been a number of charges and counter-charges in the pages of the Sunday *Times* concerning the Hungarian composer, Ernö Dohnányi, I should like to present the facts of the case, as determined by thorough investigations of the Information Control Division and Information Service Branch, United States Army, European Theatre.

Soon after the Hungarian election of November, 1945, the Hungarian Government withdrew its charges against Dohnányi of complicity or connection with the Nazi regime of Ferenc Szálasi. The accusations were found to be either untrue or flimsy. Dohnányi was completely exonerated and his name removed from the war criminal list.

Dohnányi, then in Austria, received letters from Zoltán Kodály; Edward Zathureczky, director of the Music Academy; Jenö Sugár, head of Rózsavölgyi, Hungary's largest music publisher and concert management firm; András Rékai, business manger of the Budapest Philharmonic; Imre Waldbauer, professor at the Academy, and many others, expressing pleasure at his rehabilitation and telling him how much he was missed in Hungary.

On the basis both of his exoneration by the Hungarian Government and of the testimonial letters from these musicians in the leading positions in the newly formed republic, Dohnányi was cleared by the American occupation authorities.

The recently reported demand for the extradition of Dohnányi, fourteen months after his rehabilitation, represents a drastic change in the policy of the Hungarian Government.

26 April 1948. "Presentóse Ayer el Pianista E. de Dohnanyi"
(Pianist E. von Dohnányi Presented Yesterday), *La Prensa* (Buenos Aires).

Dohnányi belongs to those whom we call the "old school" of pianists, including names like d'Albert, Rosenthal, Paderewsky and others following the lines of the great Liszt. Like them, Dohnányi plays with great sonority and warm, rich expression, which reveal a grandeur of character, always noble and profound. For each of the works he was able to create its own special atmosphere, simple and moving in every way. His left hand provides ample sonority to support the musical structure while his right touches the keys with a characteristic lightness and brings forth a clear crystal sound. This capacity enables him to achieve subtle nuances, against the full weight of a fortissimo as well as in the most pianissimo passages— clear evidence of the most rare gift he possesses. And Dohnányi succeeds

Lengyel has well pointed out that another gifted Hungarian musician came to the United States, declaring openly that music could not thrive in the Nazi-poisoned atmosphere of Hungary; also that Kodaly, while remaining in Hungary, withdrew completely from all public work and performance.

George Ruttkay, writing in "Aufbau" May 2, 1947, states also that Dohnanyi served Szalasi (later hanged as a war criminal) as Szalasi's "top musical advisor."

Mr. Schwalb, who was quoted in Mr. Elie's article of November 18, is himself authority for the statement that Dohnanyi joined Nazi cultural movements allegedly to sabotage them. This is a familiar alibi in these days of forgiving and forgetting all the sins of Axis agents and their sympathizers.

20 November 1948. Ferenc Göndör, "New Yorkba várjuk Dohnányit" (Dohnányi Expected in New York), *Az Ember* (New York).

Ernst von Dohnányi, the notorious, disreputable pianist, chief criminal music dictator of the Arrow Cross mass murderer Szálasi, has—unfortunately—already arrived in the United States of America, and, according to our information, his first concert has already taken place on 17 November in Boston in the Alumnae Hall. Moreover, if the American nation all endure this disgrace, this Hitlerian, man-slaying, Szálasi-worshipping musician might even become a permanent professor at the Wellesley College!

An article in "Az Ember" that has just reached us from Budapest depicts expertly and most moderately the misshapen features of Mr. Dohnányi. In another column of our paper one of our New Yorker friends tells—without any commentary—his frank opinion about this wretch, who has intruded unwanted into America. We ourselves have little to add to the words of these two other revelations. But, since we are informed that Hitler's and Szálasi's mutually favored Dohnányi in his infinite audacity intends to concertize even here, in New York, we wish to complete the articles of our collaborators.

In Budapest, at the Academy of Music, at Dohnányi's examinations even the most talented candidates were unsuccessful if they happened to be Jewish. Dohnányi was the leader of the "Harmonia" enterprise, which organized concerts, and, of course, no Jew was allowed to take part in them. Dohnányi was the only famous Hungarian musician who has given a musical performance in honor of Szálasi, leading it personally. Mr. Dohnányi remained loyal until his last moment to the woman- and child-murdering Arrow Crossers. This is, why he was put—after the delivery of Hungary— upon the list of war criminals. He fled to Western Austria, where not the slightest harm came to him. Should this same "Herr von Dohnázi" now come to New York to play the piano? No, we will see to this!

20 November 1948. "Herr von Dohnányi, Heraus!" (Mr. Dohnányi, Get Out!), *Az Ember* (New York).

Whether Nazi or not, this is what New York is discussing now. In Budapest it was well known that he was, and will remain, a Nazi, for this is how he was born. He was a Swabian, in the ugly meaning of the word. He spoke Hungarian with a German accent, like Miklós Horthy. He was nurtured on the dug of German culture (let the plague dry out these dugs!) His musical culture was German. His style was the one of Schumann and Brahms—only little did he swerve away from these. . . . Never in his life did he stand up for Hungarians; he thwarted Bartók and Kodály wherever he had a chance. He did not understand and did not grasp the real meaning of Hungarian music. The Hungarian peasant he knew danced in silk garments, in inns decorated with mirrors and chandeliers.

He was not a politician, but an artist, say the chimney sweepers. As for his unfortunate Hungarian manager, it is a shame that a Hungarian should have to sell such a murderous Nazi gangster! Why does not rather a German, Austrian, or Czech impresario trade with such evil-smelling merchandise?

He was a politician, otherwise how could he have kept his power under the governments of Bárdossy, Imrédy, Sztojay, and Szálasi?

1.) He was the president director of the Franz Liszt Music Academy.

2.) He was president-conductor of the Philharmonic Society.

3.) He was the musical leader of the Hungarian Radio.

He was dictator of music life, lord of life and death. He has kept these positions in his hands until the last moment. Why? Because he was one with them. They confided in him.

If he was no politician, what did he have to discuss with Szálasi? (Why had Szálasi nothing to discuss with Kodály? The dry cleaners shall not come along with the excuse that this was so because Kodály's wife was a Jewess! Lehár's wife was also Jewish, yet Hitler was very friendly with Lehár.)

If he was no politician and no Nazi, why did he run with the rabble to the West? And if he committed an error and was no criminal, why did he not return to Hungary to clear himself? Not he! He instead chose to follow the other scoundrels to Argentina. There he is in good company. Let him stay there! We don't want any of his shabby art. He doesn't deserve dollars—even pesos are too good for him. Was he a war criminal? I do not know. I do not believe so. But with his harmful Nazi sentiments he gave a bad example—many whirled after him. We wish to Dohnányi, and to everybody who has a part in his coming here, a deserved defeat. Herr von Dohnányi, heraus! [Mr. Dohnányi, get out!].

26 November 1948. Russell McLauchlin, "Von Dohnanyi Plays
Solo in His Own Works," *Detroit News.*

The first cis-Atlantic performance of a new concerto by Ernst von
Dohnanyi was played at Music Hall, Thanksgiving evening, with the wonderful old gentleman who composed it sitting at the piano. Dohnanyi is 71
years old and he plays with all the muscles and all the spirit of a brilliant
lad of 25.

The new work, about a year old, in his Concerto for Piano and Orchestra No. 2, in B Minor, Op. 42. It is rich, hearty music and it contains
so much pure Hungarian romance that, if Liszt's name were signed to the
score, everybody would believe it.

Dohnanyi's fingers flew like swallows. He is master of every technical
device. He even "played-out" a full, keyboard glissando, in the last movement. We've long known him as a great survivor of a great era—but as a
composer, only. Now we Westerners discover that, like Rachmaninoff, he
is also a Titan at the piano.

30 December 1948. Normal Nadel, "Ernst Dohnanyi Concert Major
Musical Event," *The Columbus* (Ohio) *Citizen.*

Those who heard Ernst von Dohnanyi's piano recital in the Art Gallery's Little Theater last night have had an experience to treasure. It was a
renaissance of the Romantic tradition in music.

For many in the audience, it reawakened almost forgotten musical sen-
sitivities, dormant since the early years of the century. For younger listeners, it brought an entirely new concept of the pianistic art.

This was the sort of music described in the musical histories, but seldom heard any more. Mr. Dohnanyi made it blossom anew. It was no feeble
gesture by an aged man; it was, rather, a strong, intensely vital and fresh out-
pouring of a musical style steeped in tradition. . . . Expressively, his performance left nothing to be desired. It was characterized by an intense warmth,
exquisite phrasing and a strong sense of musical design. No measure or note
was slighted. In the closing fugue of Beethoven's A-flat Sonata, for example,
he not only articulated each voice with utter clarity, but he gave each inter-
weaving melodic line a distinctive, highly individual character.

11 January 1949. "Wichita Music Lovers Defy Weather to Hear
Dohnanyi," *Wichita Falls* (Texas) *Record News.*

More than 150 Wichitans who wisely braved icy underfooting Monday
night were afforded memorable musical experience as Ernst von Dohnanyi,
celebrated composer and pianist, and [Frederic] Balazs performed brilliantly in joint concert in the college auditorium. . . . Dohnányi played,
throughout the evening, with sublime assurance which never was in any
measure demonstrative. His humility was born of exaltation derived from

the music to which his heart was given. For that reason, it was an eloquent humility, one which drew a wealth of stirring music from the piano. Every phrase was a polished unit before ever it flowed from his fingers. The result was, for the audience, complete surrender to the authoritative expression of a master.

13 January 1949. E. Clyde Whitlock, "Fire As of Old Shown Here by Dohnanyi," *Fort Worth* (Texas) *Star-Telegram.*

As an emissary from a past which already exists only in the memory of the oldsters came Ernst von Dohnanyi, Hungarian pianist, composer, conductor, to become the second composer of international acceptance to visit this city in the century of its existence. Almost a last link with an era that is gone, and a good era musically it was, Dohnanyi, with 60 years of public recognition behind him, comes to us with silvered hair, but the sap of life runs warm within him. There is nothing valetudinarian in the spirit or substance of the playing.

After a limpid and elegant presentation of the fine Haydn Variations there came in Beethoven the summit of the evening. The entire sonata, more specifically the first movement, was a memorable synthesis of eloquence, aristocratic poise and emotional nobility musically, and technically of secure facility, tonal balance and superb rhythmic rightness. In the last respect the silences paradoxically were as eloquent as the sounds, being exactly proportionate to their rhythmic values. Through all the years this observer never has experienced in the first movement so intimate a communication.

6 February 1949. "Music and Musicians," *The Kansas City Star.*

If at first you admire Ernst von Dohnanyi as a distinguished pianist and marvel at his mastery of keyboard technique, you discover you have assessed only perhaps half of his great musical talent. When he gets around to the music he wrote himself, along towards the end of one of his recitals, you are reminded that he is even more gifted as a creator then as an interpreter. . . . His poise and generalship, backed by a remarkable mind, stout heart, and indomitable spirit and strength, are combined with a vast experience to make his readings skilled and discerning. He made the much-abused Schubert "Moments Musicaux" a refreshing episode of rare depth and sincerity. . . . His own music is invariably beautiful, inventive and charming.

15 February 1952. Olin Downes, "Work by Dohnanyi Introduced Here," *The New York Times.*

The concerto is Hungarian with a vengeance if by "Hungarian" we are to mean fire, caprice, exotic dance rhythms that alternate with measures of sensuous song. Not that the work employs folk-tunes, at least any known to this reviewer, in its texture. It is not a concerto based on popular melodies. But it is inescapably in a national spirit, and perhaps in no forgiving mood.

It used to be that Mr. Dohnanyi's symphonic music was tinctured more or less strongly with Brahms. This concerto sounds as if, in America, he were more keenly conscious than ever before and reminiscent of his native land.

The concerto is scored in an unusual fashion, no doubt with purpose to leave the upper octaves clear for the tone of the solo violin. There are no violins in the orchestra; only violas, cellos, basses where the strings are concerned. But unfortunately the scoring is so heavy that the violin has to be played with special pressure of the bow for its tone to ride over the instrumentation set against it.

20 February 1952. Doris Reno, "Pianist Von Dohnanyi Proves a Hit," *The Miami* (Florida) *Herald.*

Von Dohnányi chose several of the more speaking, less dashing works from among the great numbers of his compositions, and played them with the just the right balance of gentleness and spirited bravura. . . . Von Dohnányi's is individualistic piano playing of the Romantic school—of the kind which takes only normal temperamental liberties with revered scores, and doesn't attempt to revise or restamp them, as some of our younger modern pianists tend to do. He has still great technical facility as was demonstrated, for instance, in the Liszt Rhapsodie Hongroise No. 13. . . .

Still youthful at 74, the veteran pianist was in no way outdone by any strenuousities involved in performing such a big program, and finished up as fresh as when he began.

10 April 1953. William McMahon, "Enthusiastic Crowd Hails Unit's Debut," *Atlantic City Press.*

Sharing the spotlight and enthusiasm last night were conductor Van Lier Lanning and soloist Ernst von Dohnanyi. Playing his own Concerto No. 2 in B minor, Dohnanyi threw aside his 76 years like an old cloak and tackled the composition with the gusto of a youngster on his first concert date, but with the sureness of great artistry and experience. Some pianists tackle an instrument like an enemy; others caress it. Dohnányi commanded it; and it obeyed.

His work, heard here for the first time, is both modern and fundamental, never sacrificing traditional structure, and workmanship, even when it is jumping into modern-day harmonies and tempos. . . . Dohnanyi received an ovation at the climax of his composition.

10 November 1953. Paul Affelder, "Dohnanyi Proves Revelation as Soloist in Original Work," *Brooklyn Eagle.*

Those who attended the National Orchestral Association's opening concert of the season last evening at Carnegie Hall were treated to a startlingly pleasant surprise. The big event of the program was to be the first New York performance of the Piano Concerto No. 2 in B Minor, Op. 42, by the noted Hungarian pianist-conductor-composer, Erno Dohnanyi, who was also to be the work's soloist. Immense interest was manifested not only in the concerto, but in Dohnanyi himself, since he had not been heard here in a quarter of a century.

But Dohnanyi, who has been living in this country for the past five years, and who now teaches at Florida State University in Tallahassee, was 76 last July, and no one—least of all this reviewer—expected very much in the way of pianistic prowess from one of his years, even though he was once one of the world's most phenomenal keyboard virtuosi.

How wrong we were! Not only did the concerto turn out to be one of the most attractive new orchestral works to reach here this year, but it was performed with the vigor, the tonal wealth and the technical mastery of a man half his age.

Nor has Dohnanyi, the composer, been a bit sparing of Dohnányi, the pianist. It is perfectly safe to say that few artists before the public today would be anywhere near equal to the technical and musical demands of this concerto, yet this remarkable septuagenarian dashed it off with complete ease.

One is not likely to hear such brilliant execution of extremely difficult passage work in months of concert-going. There is no question about it; Dohnanyi is still the wizard of old.

10 November 1953. Jay S. Harrison, "Concert and Recital: National Orchestra," *New York Herald Tribune.*

The Hungarian composer Ernst Von Dohnanyi is seventy-six years old and he has not since the late twenties made a local concert appearance. It was thus the privilege of a large audience, assembled last night in Carnegie Hall for the opening of the National Orchestra Association's twenty-fourth season to welcome Mr. Dohnanyi back as soloist in the New York premiere of his Piano Concerto No. 2, in B minor. . . .

Mr. Dohnanyi's concerto, completed in 1947, is in the grand style—broad, lyric, impassioned and lovely. There is nothing small about it, nothing petty or mean. Indeed, it is so obviously and sincerely made of the heartiest sentiments that it is quite impossible not to be warmed by the glow it casts off. . . .

In its rendition, the concerto went like the wind. How, at the age of seventy-six, Mr. Dohnányi is able to careen so glibly about the keyboard is no question this writer can answer. But the fact remains that the composer darted to and fro as though he had just graduated cum laude from a conservatory and was prepared to tackle single-handedly the entire virtuoso repertoire. Hearing Mr. Dohnányi play made the youngsters on the scene feel ancient and worn.

10 November 1953. "Dohnanyi Returns for Concerto Bow,"
The New York Times.

After an absence of almost twenty-seven years, the Hungarian composer, Ernst Von Dohnanyi, returned last night to the New York concert stage at Carnegie Hall. He returned to play the solo part in the first local performance of his Piano Concerto No. 2 in B minor, a work he completed in 1947, while living as a "displaced person" in Austria.

He played the concerto with the ensemble of the National Orchestral Association, under the direction of Leon Barzin, and the performance was clearly an occasion of much good will. The 76-year-old composer was warmly greeted by the audience. The young instrumentalists paid him the honor of declining to rise when he asked them to share the applause, and in his many bows it seemed that the composer could not shake Mr. Barzin's hand often enough. . . .

The concerto . . . evoked so much applause that the composer was recalled to the stage five times.

Appendix D. Works List

Titles of published works are printed in bold type.

1884

Gebet [Prayer] for piano

1885

Six untitled pieces for violin and piano in F Major, C Minor, B Major,
    E Major, F Major, and E Minor
Adagio in A Major for violin and piano
Untitled piece for violin and piano in A Major
Untitled cello sonata in D Minor

1886

Etude in D Major for piano
Etude in C Major for piano

1887

Bagatelle in C-sharp Minor for piano
Bagatelle in D Major for piano
Bagatelle in A Minor for piano
Tarantella in E Minor for piano

1888

Cello Sonata in G Major
Mazurka in C Major for piano
Impromptu in A Major for piano
Scherzo in A Major for piano
Waltz in C-sharp Minor for piano
Pastorale in A Minor for piano
Tarantella in E Minor for piano

Scherzino in A Minor for piano
2 kleine Scherzandos [Two Small Scherzandos] for piano

1889

Piano Quintet in B-flat Major
String Quintet in G Major
String Quartet in D Major
"*Grand*" Cello Sonata in C Major
Mazurka in B-flat Minor for piano
Mazurka in B-flat Major for piano

1890

"*Grand*" String Quartet in G Minor
6 Fantasiestücke [6 Fantasy Pieces] for piano
Piano Sonata in A Major
Piano Sonata in G Minor
Bagatelle in D Major for piano
Tarantella in C Minor for piano
Piano Sonata in B-flat Major
Canon in C Major for piano

1891

Romance in A Minor for piano
Fantasiestücke [Fantasy Pieces] in A Major for piano
Die Bergknappen [The Miners], Romantic Opera
Ave Maria for tenor and bass soloists, solo violin, and string orchestra
Lied for voice, cello, harmonium, and piano
Heda: Six Pieces for Piano (based on the name "Heda")
Novelette in E Major for piano
Üdvözlő dal [Song of Welcome] for choir, string orchestra, piano, and harmonium

1892

Mass in C Major for alto and tenor soloists, choir, string orchestra, and organ
Overture in B-flat Major
"Die verlassene Fischersbraut" [The Fisherman's Abandoned Bride] for voice and piano
Zwei Liedchen [Two Little Songs] for voice and piano
"Das verlassene Mägdlein" [The Abandoned Maidservant] for voice and piano

Fantasy in C Major for organ
"Du schönes Fischermädchen" [You Pretty Fisher-Maid] for voice and
     piano
"Das Blumenmädchen" [The Flower-Maid] for voice and piano
"Wie dunkel und still" [How Dark and Still] for voice and piano
Pater noster for choir
Impromptu in F Minor for piano
"Wilder Ritt" [Wild Ride] for voice and piano

1893

"Reue" [Regret] for voice and piano
Piano Quartet in F-sharp Minor
String Quartet in A Minor
String Quartet in D Minor
"Ich sehe, wie in einem Spiegel" [I See It as in a Mirror] for voice and
     piano
O salutaris hostia et Ave verum for men's choir
Veni sancte spiritus for men's choir
Kyrie for choir and orchestra
Királyi hymnus [Royal Hymn] for choir
Der 6. Psalm [The Sixth Psalm] for two choirs
String Sextet in B-flat Major

1894

Romance in F-sharp Major for piano
"Auf Wiedersehen" [Goodbye] for voice and piano
"Ein Blick in deine Augen" [A Glance in Your Eyes] for two voices and
     piano
"Wiegenlied" [Lullaby] for voice and piano
Minuet in D Minor for string quartet

1895

Piano Quintet No. 1 in C Minor, op. 1
Untitled violin duet in G Major

1896

String Sextet in B-flat Major (revised; originally composed in 1893)
Symphony in F Major
Zrínyi Overture
Var. (Hymnus Erkel) [Variations on Ferenc Erkel's *Hymn*] for piano

1897

Vier Klavierstücke, op. 2 [Four Piano Pieces]
Cadenzas to Beethoven's Piano Concerto No. 4 in G Major, op. 58
Walzer, op. 3 [Waltz] for piano, four hands.
Variationen und Fuge über ein Thema von E. G., op. 4 [Variations and
    Fugue on a Theme by E(mma) G(ruber)] for piano
Walzer aus dem Ballett "Naila" von Leo Delibes [Waltzes from the Ballet
    Naila by Leo Delibes] for piano

1898

Piano Concerto No. 1 in E Minor, op. 5
String Sextet in B-flat Major (revised; originally composed in 1893 and
    revised in 1896)
Intermezzo in G Minor for piano
Gavotte und Musette [Gavotte and Musette] in B-flat Major for piano

1899

Passacaglia, op. 6 for piano
String Quartet No. 1 in A Major, op. 7
Cello Sonata in B-flat Major, op. 8

1900

Albumblatt [Album Page] for piano

1901

Symphony No. 1 in D Minor, op. 9

1903

Serenade, op. 10 for violin, viola, and cello

1904

Vier Rhapsodien, op. 11 [Four Rhapsodies] for piano

1905

Concertstück, op. 12 [Concert Piece] for cello and orchestra
Winterreigen, Zehn Bagatellen, op. 13 [Winter Round Dance, Ten
    Bagatelles] for piano

1906

"Waldelselein" [Little Elsa of the Woods] for voice and piano
Cadenzas to Mozart's Piano Concerto in G Major, K. 453

1907

Sechs Gedichte von Victor Heindl, op. 14 [Six Poems by Victor Heindl]
for voice and piano
String Quartet No. 2 in D-flat Major, op. 15
Im Lebenslenz: Sechs Gedichte von Wilhelm Conrad Gomoll, op. 16 [In
the Springtime of Life: Six Poems by Wilhelm Conrad Gomoll] for
voice and piano
Humoresken in Form einer Suite, op. 17 [Humoresques in the Form of a
Suite] for piano

1909

Der Schleier der Pierrette, op. 18 [The Veil of Pierrette], Pantomime
Stücke und Tanze, op. 18, no. 1 [Pieces and Dances] from *Der Schleier
der Pierrette* for orchestra
Walzer Pierrette [Pierrette Waltz] for 3 pianos
Suite für Orchester, op. 19 [Suite for Orchestra]

1910

Der Schleier der Pierrette: Hochzeit-Walzer, op. 18, no. 4 [The Veil of
Pierrette: Wedding Waltz] for piano
Hochzeitsmarsch [Wedding March] from *Der Schleier der Pierrette* for piano
quintet
Hochzeitsmarsch [Wedding March] from *Der Schleier der Pierrette* for violin
and piano

1911

Der Schleier der Pierrette Hochzeit Walzer, op. 18 no. 4 [The Veil of
Pierrette Wedding Waltz] for piano, four hands
Tante Simona, op. 20 [Aunt Simona], Comic Opera
Violin Sonata in C-sharp Minor, op. 21

1912

Drei Orchesterlieder auf Gedichte von W. C. Gomoll, op. 22 [Three Orchestral Songs from Poems by W. C. Gomoll] for voice and orchestra

Drei Stücke, op. 23 [Three Pieces] for piano
"Am Bach" [At the Brook] for voice and piano

1913

Suite nach altem Styl, op. 24 [Suite in Olden Style] for piano
*Fugue für eine vorgeschrittene linke Hand oder für zwei zurückgeschrit-
ten Hände* [Fugue for One Advanced Left Hand or Two
Unadvanced Hands] for piano

1914

Variationen über ein Kinderlied, op. 25 [Variations on a Nursery Song]
for piano and orchestra
Piano Quintet No. 2 in E-flat Minor, op. 26

1915

Cadenzas to Beethoven's First, Second, and Third Piano Concertos
Violin Concerto No. 1 in D Minor, op. 27

1916

A tékozló fiú [The Prodigal Son], pantomime, arranged for piano
Sechs Konzertetüden, op. 28 [Six Concert Etudes] for piano
Bölcsődal [Lullaby] for voice and piano

1917

Variationen über ein ungarisches Volkslied, op. 29 [Variations on a Hungarian Folksong] for piano

1919

Sonatas for Piano by Ludwig van Beethoven, edited by Bartók and
Dohnányi
Fantasie for Piano in D Minor by Wolfgang Amadeus Mozart, edited by
Dohnányi
J. S. Bach: Kleine Präludien [Johann Sebastian Bach: Little Preludes] for
piano, edited by Dohnányi

1920

Pastorale: Mennyből az angyal . . . ungarisches Weihnachtslied [Pastorale
on the Hungarian Christmas Song "An Angel from Heaven"] for
piano

Valses nobles für Pianoforte von Fr. Schubert [*Valses nobles* for Piano by Franz Schubert], arranged by Dohnányi

Rondo alla Zingarese von J. Brahms [Rondo alla Zingarese by Johannes Brahms], arranged for piano

Hitvallás—Nemzeti Ima [Credo—National Prayer], melodrama for narrator, choir, and piano

Hitvallás [Credo] for tenor and choir

1921

Nemzeti Ima [National Prayer] for choir

Ivas Turm, op. 30 [Iva's Tower], Romantic Opera

Fanfare and *Hiszekegy* [Fanfare and Hungarian Apostles' Creed] for brass choir and timpani

"Magyar jövő himnusz" [Hungarian Future Hymn] for choir

1922

Magyar népdalok [Hungarian Folksongs] for voice and piano

1923

Ünnepi nyitány/Ungarische Festouverture, op. 31 [Festive Overture/Hungarian Festive Overture] for two orchestras and brass band

1924

Ivas Turm [Iva's Tower], Romantic Opera (revised; originally composed in 1921)

Ruralia Hungarica, Sieben Stücke, op. 32a [Ruralia Hungarica, Seven Pieces] for piano

Ruralia Hungarica, Fünf Stücke, op. 32b [Ruralia Hungarica, Five Pieces] for orchestra

Ruralia Hungarica, Drei Stücke, op. 32c [Ruralia Hungarica, Three Pieces] for violin and piano

Ruralia Hungarica: Andante rubato, op. 32d [Ruralia Hungarica: Andante rubato] for cello (or violin) and piano

1925

Léo Delibes: Valse "Coppélia" [Léo Delibes: *Coppélia* Waltz], arranged for piano

1926

String Quartet No. 3 in A Minor, op. 33
"Widmung" [Dedication] for voice and piano

1927

Változatok Bókay bácsinak egy témájára [Variations on a Theme by Uncle Bókay] for piano
Der Tenor, **op. 34 [The Tenor], Comic Opera**

1928

Waltz for Piano by Johannes Brahms, arranged by Dohnányi
Johann Strauss: Two Waltzes: "Schatz-Walzer" (from *Der Zigeuner-baron*) and "Du und Du" (from *Die Fledermaus*), arranged for piano
Schubert: Fantasy for Four Hands in F Minor, op. 103, arranged for orchestra
"A múzsa csókja" [The Muse's Kiss], Ballet

1929

A legfontosabb ujjgyakorlatok biztos technika elsajátítására a zongorán [Essential Finger Exercises for Obtaining a Sure Piano Technique]
Himnusz Szent Imre királyfihoz [Hymn to the Royal Prince Saint Imre] for men's choir

1930

Köszentő [Congratulation] for choir
Missa in dedicatione ecclesiae, **op. 35 for soloists, double choir, and orchestra**

1931

J. B. Cramer: Selected Studies for Piano, edited by Dohnányi
Diákok dala [Students' Song] for men's choir
Magyar karácsonyi énekek [Hungarian Christmas Songs] for voice and chamber orchestra

1932

Murányi Vénusz [Venus of Murány], opera *(unfinished)*
Magyar induló [Hungarian March] for voice and piano. Separate arrangements for mixed choir, for male choir, and for orchestra

1933

Symphonischen Minuten, op. 36 [Symphonic Minutes] for orchestra

1935

Sextet in C Major, op. 37 for piano, violin, viola, cello, clarinet, and horn

1937

Die heilige Fackel [The Holy Torch], Ballet

1938

A Himnusz és a Rákóczi induló [Hymn and Rákóczi March] for orchestra
Himnusz [Hymn] for men's choir

1941

Cantus vitae, op. 38 [Song of Life], symphonic cantata for soloists, choir, men's choir, children's choir, and orchestra

1943

Suite en valse, op. 39 [Waltz Suite] for orchestra

1944

Symphony No. 2 in E Major, op. 40

1945

Suite en valse, op. 39a for two pianos, four hands
Six Pieces, op. 41 for piano

1947

Valse boiteuse, op. 39b [Limping Waltz] for piano
Piano Concerto No. 2 in B Minor, op. 42

1950

Violin Concerto No. 2 in C Minor, op. 43
Twelve Short Studies for the Advanced Pianist

1951

Three Singular Pieces, op. 44 for piano

1952

Concertino, op. 45 for harp and chamber orchestra

1953

Stabat Mater, op. 46 for soloists, boys' choir, and orchestra
American Rhapsody, op. 47 for orchestra

1954

Schubert: Valses nobles, arranged for two pianos, four hands

1957

Symphony No. 2 in E Major (revised; originally composed in 1944)

1958

Aria, op. 48, no. 1 for flute and piano

1959

Passacaglia, op. 48, no. 2 for solo flute

1960

Tägliche Fingerübungen für fortgeschrittene Pianisten [Daily Finger Exercises for Advanced Pianists]
Untitled trio for three flutes *(unfinished)*

INDEX

ILONA VON DOHNÁNYI (1909–1988), Ernst von Dohnányi's widow, was a journalist and historical novelist who also wrote biographies of the composers Vincenzo Bellini, Gaetano Donizetti, Gioacchino Rossini, and Robert and Clara Schumann. Her previous publications about her husband include *From Death to Life* and *Message to Posterity from Ernst von Dohnányi.*

JAMES A. GRYMES established the Ernst von Dohnányi Collection at Florida State University. His research has appeared in such journals as *Music Library Association Notes* and *Studia Musicologica Academiae Scientiarum Hungaricae,* and he is the author of *Ernst von Dohnányi: A Bio-Bibliography.*